Managing Change, Organisational Behaviour and Human Resource Development

Changing Contours of Administration Since Independence Golden Jubilee Volume Series - 16

Managing Change, Organisational Behaviour and Human Resource Development

Editors
Rakesh Hooja
Girish K. Srivastava

Series Editor
Rakesh Hooja

The HCM Rajasthan State Institute of Public Administration, Jaipur

RAWAT PUBLICATIONS
Jaipur • New Delhi • Bangalore • Mumbai • Hyderabad • Guwahati

ISBN 81-316-0232-X

Published by
Prem Rawat for **Rawat Publications**
Satyam Apts, Sector 3, Jawahar Nagar, Jaipur 302 004 (India)
Phone: 0141 265 1748 / 7006 Fax: 0141 265 1748
E-mail: info@rawatbooks.com
Website: www.rawatbooks.com

New Delhi Office
4858/24, Ansari Road, Daryaganj, New Delhi 110 002
Phone: 011 2326 3290

Also at Bangalore, Mumbai, Hyderabad and Guwahati

Typeset by Rawat Computers, Jaipur
Printed at Chaman Enterprises, New Delhi

Contents

Part III
Human Resource Development

Series Editor's Introduction

RAKESH HOOJA

It is most likely that all possible types of developmental, governmental, regulatory and administrative initiatives have been tried out in some part or the other of India over the last 60 years since the country gained independence. With governments of different ideological hues having remained in power at difference points of time in different states of the Indian Union and at the Centre, and with different ideas about development, governance, planning, state welfarism, market-orientation, administration, nation-building etc., having been fashionable or accepted in different time frames, as well as a willingness to try out and emulate what was being attempted in countries of the West, or of the Soviet bloc, or in other developing areas, all forms of administrative and governmental action and all types of development schemes, as well as types of organisational arrangements, have been tried out somewhere or the other in India and have been commented upon by experts, scholars, researchers, practitioners, journalists and the ordinary laymen. In fact, Public Administration is a well-established discipline in India and has been regularly analysing changes in the field, as also in administrative thinking, and in policy making, over the years.

These debates, discussions, descriptions, analyses, comments, opinions, findings and administrative prescriptions have been duly covered in the various articles published in the two journals of the HCM Rajasthan State Institute of Public Administration (HCM RIPA), which contain useful and valuable reference material.

It is in this context that we have undertaken this project of preparing thematic volumes, which would indicate some of the important *Changing Contours of Indian Administration Since Independence*. We wanted to look at how concepts, approaches, organisational structures, procedures, policies, programmes, projects, working styles, and modes of observation, analysis and evaluation, have all emerged and undergone change over time.

Accordingly, to celebrate 50 years of HCM RIPA, we felt it appropriate to select the best and most appropriate articles from the issues of *Prashasnika* which is being published for the last 35 years and from *Development Policy and Administrative Review* that was brought out for 11 years. Deliberately wanting the articles selected for inclusion in this series to retain the flavour of the period in which they were written and to reflect the thinking and practice of that time, we have chosen not to modify the selected articles, except in some cases to slightly change the titles of the articles. The words, descriptions and analyses are of the authors as they had originally written the pieces. However, the articles selected have their intrinsic value, and by putting them together into separate thematic volumes, we have, hopefully, enabled readers to visualise how certain administrative concepts, or governmental and developmental programmes (or experiments) and policies, have been initially conceptualised and implemented, and have subsequently evolved over time. We have also attempted to provide a judicious blend of the theoretical and the practical in each book as also in the series as a whole.

Having gone through the back issues of *Prashasnika* and of *Development Policy and Administrative Review*, we have selected the following as the themes for each of the separate volumes:

1. Development Administration and Rural Development
2. Training, Civil Services and Personnel Administration
3. Panchayati Raj, Participation and Decentralisation
4. Administration of Health and Education Sectors

5. Welfare and Tribal Development Administration
6. Administration of Public Sector Enterprises and Industrial Development: Changing Trends Since Independence.
7. Administrative Theories: Approaches, Concepts and Thinkers in Public Administration
8. Prashasnik Parivartan or Administrative Change (in Hindi)
9. Plan and Project Formulation and Implementation: Theoretical and Applied Aspects
10. Urban Development and Administration
11. Governance and Reforms
12. District Level Administration and The Role of the Collector
13. Administration of Desert, Drought Prone and Dry Farming Areas
14. Administration of Water Management and Command Area Development
15. Administration for the Empowerment and Welfare of Women
16. Organisational Behaviour, Managerial Change and Human Resource Development
17. Land Use Revenue Administration and Land Reforms
18. Criminal Justice and Police Administration
19. Financial Management and Economic Administration in Government

Other titles may be added as we go along.

I have received able support from my colleagues on the Series Editorial Board, namely, Dr Ramesh K. Arora, Shri S.N. Lathi, Mrs Pankaj Patni and Shri K.K. Parnami (and earlier Shri Suneel Dhariwal, Shri Sandeep Varma and Shri S.C. Soni), in finalising the themes for the individual volumes and identifying the possible thematic volume editors. Shri Parnami got a cumulative index prepared of all the matter published in our two journals without which this exercise could not have been started. We are also gratified that the two publishers, Subodh Bhushan Gupta of Aalekh Publishers and Pranit Rawat of Rawat Publications respectively agreed to jointly co-publish the books with HCM RIPA at no cost to HCM RIPA, and to distribute them. The editors of each volume also are to be thanked for their efforts at meticulously culling out and selecting the best and most relevant articles for our consideration for inclusion in the respective volumes, and for their writing appropriate volume introductions.

It is hoped that this series of volumes shall prove to be a useful source of reference contributing to better understanding of the themes covered and acting as a stimulus for further reflection to all those interested in Indian administration, and that readers shall enjoy and appreciate reading the books as much as we in the Series Editorial Board, and the volume editors, did while preparing the books for publication.

Introduction

Managing Change, Organisational Behaviour and Human Resource Development

RAKESH HOOJA AND GIRISH K. SRIVASTAVA

Management is the process of effectively administering and coordinating resources to achieve the goals of an organisation. Effectiveness is achieved only when the organisation pursues appropriate goals. Efficiency is achieved by using the fewest inputs (such as people and money) to generate a given output. In other words, effectiveness means "doing the right things" and efficiency means "doing things right" (Drucker, 1967).

The concept of management is both dynamic and evolving. It has multi-dimensional facets. In terms of duty, management is identified as a distinct duty of planning, organising, coordination, controlling, staffing and directing the organisations. In terms of responsibility, management is getting things done through other people according to what is wanted by those who are responsible for managing and rather than what these other people want. This means that a manager is one who takes the responsibility of getting work from others. It is not necessary that the manager should himself do the work or know about the details of its execution. What is necessary is that, he or she should have the capability of taking work from others. One is a manager because he is accountable to his superiors for others' (subordinates) performance. Therefore, management involves distinct responsibilities along with the specific duties. As a technique, management is leadership that is reflected in the way of managing persons and taking decisions. Thus, leadership styles in fact reflect the style of management.

The old concept of administration/management to rule over others has now been replaced by the concept of 'serving others'. Hence, the quality of service rendered by governmental/non-governmental organisations reflect the quality of management of change in values, technology, individuals and environment. In the management of change, organisations are pivoted to shape their destiny rather than allowing them to drift with circumstances. It is here that management must inject rigour and effectiveness. Management is not just development of things, it is mainly the development of human resources that concern people, interpersonal relationships, small groups, intergroups, and organisational norms and values (Argyris, 1971).

The present edited volume discusses these issues in twenty-five chapters in three major sections, viz., managing change in government, organisational behaviour, and human resource development.

Managing Change in Government

Management is not about the preservation of the status quo; it is about maintaining the highest rate of change that the organisation and the people within it can stand (John Harvey-Jones, 1988). Having entered the new millennium, the saying that "the only certainty is change" is truer than ever before. Change is coming from all directions. Diversity in the workforce has become the rule rather the exception; organisations are being restructured and redesigned to be lean, flexible and adaptable to change; and managers in all areas and at all levels of the organisation are expected to be proactive, team-oriented, and focused on results (Pamela S. Lewis, Stephen H. Goodman, and Patricia M. Fandt, 1998). Thus, managing change in government also assumes importance. This has been amply underscored by scholars like Peter F. Drucker (1964) and Warren G. Bennis (1969).

Managing change is nothing new in itself. What management is now having to live with is discontinuous change rather than steady or incremental and gradual change. The reasons for change are variegated, including geo-political developments, globalisation, privatisation, fundamental shifts in public aspirations, the environmental revolution, reengineering the shift from hierarchical management to team-building, "adhocracy" (a la Alvin Toffler), a willingness to break hollowed moulds of behaviour, quality revolution, new production technology and its indispensably, close attention to the customer. In most situations, a conjunction of these factors propels organisational change.

The greatest personal skill needed, under changing environment, will be to manage radical change and the top management jobs will become major areas of thought, experimentation, and innovation (Drucker, 1980). Organisation is a social system deliberately established to carry out some definite purpose (Caplow, 1983). Organisations only change when people manning them change, and people will only change when they sincerely accept that change is sine qua non to goal-oriented progress. People and top management support is important for change since unless and until top management and people do not change their ideas and values in tune with the demands of time, change in an organisation is inconceivable. Thus, all these issues lead to change management strategies for getting things done and achieving optimal results from limited resources.

Section one of the present volume provides the conceptual perspective and application of various managerial approaches and tools and techniques that help in managing the changing environment. This section contains eleven papers.

The first paper by K.B.C. Saxena, an eminent former faculty at IIMB, who has written a lot on reengineering public administration in India and developing countries, covers the application of the modified concept of business process reengineering (BPR) to public administration which has been given the name "Public Administration Reengineering" (PAR). Under this concept, Saxena has discussed a set of principles, viz., create customer focus, rethink functions and processes, simplify and discard activities, measure the organisational performance, set audacious objectives, empower people, and utilise IT as an enabler of PAR.

He believes that PAR will bring radical change in thinking amongst the public administrators which ultimately will benefit society in the context of improved responsiveness to public demands, improved quality of service, reduced delivery/response times and reduced cost of operations.

Pradip N. Khandwalla, former Director IIMA, in his paper discusses the need for creativity and various interpretations of the concept. In this paper, he has focused on demystifying the various abilities associated with creativity and techniques for stimulating creative thinking for solving many complex problems and providing a series of solutions to a given problem.

Then comes the paper by Ramesh K. Arora on "New Public Management: Emerging Concerns". It focuses on the traditional administrative and managerial theories and the factors that led to opting for new public management practices. He has also discussed the most common attributes of new public management (NPM) in his paper.

N. Vittal, former Central Vigilance Commissioner (CVC), discusses the need for better governance through accountability and transparency. He advocates that bureaucracy needs to be de-politicised and that the rule of law must be observed in letter as well as spirit for ensuring better governance. He has set forth a number of ideas to curb corruption, viz., strengthen the judiciary, application of PERT or CPM and ABC analysis concepts in courts, computerisation in banking sector, ensuring building a culture of accountability in the system, use of citizen's charters, use of information technology, which will help to move towards better governance.

The next paper is on "Administrator as Manager" in which I.C. Srivastava has discussed the new role of an administrator. In the wake of globalisation and predominance of market economy all over the world, coupled with economic liberalisation, the concept and content of governance has undergone a sea change. Under these circumstances, the role of administrator which was earlier power-centric, bureau-oriented and bound by rules and precedents, has now slowly started moving towards managerialism which means that the practices of management are bound to be used for making good governance a reality.

"Management in Government" is the title of the next essay written by B.R. Virmani. In this paper, he discusses some of the concepts, issues and problems of management in government. He has laid substantial emphasis on the need to understand how government administrators structure their work environment, work strategies and work style, and also on the need for training for the development of government administrators.

N.K. Kulshrestha, in his paper on "Managerial Excellence for Effectiveness", has focused upon areas of excellence, approaches and parameters of excellence. He has also advocated the need to apply the six essential skills for managerial excellence on the basic foundation of strategy and structure in an organisation.

In the next essay, Girish K. Srivastava has emphasised the necessity of introducing an efficient and effective inventory management system in government departments. He has discussed several inventory management and control techniques, which may be applied in government departments. By using these techniques and managerial approaches, government departments would be able to perform their works/services in an efficient and economic manner, and thus unnecessary blocking of funds in inventories can be avoided.

Then follows Hans C. Blaise's paper, in which he has examined the need of developing management competence and sharpening the public administration professionals for development in developing countries. He has discussed several issues, e.g., contribution of management specialists, attention on programme management, integrating generalist rather than gentleman generalist, professional education and practices, sophisticated management technologies that are required for a nation's development.

The paper by R.H. Joshi is related to augmenting managerial effectiveness through the adoption of attitudinal model. In this paper, he discusses several attitudinal inputs which, if applied or taught in training programmes, are likely to enhance managerial effectiveness. The adoption of the model for regular and consistent practice will certainly contribute in strengthening leadership qualities to a great extent which in turn would result in developing managerial effectiveness.

The last paper in this section is on Improving Individual Effectiveness in Government in which N. Vittal briefly describes three main factors that kill an individual's initiative to contribute to governmental effectiveness. These factors are: perception of rules and regulations, departmental culture which makes an individual not to look at the issues in a wider perspective but from the limited tunnel vision of the department, and jealousy on the part of the peer group and sometimes even superiors against an individual government servant who turns out to be outstanding. All these observations if properly understood in true and positive sense will help in increasing governmental effectiveness and will also help to come out of this 'Indian crab' situation.

Organisational Behaviour

Organisation and management are facing challenges emanating from global competitiveness, the information age, automated decision-making, information superhighway, quality service revolution, diversity and ethics. Human behaviour cannot remain untouched by these changes. Human behaviour at work is much more complicated and diverse than is suggested by the economic-security working condition approach. The new perspective assumes that employees are extremely complex and that there is a need to understand these complexities for managing people effectively. Each organisation is facing human-oriented problems. The traditional resource based organisation of the past is rapidly giving way to the emerging knowledge-based organisation. Thus, it becomes essential to understand organisational behaviour issues for better and effective management of organisation. The only suitable competitive advantage in today's environment is provided by the people. How to effectively manage human resources has become the key challenge not only to compete but also to survive. Managers must understand and be able to apply innovative techniques to better manage their human resources. This is why the study and application or organisational behaviour becomes so important in the years ahead.

Organisational behaviour (OB) is concerned with the study of what people do in an organisation and how that behaviour affects the performance of the organisation. Thus, it involves the study and application of the human side of management and organisations. OB is understanding, prediction, and management of human behaviour in an organisation. It deals with human dimensions of management. Current environmental challenges and the paradigm shift facing management lead to the need to study organisation behaviour.

The second section of the present volume gives the perspective, background, methodology and approach to this field. This section contains eight papers.

It begins with a paper by M.L. Mehta, a former chief secretary of Rajasthan. In his essay, Mehta has highlighted basic concepts and approaches to motivation. Motivation is the key to better man-management and, therefore, to better performance. That is why all executives are concerned with motivating their personnel to perform better. Every executive must develop and strengthen his motivational strength with his subordinates as that is the key to his success. Motivation is the magic touch for good performance and maximising human resource potential. Mehta has discussed three approaches, viz., carrot and stick approach, scientific management approach, and human relations approach, and seven theories related to the approaches.

Jagdish C. Kukar, in his paper on "Work Motivation", has also focused upon the various approaches to motivation and different types of motives that motivate people. He observes that motivation is the basic task of leadership and that managers as leaders have an important role to play in creating a motivating and supportive environment in their organisations.

"The Styles of Leadership" is the title of next essay written by G.P. Pilania, a former eminent police officer who has now taken to politics. The author is of the view that leader needs to focus on the needs of the organisation and not on the needs of the individual. Leadership is the process of influencing the activities of an individual or a group in efforts towards goal-achievement in a given situation. He has discussed various leadership studies and has suggested a typology of leadership styles that stands out from these studies. Finally, he concludes that there is no 'the best' style of leadership for all purposes which is universally successful but it would vary from situation to situation.

Asha Hingar has discussed theories of leadership providing a broad conceptual overview. She recommends that an administrator should attempt to adopt a style that is compatible with the needs and expectations of the subordinates and is appropriate in the given situation, but one should also recognise that this style might vary from group to group, or even from individual to individual, and from situation to situation.

In the next paper Rakesh Hooja sets forth a set of eleven questions which he feels are relevant while discussing leadership in its administrative context. This is followed by a discussion of leadership traits, leadership skills and leadership styles, many of which have been listed by Hooja while identifying the attributes of a good or successful leader.

Kamlesh Gupta's paper follows in which he has examined some aspects of decision process in administration. He explains five general steps inherent in the process of rational decision-making.

In the next article, Anita has looked at key result areas for trainers, for training institutions, and for training interventions and come up with ideas about training for organisational development through self-development.

The last paper in this section is by H.C. Suman on the anatomy of conflict and its management. The author is of the view that the conflict is a situation in which the interests of groups or individuals are perceived to be incongruous or in which there is a lack of adjustment between the individuals or groups and the job requirements or the circumstances in which it is performed. He has discussed consequences of conflicts, issues and sources of conflicts and finally the process of conflict resolution. He further observes that successful conflict resolution requires time, thought, patience and courage of conviction.

Human Resource Development

Human resource management involves all management decisions and practices that directly affect or influence the people or human resources who work for the organisation. Training function of human resource management is popularly known as human resource development. Human resource development (HRD) function is very much important in organisation. It helps organisation in maintaining competitiveness and preparing for the future. HRD is a philosophy that values human beings and promotes their development.

The third section of the present volume, which is on human resource development, includes a total of six essays.

This section commences with a paper by Udai Pareek, an eminent HRD expert and former professor at IIMA, who has written a lot on various aspects of human resource development. In this paper, he has demystified the subject of human resource development. He has discussed six units of human resources, viz., persons, job or roles, dyads, teams, inter-teams and the organisation, and has then dealt with concepts of the development of these units. He stresses on the development of these six foci or targets of HRD along with HRD systems and activities. He has also suggested six HRD systems, viz., appraisal systems, career systems, training system, work systems, cultural systems, and self-renewal systems which are important parts of development of HRD in an organisation. He suggests that HRD-related research is important for HRD effectiveness. It helps in analysing data and information generated by the HRD sub-systems.

In the next article, Asha Hingar and Sangeeta Sharma have discussed three approaches, viz., structural approach, organisational climate approach and the training approach, to human resource development.

"HRD Climate in Public Enterprises: A Case Study" is the title of next paper contributed by C.M. Mahajan. The author is of the view that there is a need to institutionalise the system of HRD in all public enterprises in order to improve their working as well as make them operationally more productive. A positive, forward looking HRD policy is important for the efficiency and effectiveness of public sector employees.

R.P. Jaiswal discuses job selection, job satisfaction and career commitment on the basis of a research study of male and female scientists and engineers. He has analysed reasons for job selection, motivating factors for job selection, job satisfaction, and career commitment issues. Apart from other reasons, facilities related to salary, promotion, transfer, placement, interpersonal relationship with seniors and subordinates contribute to a large extent in making a person committed to his work.

Meena Sogani and Sangeeta Sharma in the next article discuss the role of academic institutions in human resource development. Human resources play a distinct role in the process of conversion of inputs into outputs. Values and excellence are required in human beings for balanced growth. A planned intervention through academic institutions acts as motivators of each individual's growth. They have recommended the formulation of an integrated educational policy in terms of re-analysis of contents of syllabi, revision of texts based on goal-orientation, and developing infrastructure supported by appropriate audio-visual aids.

The last article in this volume is contributed by J.P. Singh on "Human Resource Development (HRD) Organisation Development (OD) Interface". In his paper, he has discussed the concept of HRD and OD and made a comparison of HRD and OD through the Input-Throughput-Output Model. Apart from comparison of these two concepts, he discusses certain commonalities between OD and HRD. He is of the view that both (OD and HRD) focus on behaviour of the people in an organisation rely on the behavioural science knowledge about people, make an assumption that people like to change, and aim at bringing about behavioural change in the organisation

The papers presented in this volume were written at different points of time as they reflect the development of various concepts and themes which have been taking place in the area of managing change, organisational behaviour and human resource development. Hopefully, our enlightened readers will be able to better appreciate the dynamics of organisation behaviour and its juxtaposition with human resources and other forces that propel and guide change through the articles collected in this book.

Select References

Anita, (ed.) *Readings in Organizational Behaviour*, Jaipur: HCM RIPA (1990).

Argyris, Chris, *Management and Organizational Development*, New York: McGraw-Hill Book Company (1971).

Bennis, Warren G., *Organizational Development: Its Nature, Origin and Prospects*, Mass: Addison-Wesley Publishing Company, Reading (1969).

Caplow, Theodore, *Managing an Organization*, New York: Holt, Rinehart and Winston (1983).

Drucker, Peter F., *Managing for Results*, London: Harper & Row (1964).

——, *The Effective Executive*, New York: Harper & Row (1967).

——, *Managing in Turbulent Times*, London: Heinemann (1980).

Harvey–Jones, John, *Making it Happen*, Glasgow: William Collins (1988).

Hooja, Rakesh and Ramesh K. Arora (eds.), *Administrative Theories: Approaches, Concepts and Thinkers in Public Administration,* Jaipur: Rawat Publications. (2007).

Lewis, Pamela S., Goodman, Stephen H., and Fandt, Patricia M., *Management: Challenges in the 21st Century*, Ohio: South-Western College Publishing (1998).

Mehta, M.L., Kukkar, Jagdish C. and Hooja, Meenakshi, *Motivation* (Training Reprint 3/2005), Jaipur: HCM RIPA (2005).

Part I

Managing Change in Government

1

Reengineering Public Administration

K.B.C. SAXENA

The last two decades or so have witnessed a remarkable change in the structure and culture of government and public service organisations in the industrialised countries. There is an increasing demand by citizens for social action and public services that have to be funded and monitored by government, coupled with their unwillingness to pay more taxes. Further, the need for government regulation of economic and social development and the growing complexity of the society is confronting public administration with a great deal of complex problems and tasks, such as improved health care for the aged and housing for the lower income groups, etc. Solving these problems need more resources, which the public sector has to provide only through "working better and costing less".

As for developing countries, many of them such as India have made economic management their prime agenda. They are going through a process of restructuring their economy to emphasise competition, integration with global markets and an increasing level of privatisation. Such restructuring has also brought out the need to review the role of government in economic activities. Increasingly, the role of government is moving away from producing goods and services through public enterprises, to that of creating an enabling economic environment through policy changes and more effective policy implementation. To realise this goal, there is a strong need for the public administration in these countries to be efficient and cost-effective.

Unfortunately, the public administration in developing countries is, in general, highly bureaucratised and extremely centralised, based on an authoritarian legal system (Avegerou, 1990). It has been shaped under conditions of domination from outside centres (under colonial regimes or under the influence of 'protecting' superpowers), and has been assigned a significant and highly political role of planning and implementing the development process. Many developing countries are, in general, characterised by a combination of factors such as population growth, weak infrastructure, foreign indebtedness, asymmetric world relations and increasing inequalities between individuals, groups and regions, which hamper their socio-economic development. Therefore, efficiency and cost-effectiveness of public administration is of utmost importance in order to effectively manage the development process.

Thus, public administration in both industrialised as well developing countries is increasingly entrusted with the responsibility of high performance level as well as cost-effectiveness. At the core of this dilemma is the increasingly felt need for a *radical transformation* of public administration than in the earlier periods. Whereas the concepts of unity, cooperation, coordination and increased size have guided the attempts to change the public sector in the 1960s to 1980s, the present themes guiding public sector change are of decentralisation, desegregation, competition and markets, efficiency strategies, reduction in size of units, emphasis on 'proper' management practices, customer orientation and performance measurements. *Reengineering* is an approach to facilitate such a transformation, and such efforts are already in progress in many industrialised, newly industrialised and less-developed countries such as Australia (Parker, 1994), the Netherlands (Snellen, 1994), UK (CCTA, 1994), USA (Carr and Littman, 1990; Gulledge et al., 1994; Katz, 1994; Osborne and Gaebler, 1993) Singapore (Neo, 1994) and Slovenia (Bavec, 1992).

Business Process Reengineering

Engineering may be defined as the systematic design and building of a 'process' or 'artifact' from a concept that has been converted into an implementable specification with the application of science and mathematics. *Reengineering* thus involves taking an already existing process or artifact and improving it in its critical, contemporary measures of performance, such as cost, quality, service and speed.

Business process reengineering (BPR) refers to an integrated programme and perspective on organisational change focusing on *business processes* rather than *business functions,* in order to significantly improve their performance. In this context, a business process refers to a set of inter-related work activities and value-added tasks that convert business inputs into business outputs. A process corresponds to a natural business activity and often cuts across traditional functional structure of organisations. Examples of such processes could be product development, service delivery, or order fulfilment.

The traditional functional (hierarchical) view of organisations optimises individual business functions (such as finance, production, marketing, etc.) sometimes at the expense of the entire business. The narrow scope of a function attacks symptoms (of a problem) in one function but misses the causes rooted in another. It can also fail to prioritise problems which although small for any individual function, might be large in aggregate. As a result, operational improvements occur piecemeal and independently of one another. Consequently, their impact is substantially lower than is often required.

BPR has been perceived as a business process focussed initiative involving simultaneous change to organisational design, culture and information technology (IT), to enable radical performance improvements. BPR is not merely downsizing, restructuring, computerisation, continuous improvement, although all these can be parts of BPR. Benefits from a BPR exercise can be expected to include (Saxena, 1998):

- clearer focus on the customer's needs,
- reduced cost of operations,
- improved quality of service,

- reduced delivery/response times, and
- improved responsiveness to customer demands.

In summary, the major benefits to an organisation of undertaking BPR can be:

- a radical improvement in current process performance,
- better alignment of business process with strategic objectives and key performance indicators,
- focus on outputs that the customer wants rather than inputs to the organisation, and
- Increased job satisfaction leading to better individual performance.

Thus, BPR aims to refit or revamp an organisation to survive today's economic downturn and to emerge, refreshed and revitalised, to meet its social obligations and accept its economic challenges into the next century. It provides a way to enhance the efficiency as well as effectiveness while resources are declining.

Public Administration Reengineering

BPR is common in the private sector, and the public sector cannot insulate itself from new management cultures that evolve from innovative practices. However, because of the differences in the nature of private and public sectors, the BPR concepts as applied in the private sector may need some modifications before they could be applied in the public sector. We would refer to the application of these modified reengineering concepts to public administration as "public administration reengineering" (PAR).

PAR involves a total replanning and concurrent redesign and implementation of administrative processes, organisational structure and the supporting information system in direct or indirect response to external forces in order to achieve some objective (such as cost-effectiveness, time service quality or customer satisfaction), which are usually not easy to achieve given the current conditions of the public organisations (Saxena, 1996).

PAR is particularly relevant in those areas which involve extensive contact with the public, with record keeping and/or claims processing following customer contact or involving financial transactions. This is because the statutory basis, authorisation or rationale of many of these services will often specify the outcome sought, but allows the organisation concerned considerable freedom to determine how the service outcome is to be achieved. These are areas where the basic business transactions are similar, so giving scope for a repeatable process. The work is usually of a relatively routine nature and the amount of discretion to take decisions can justifiably be limited.

However, reengineering public administration requires innovative management and a willingness to change. Unfortunately, the nature of public administration itself is so different from business administration that it may inhibit the reengineering effort. For example, consider the following characteristics of public administration (Morgan et al., 1994; Osborne and Gabler, 1993):

- Public administration is more resistant to change, being highly bureaucratic in terms of an over-commitment to regulation and enforcement of precedent and rules.
- Public administration institutions are typically paid out of an allocated budget, which is not based on their results and performance. Thus, there is apparently no pressure on them to perform better.
- Public administrators' and managers' pay has traditionally not been related to performance. Promotion, rewards and recognition systems in public administration are, by and large, based on seniority classification systems for positions rather than any pure merit-based classification. This may demotivate those managers who are willing to be champions for reengineering projects.
- Public administrators and managers are not free to enact management in the way managers in a business are. This is often due to political control, as politicians do not necessarily restrict themselves to policy making: they often wish to involve themselves in the execution of policy.

Principles of Public Administration Reengineering

PAR is not an easy concept to apply due to the absence of forces which promote mechanisms for change in the private sector environment. However, whatever the scale, there will be a set of common principles in a PAR exercise, which are listed below:

Create Customer Focus

A common assumption in reengineering is that every organisation has customers and if their needs are not met, they may be able to go elsewhere, or create pressure for change. However, in public administration, customer is a more problematic concept. The benevolent paternalism of traditional government bureaucratic provision has not sought the voice of the 'customer' in the past. Given that the public sector provisions were supplying monopoly or near monopoly services, there was in fact no incentive to do so because no challenge of having to retain or attract customers existed. However, in the last decade, government provisions in countries such as UK and USA have seen the effects of two forces. On one hand, there has been the growth of *consumerism,* and the fact that people accustomed to the modern 'supermarket' range also want more choice and better service in government provisions, politicians have been swift to respond to this. On the other hand, there has been the reshaping of government provisions, organisationally, to give greater financial accountability and measures of performance. Even, in India, the recent court judgments related to services provided by Indian railways and health care agencies show that public service agencies are increasingly deemed accountable for the quality of their 'services'. Thus, the customer might have been a problematic concept in public administration of the past, we see this as being less and less the case as we move into the future. Once the customer is identified, there will be a need to focus on what is of most importance to the customer and necessary to the running of the organisation, including public accountability requirements.

Rethink Functions and Processes

Traditionally, all public organisations are structured as a hierarchical bureaucracy. Therefore, the move from a functional to a process-oriented organisation needs to be planned and managed. This will be based on the value-adding service activities provided for the customer rather than for the top bureaucrats of the functional departments.

Challenge Organisational Principles

Assess reasons for, and ask what is the cost and value of activities.

Simplify and Discard Activities

Keep only those processes which add value and those which are absolutely necessary.

Measure the Organisational Performance

The most common basis for defining performance of a public administration process is the concept of 'value for money'. Value for money is most easily defined as the economic acquisition of resources and their efficient utilisation in the realisation of the purposes of the organisation—with the simultaneous achievement of economy, efficiency and effectiveness. Here, *economy is* defined as the resources used at the lowest possible cost; *efficiency* as the ratio of actual input to actual output; and *effectiveness* as the extent to which the impacts of a policy or programme meet its objectives. These three concepts are essentially interdependent and the relationship between them is shown as follows:

Performance indicators have two main roles. First, they can provide managers and administrators with information necessary to make decisions which reflect economy, efficiency and effectiveness, thereby assisting them in judging how far their objectives have been achieved. Their second role is to provide those outside the organisation, including the auditors, with a basis for judging performance and establishing accountability.

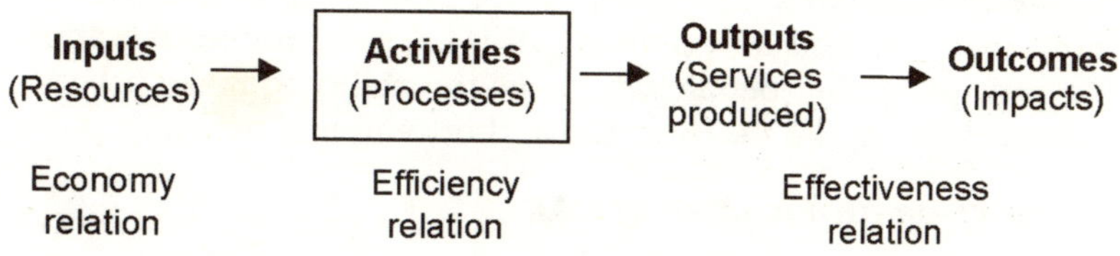

Unfortunately, when public organisations set out to measure performance, their managers usually measure their volume of outputs such as how well they carry out some administrative processes, how many people they serve, how fast they serve them, etc., (Osborne and Gaebler, 1993). But, outputs do not guarantee outcomes. For instance, a primary school might pump out more and more successful students. But if these students are not able to achieve the minimum levels of learning (MLL), what good is the education imparted by the school?

Output measures can also be useful as they help the organisation get a handle on how they can improve their management. In addition, the outcomes desired by any organisation are often very difficult to measure or will not become evident for a long time. In such cases, organisations often output choose measures that appear to be reliable proxies for the ultimate outcome. The problem comes when organisations measure only outputs and none of the outcomes—as too many do.

Therefore, compare the outcome as well as the output of a process to determine actual achievement against the target set. Also benchmark performance, i.e., compare the process performance with the achievements of others.

Set Audacious Objectives

Set performance targets out of reach but not of sight, such as cutting of overhead costs by 50 per cent within 12 months. Ideally, these targets should not be achievable by current improvement approaches alone, thus forcing more innovative thinking.

Empower People

Empowerment refers to the ability of an individual or a team to work in their own way within agreed time-lines and with agreed resources to achieve a goal set by the leadership of the organisation (Morgan and Murgatroyd, 1994). The philosophy behind this principle is that people who have the ability to make process improvement should be given the authority to make them.

Utilise IT as an Enabler of PAR

Public administration in most countries shares a belief that the advances in IT represent a major opportunity to accelerate development and a crucial component of their ability to compete. Therefore, there is hardly any need to demonstrate here the importance of IT in public administration. Public administration and services are highly *information intensive* and therefore IT could play a crucial role in improving cost-effectiveness. Unfortunately, IT use in public administration typically lags behind business application. For instance, the tightening of the national budget and an accelerated pace of policy changes would increase the demand for policy analysis, transparence, expenditure control, and programme monitoring and evaluation (Bavec, 1992). This would also heighten the need to reduce transaction costs between the public and private sectors and to modernise major public transaction processing systems such as customs, tax administration, land records administration and state treasury administration. IT use in these areas would provide substantial downstream effects and clearly increase the effectiveness of government operations.

IT system can be a powerful agent both for and against change. They have the potential to simplify a process, automate the mundane, and to give rapid access to relevant information. Requirements change, however, and those same systems which had previously been beneficial may no longer meet customer's needs. A PAR exercise will highlight activities that support the customer's requirement and those that the organisation itself requires to manage its operations.

No technology stands out as essential in PAR, the use and type of technology is dependent on the requirements of the future process-oriented public administration. However, given the frequent need to improve timeliness and reduce the time taken to carry out a task, telecommunication networks, including computer-to-computer links such as Electronic Data Interchange (EDI), are often essential in achieving a major improvement. Organisational databases, groupware allowing simultaneous access to a piece of work, cross-functional information systems, etc., will also have a part to play when designing new system to support a process-oriented administration.

PAR does not necessarily require 'leading edge' IT systems to be useful. The administration will require cost-effective and rapid access to accurate and relevant information in two areas: those that add value to the process of fulfilling the customer requirement and those that provide support to the business to enable it to function. IT of particular value is that which can support network relationship, that is, communicating across organisational boundaries with customers, suppliers and business partners.

Applying Public Administration Reengineering

PAR is most effective when integrated into a radical reappraisal of administrative activities. This begins with revisiting the objective of the public organisation and asking the following questions:

- If starting again, what would we do differently?
- How and why do we add more or less value than our competitors (if any)? Or, if no competitors, do we add sufficient 'value' for the money spent for it?
- What is the current assessment of customer requirements and the trade-offs they make between service, functionality, quality and cost?

Having obtained the answers to above questions, the reengineering of administrative processes is carried out by:

- Eliminating unnecessary tasks or processes and reducing any delays introduced by multiple authorisations, inspections and hand offs between departments;
- Automating workflow to minimise delays between processing stages; and
- Reducing the amount of paper handling by promoting the use of electronic communications both internally and with customers and suppliers.

Finally, management approaches need to be reconsidered in the light of the proposed changes:

- Increasing staffing flexibility by creating a multi-skilled workforce.
- Reducing duplication of effort and investment by forming stronger partnerships with customers and suppliers, sharing key information and undertaking joint development.
- Devolving more responsibility and authority.
- Outsourcing essential tasks which add no value but divert time and resources.

Examples of PAR Applications

Public administration interchanges a majority of data internally between ministries, government agencies and the public sector, but data interchange with the private sector is still minor. Also, public administration makes extensive use of official statistics for supporting its decisions.

Therefore, most of the existing use of PAR is mainly in automatic compilation of statistics, automatic transaction processing or automatic case management. Some of these examples are summarised below to give an idea of the need and benefits of PAR, both in industrialised as well as developing countries.

- *Improvement of Statistical Compilation Process through Automated Statistical Compilation within the European Union.* With the emergence of European Union, there is an increasing demand for reliable statistical information to support decision-making on social, financial and economic issues. Thus, the national and regional statistics organisations (such as Eurostat) are under pressure to enhance the efficiency of the process of collecting and disseminating statistics between economic agencies, regional and national administrations, European institutions and end users. On the other hand, the various economic agencies are becoming increasingly reluctant to complete specific statistical questionnaires in an age when all their other productive, operational or administrative activities are highly automated. Obviously, the data required for statistical purposes can derived from or communicated by the inter-organisational transactions in the electronic form (such as EDI messages) if the statistical needs are taken into account in the various commercial sectors where EDI technology is operational and related messages are being designed. A number of such projects are either in operation or being planned within the EU to explore this aspect further.
- *Improvement of Case Management Process by Automated Decision-Making in the Dutch Government.* Most ministries of the Dutch government have improved the handling of relevant cases pertaining to residents/citizens through automated decision-making (Snellen, 1994). The extent to which the decision-making is automated depends on the type of IT system used by a ministry. For example, the following ministries use automated systems for the production of the text of a decision:

Ministry	*Application*
Foreign Affairs	Decisions on personnel affairs
Economic Affairs	Decisions related to grants and subsidies
Justice	Decisions on minor traffic offenses
Social Security and Employment	Decisions of personnel affairs
Traffic and Water Authority	Generation of car licenses

The following ministries use automated system for the assessment of the data on the basis of the criteria of the applicable regulation. These systems at least partly take over the process of legal reasoning in automatically assessing the factual data.

Ministry	*Application*
Housing, Physical Planning and Environment	Requests for rent allowances
Traffic and Water Authority	Permits for houseboats, accreditation for garages as official car inspections
Education and Science	Requests for study grants for minor and part-time students
Finance	Establishing fiscal obligations as to income tax and value added tax
Welfare, Health and Culture	Contributions of parents whose children are raised outside the home
Social Security and Employment	Assessment of requests for overtime work
	Finally, the following ministries use some information systems which assemble at least part of the necessary data in an automated way
Finance	Import declaration
Defence	Draft
Welfare, Health and Culture	Determination and publication of prices of medicines

- Thus, the improvement in terms of case management processes is of varying degrees. The earlier systems automated the administrative processing of cases. Later on, systems were developed which assessed cases without interference from officials (e.g., rent allowance) or which selected cases on the basis of their complexity and directed them to specialised officials (e.g., taxes). At the highest level were expert systems in which expert knowledge was codified to take over the decision-making from specialists in a certain area.

- *Reengineering of Singapore's Trade Clearance Process.* Singapore has the strategy of acting as an international trading hub. International trade is characterised not only by the physical movement of goods across national boundaries, but also by the unwieldy, voluminous, and costly paper work that accompanies it, containing data that facilitate the physical good movement, show ownership and meet governmental requirements. The Singapore government requires that trade documents be prepared and submitted to a number of government agencies for clearance before goods may be imported or exported. There are 20 government agencies requiring documentation for specific categories of goods, although up to three agencies' approval is the norm for any one commodity. The documents are in paper form and are often hand-delivered to, and collected from, the agencies in many geographically dispersed locations. Moreover, even though much of the information contained in these documents is common, each agency has its own format: with the consequence of entering the same information several times on different forms by the trader. As the average number of trade documents is about 10,000 per day, the whole process is complex, time-consuming and may be even irritating both for the trader as well as the government. To overcome this problem, the Trade Development Board (TDB), which is the government agency for promoting international trade, reengineered its trade clearance with the help of Trade Net, an EDI system that allows traders to send trade documents *electronically* to TDB as well as other government agencies simultaneously (Neo, 1994). With the reengineered process, trade permits are now approved in 15 minutes rather than two days. Similarly, trade statistics are now available in two weeks (down from four weeks) for internal management reviews and four weeks (down from six weeks) for public release. Also, the number of staff in TDB's documentation department dropped from 134 in 1988 to 88 in 1992, though all this staff was redeployed for other work. This reengineering of the trade clearance process became possible as TDB extended its own vision of not merely acting its traditional role of trade controller but also of trade facilitator.

- *Reengineering of Customs Administration Process in the European Union.* Customs administration in most countries used to be a heavy-handed instrument of government, very often militarily organised, to safeguard borders in order to make it difficult to import goods, and used mainly as a tool to fuel the government's budget. This strategy has now changed, in general, in the modern customs administrations in the countries when they changed to a free-market economy in European Union as well as in countries of Eastern Europe and former Soviet Union (who are now moving from a state-controlled economy into a free-market economy). Now, they are talking of a customs service as an instrument to develop the economy (for example, still levying a certain amount of duties to safeguard virgin firms or industries, or industries having higher labour costs than others), to safeguard the people, for instance, concerning health, weapons, drugs, and also to safeguard animal species, environment, etc.). With this change in the strategic role of customs departments, the customs administration process has changed too. In the past, every shipment to be imported had to be inspected in order to control the correct application of duties, which were different for the different kinds of merchandise, and to combat smuggling of unwanted items. Nowadays, this old process has been reengineered into a more efficient process in most industrialised countries, because otherwise importations and therefore the international trade would come to a standstill (because of its immense growth during the last few decades).
- In the new customs administration process in European Union, instead of stopping a shipment for controls at the point of entry, viz., border, airport or seaport, customs

depends on its clients' own declaration of goods required by international legislation for other purposes. The merchandise passes the border with a very simple formality done in seconds, only meant to check that the shipment is later really declared to customs. When the merchandise arrives at the factory or any other importers' premises within the country, customs is informed. If it does not want to inspect it, this is considered to be imported. The items then will have to be entered into the books of the firm and declared periodically to customs, who will audit the books from time to time to find out if everything has been done correctly. Another change made in the new process is the method of differed payment, in which the importer may take the merchandise away without paying the customs duty and sell it, and pay the duty later. This change is very important for those countries where credits are very expensive because the importer can pay the duty out of the payments received from the buyers. These changes in the new process are based upon new legislation and do not need use of information technology (IT).

With the use IT, the customs administration process could be made even more effective. For example, IT-based systems are being used by the UK Customs Directorate for automatic compilation of trade statistics and generating single European market declarations. Use of EDI in these systems enables the establishment of an *integrated customs clearance system* with the following operational scenario. Customs wants to be in the possession of consignment data prior to the arrival of the actual goods. This is achieved by a pre-arrival cargo reporting facilitated by the EDI system. With a pre-arrival lodgement of the goods declaration, the customs procedure of clearance could start well in advance. Customs can then screen these data carefully against its own selection criteria within the automatic selectivity programme. Customs may then decide as to whether the cargo should be subjected to full examination, partial examination, or no examination upon arrival at its port of destination with a pre-arrival notification of customs status.

Critical Success Factors for PAR

A critical success factor (CSF) is an element that makes a vital contribution to the success of a project, if missing, it is likely to lead to the failure of the project. Ensuring that the critical success factors are all addressed might be considered an organisational prerequisite for a PAR exercise. The CSFs for a PAR exercise are:

- The desire to change the status quo—a willingness to rethink all aspects of the administration process;
- Sustained drive, commitment, patience and active involvement at the highest level;
- Clear and consistent strategic focus and long-term vision shared across the organisation;
- Demanding goals—out of reach but not out of sight;
- Good planning and management;
- Participation with all those who have a stake in the successful outcome of the exercise;
- Effective communication throughout the PAR project;
- Continuous measurement of performance against targets.

Conclusion

This paper has extended the reengineering concept to public organisations as public administration reengineering (PAR), which is an approach to bringing about radical change. It provides public organisations with a means of delivering major improvements identified in their goals and objectives. We believe that PAR is certainly within reach for many developing countries, in particular India, if the public administration in the country can be properly motivated (or enlightened!). It is hoped that the paper will stimulate thinking in this direction among the public administrators and will enable them to reap the benefits of PAR.

References

Avegerou, C. (1990) "Computer-based Information Systems and Modernization of Public Administration in Developing Countries", in *Information Technology in Developing Countries,* by S.C. Bhatnagar, and N. Bjorn-Andersen, (eds.), Elsevier Science, pp. 243–50.

Bavec, C. (1992) "EDI Strategy in the Public Administration in Slovenia". Proc. Fifty International EDI Conference, Bled, Slovenia, September, pp. 179–86.

CCTA, (1994) *BPR in the Public Sector: An Overview of Business Process Reengineering,* Her Majesty Stationery Office, London.

Carr, D.K. and Littman, I.D. (1990) *Excellence in Government: Total Quality Management in the 1990s,* Coopers & Lybrand.

Gulledge, T.R., Sibley, E.H., Hill, D.H. and Sullivan, L.M. (1994) "Functional Process Improvement Implementation: Public Sector Reengineering", Proc. 13th IFIP World Computer Conference 94, Vol. 2, Elsevier Science, pp. 475–80.

Katz, R.H. (1994) "Reengineering Government Through Information Technology: The Performance Review", Proc. 13th IFIP World Computer Conference 94, Vol. 2, Elsevier Science, pp. 373–79.

Morgan, C. and Murgatroyd, S. (1994) *Total Quality Management in the Public Sector,* Open University Press.

Neo, B.S. (1994) "IT-Enabled Business Reengineering: A Study of Singapore's Trade Clearance Process", in *Business Process Re-engineering: Information Systems Opportunities and Challenges,* by Glasson, B.C. et al., (eds.) North-Holland, pp. 422–33.

Osborne, D. and Gaebler, T. (1993), *Reinventing Government: How the Entrepreneurial Spirit is Transforming the Public Sector,* Penguin Books.

Parker, B. (1994) "Business Reengineering and Management Alignment: A Re-engineering and Management Alignment: A Review of Structural Reengineering in the Public Sector and the Problem of Management Alignment with Enterprise Objectives", in *Business Process Reengineering: Information Systems Opportunities and Challenges,* by Glasson, B.C. et al. (eds.), North-Holland, pp. 459–68.

Saxena, K.B.C. (1998) "Gaining Competitive Edge through Strategy-driven Business Process Reengineering", *Management Review* (March).

Saxena, K.B.C. (1996) "Reengineering Public Administration in Developing Countries", *Long Range Planning,* Vol. 29 No. 5, pp. 703–11.

Snellen, I.Th.M. (1994) "Automation Policy Implementation: Reengineering from within Public Administration" in *Business Process Reengineering: Information Systems Opportunities and Challenges,* by Glasson, B.C. et al., (eds.) North-Holland, pp. 545–56.

2

Creativity

PRADIP N. KHANDWALLA

There are many definitions of creativity, each emphasising a different facet of creativity. Those who emphasise outputs of creative effort, describe creativity as the discovery of something that is novel, but also useful or relevant or economical or elegant or valuable. Thus, a ballpoint pen that lasts forever, or at least much longer than current options, would be classified as an act of creativity. A novel hypothesis that explains, say gravity, would be a creative act. A poem that successfully combines both naturalism and surrealism, may also be considered as an act of creation. The merely trivial is not creative, nor the merely novel. The product or outcome of a creative effort must be both significant and strikingly different from the beaten track.

Some others have stressed the creative process. In this view, creativity is divergent thinking, the seeking of relationships between previously unrelated concepts or frames of reference, of exploring the under-known. The outcome of this effort may or may not be creative, but the effort reveals the characteristics of the creative process: wide search or exploration, leaps of imagination, incubation, sometimes strikingly fresh insights. Therefore, we say that the sciences and the arts are generally more creative pursuits than factory work or vocational training; or that research and development is a more creative activity than accounting and control. That is, problem solving in the sciences, the arts or R and D generally exhibits greater divergent thinking than problem solving relating to factory work, vocational training or accounting and control. (This does not, of course, mean that one cannot be creative in factory work or in accounting; only that, because of the routinised nature of the work, the individual is not required to be imaginative).

Still others identify creativity with certain states of being. For example, Abraham Maslow, the high priest of humanist psychology, has identified creativity with openness in expressing feelings, receptivity to ideas, concern for other's desire to grow as a person and actualise one's potential and so forth. Other psychologists have compared creative and non-creative persons from the same profession. They have identified a number of additional personality traits and abilities that distinguish the creative from the non-creative persons, like the greater love of complexity of the creative; their more bizarre fantasy life, but simultaneously, a high degree of practicality; their greater independence of judgement. The ability to come up with many, varied and uncommon ideas or solutions also seems to distinguish the creative from non-creative persons.

Each one of these views of creativity is flawed. If one judges creativity only in terms of the novelty and usefulness or elegance of a product, one may sometimes find that this creative product may have been discovered or produced, either accidentally or by a non-creative process. Today, innovations are increasingly institutionalised. For example, many researchers discover something or the other, simply by taking a problem area and by applying to it the scientific method. Indeed, Maslow has contemptuously disposed off universities and scientific establishments as havens of the mediocre. If one judges creativity by the creative process instead of the creative product, tile dreamer would be the champion creative, for the extent of imagination and divergent thinking, combinatorial play, the relating of remote ideas and so forth that characterise the creative process, are at their flood tide during dreaming. If creativity is to be judged, in terms of the characteristics of the creative person, such as lack of inhibitions, receptivity, curiosity, idea flow, etc., the child would outrank the Einsteins, Tagores, and Picassos of the world.

I suspect creativity has to do with the employment of a playful and exploratory, rather than a mechanical process of problem solving, by a person who is open, curious and imaginative, rather than by a person who is inhibited and conventional, to find solutions or designs that are novel (and yet useful) rather than merely run-of-the-mill.

Let us explore briefly creativity as a mental ability and distinguish it from another famous mental ability, namely, intelligence, as it is measured in contemporary IQ tests. The best way to appreciate the difference between creativity and intelligence is to do a test of each. Given ahead is a 5-minute "test", that will give you a feel for the difference between intelligence and creativity, as they are measured nowadays.

Test

1. Find the word that does not fit with the rest
   MBAOBY DNOONL COWSOM ATR
2. Guess the word given the following four clues
   Law Chair Bangle Sword
3. Write the 3-letter word that means the same as the words outside the brackets:
   PROHIBIT (...) DRINKING PLACE
4. Complete the following sentence humorously:
   One moonlit night, while strolling in a garden ...
5. Find the missing number:

2	9	0	8
4	10	5	4
3	5	2	2
3	14	3	–

6. Give striking alternative titles to World War II.

Creativity Versus Intelligence

Notice that possible solutions are much fewer in the three IQ items. 1, 3 and 5; to solve them mostly logic and vocabulary rather than imagination are required; and that solutions once found, fit the problems rather snugly. In the creativity items, a number of other mental capabilities get exercised, such as associative thinking as in item 2, wide search as in item 4, and an enormous degree of compression of thought required in item 6 that must, however, be expressed aesthetically. Also there is no certainty at all that the solutions are the best possible or even good. As is obvious, the degree of convergent thinking needed is much higher for the IQ problems than for the creativity problems, while the degree of divergent thinking needed is much higher for tackling creativity as compared to IQ problems They represent quite distinctive sets of abilities, and indeed research suggests that those who are high IQ scorers are not necessarily creative and vice versa. The ranks of the uncreative and the stupid are alarmingly large, and rare indeed are humans that are both creative and intelligent. No more than one in ten thousand may be exceptionally creative and intelligent.

Creativity Abilities

Creativity is not one ability at all, but a whole cluster of abilities. These are described as follows:

The first is called ideational fluency. It measures a person's ability to come up with a number of solutions to a given problem. For example, if I ask a group of persons to list the number of uses of bricks, some might come up with five uses, others with 15 or 20. Those that come up with a large number of uses, would be called ideationally fluent persons. Ideationally fluent persons tend to come up with a greater variety of solutions, as well as with a larger number of unusual solutions, than persons that are ideationally not fluent.

The ability to provide a large variety of solutions, to respond to a problem from a variety of viewpoints, and to use a variety of approaches in problem solving is another important ability. It is called flexibility. In the brick example, one person may have listed several uses of bricks, but all of these uses may be connected with its use as a construction material—build houses, build bridges, build wells, build walls, etc. Another person may list a large variety of uses, such as bricks as weapons, as stepping stones in mud, as doorsteps, as engraving material, as supporters for shelves, etc.

The third creative ability is originality, or the ability to come up with unusual but appropriate responses. For bricks, their use as hiding places for jewellery, or their use as dumbbells, or their use as substitutes for pillows by placing them under the mattress, may be considered unusual, and therefore, original responses. A related ability is the ability to come up with novel relationships between ideas or two frames of reference. This is the sense in which Koestler understands creativity. It is the faculty that helps an Edison leap to the realisation that what you need to turn electricity into light is not a good conductor of electricity as his contemporaries thought, but a bad conductor—a new relationship between current, impedance and incandescence. Or the faculty that helps one see the possibilities for perspective painting, by measuring the angles subtended in the eye by objects. And finally, it is the faculty that helps a poet to see neckties as tethers of civilisation, or rivers as arteries of God, or a dewdrop as the abode of Vishnu.

A fourth ability is to notice the unexplained, the unsatisfactory, or the incongruent—in other words, the ability to sense problems. Scientists often dismiss data inconsistent with their pet theories as "noise". It is the inquisitive scientist, curious about—"noise", that sometimes makes remarkable discoveries. Alexander Fleming, the discoverer of penicillin, is a case in point. Many scientists had observed that fungus forming in a bio-chemical culture inhibits the growth of bacteria. But they failed to grasp the significance of this "noise" in their experiments. It was Fleming who wondered about this and ultimately saw the significance of this for treating infections.

A fifth ability is the ability to go to the roots of a phenomenon by unravelling its causes. and equally, to visualise its consequences. This, of course, is a vital ingredient of scientific creativity. But I suspect it may be equally important in artistic creativity, where the ability to discern the mental associations of an object, and its potential as a metaphor in a work of art may be vital—to see, for example, modern city life as a spiritual waste land, as in Eliot's *The Waste Land,* or, since death reminds us of tears, and tears of dewdrops, to use dew to convey pain at the death of a child as in the following lovely haiku:

Dew evaporates
and all our world
is dew ... so dear,
so fresh, so fleeting.

The ability to elaborate on a theme has also been recognised as a significant creative ability. It is the difference between a legend and Shakespeare's dramatic version of it, or an insight that capitalist economies get stuck with recessions and the full-fledged Keynesian general theory of economic equilibrium, or the idea that man has considerable creative potential and a full-fledged training programme for increasing creativity, or the difference between the notes of raga and its alaap. The ability to elaborate is indispensable in putting a creative idea to work.

An ability of considerable importance, is the ability to go behind the surface features of a problem, and see what the "real" problem is. A group of psychologists, called gestalt psychologists have held it to be mainly responsible for producing original insights. Consider the problem faced by an ambulance, blocked on a long narrow bridge by a flock of sheep. So long as one defines the problem as how to get the ambulance to overtake the sheep, there would be no really effective solution. It is only when one defines the problem, as one of getting the ambulance ahead of the sheep, that a solution at once dawns—the flock can be turned around and driven past the stationary ambulance.

Obviously, these abilities—ideational fluency, flexibility, originality, problem sensitivity, the ability to grasp the causes and visualise the consequences, the ability to elaborate, the ability to restructure problems—are not generally found in equal measure in the same individual. The individual who can ideate fluently, may not be very original, and vice versa. It is, therefore, inappropriate to categorise a person as creative or uncreative, without specifying the dimensions on which he has high ability and the ones on which he has limited ability. If we are comparing two individuals, we should be very careful before we brand one person as less creative than the other. The chances are that the former may well be superior in at least one of the creativity related abilities.

Techniques of Creativity

A number of techniques have been developed to stimulate creative thinking. Some of these are based on the idea that if we can defer evaluation of the ideas we produce, that is; separate out the phase of idea-evaluation from the phase of idea-production, we can greatly increase the number of ideas we produce. Thereby, we increase substantially, the chance of coming up with a really brilliant idea. Some other techniques are based on the idea that if we can subject the mind to certain kinds of constructive strain, it is likely to leap to an original insight or idea.

The most widely used technique for generating creative ideas is the one called brainstorming. It was the brainchild of one Alex Osborn, an advertising executive. The basic steps are:

1. A problem is presented to a brainstorming panel by the leader. The problem should be stated as clearly as possible, so that there is no misunderstanding about what it is. The more precise the problem, the better.
2. The leader requests one idea at a time, from each member of the panel. It goes on for several rounds.
3. During the idea-generation, the rule is that no one is to criticise anybody's idea. Hitchhiking, or basing an idea on someone else's idea, is encouraged.

Research has shown that ideas produced by this deferred evaluation technique, are not only more numerous but also of better quality, than the ideas produced by an equivalent sized group, in which the deferred evaluation principle is not used. In fact, research suggests that individuals brainstorming alone, tend to produce more and better ideas than a brainstorming group consisting of the same number of individuals. This technique is highly recommended as being eminently practical and productive.

A technique that combines the convergent thinking principle of forming categories with the brainstorming principle of generating many alternative solutions, is the technique of attribute analysis, ascribed to Crawford. The steps are:

1. Given an object that we wish to design, be it a tangible object or an activity, we first identify its major attributes. If we are trying to design a better chair, for example, we may identify comfort, durability, ease of moving and attractiveness as, say, the major attributes.

2. Next, we take up each attribute and generate as many alternative ways of securing the attribute as we can. For example, to make a chair more comfortable, we may consider upholstering it, making it adjustable as to length, direction, level, etc., curving the back to provide support to the spinal column, giving it supporting handles or support for the feet, and so forth. It is easy to see that if we generate even four alternatives, for each attribute, we have generated $(4)^4$ or 256 alternative designs for a chair. After generating these alternative designs, of course we need to evaluate them in terms of criteria such as cost, marketability, etc.

Both these techniques, that is, brain-storming and attribute analysis, guarantee the generation of many solutions. The problem then becomes one of choosing, one or a few solutions for more intensive testing. One simple technique is to establish criteria of evaluation, and then have each member of group of experts pick out, say, the three solutions he or she thinks are most promising. These votes are pooled and the solutions receiving the most votes are taken up for more intensive investigation.

A very unusual technique for solving many complex technical problems is the technique of synectics, invented by Gordon, an advertising executive and later a management consultant. The technique is based on the principle that constructive psychological strain can lead to original solutions to problems. This is another group problem solving technique. This constructive psychological strain is generated by a number of processes:

1. After the problem is explained to the group, members are asked to explain the problem as they understand it. For example, if the problem is one of estimating petroleum reserves thousands of metres underground, one member may state that the problem as he understands it is one of making rocks tell us how much oil they contain.
2. The leader invites social or biological analogies, pertinent to the problem as understood, if it is a physical or a technical problem, and analogies from the physical sciences, if it is a problem concerning a living system. Thus, one may look into the structure of the whale to explore a problem connected with submarines, and the processes of the computer to understand better the brain. In other words, there is a

deliberate attempt to gain insight, by searching into analogous but otherwise very different terrain.

3. To generate insights through empathy, the leader may request personal analogies. Thus, if one is looking into the causes of metal fatigue, the members are asked to imagine themselves to be metal in a jet plane flying at a high altitude, and report what they feel-see-hear-smell-taste. This subjectification of an object of enquiry, sometimes, yields discoveries.
4. Synectics problem solving goes through phases of imaginative exploration, such as through various personal and other analogising and phases of imaginative compression through book titles or symbolic analogies. After there has been a good deal of exploration, the leader may seek to crystallise the images and ideas generated, by inviting group members to come up with poetic or paradoxical phrases, that could serve the same function as book titles. Suppose the original problem had been the control of hurricanes and a very elaborate exploration of a war had ensued, in order to gain insights into what happens when air masses with different moisture contents and pressures collide. The leader, at this point, may request members to provide alternative book titles to a battle. A number of titles could be generated, such as 'greatness decimated' or 'migration to hell', or 'vulture's paradise' or 'sin immortalised' or 'dicey chastity', or 'finished hate'. One or more such book titles could trigger further poetic exploration in search of a technical solution.

During the process, any evaluative remarks are, of course taboo. The imagination is continuously stretched, by going from the familiar to the unfamiliar and from the strange and unfamiliar to the familiar. The technique has been successfully employed in finding solutions to a number of intractable technical problems.

Synectics is a difficult technique, but its principle of constructive psychological strain is most practical. Basically, it consists of mechanisms that bend and stretch the mind in every direction, through the stuff of poetry. It is a technique for churning the mind, so that novel visions and insights rise to its surface.

Another technique that can be usefully combined with any of the other three techniques described earlier, is the one of checklist of questions. This was also developed by Osborn, the creator of brainstorming. This consists in subjecting a tentative solution to a barrage of questions. Some of these are quite straight forward questions, such as, how can we modify the solution to make it more economical; or can we find other uses of the solution; or can we get to the solution through other cheaper means; or what could we add or delete from the solution to make it more elegant, more practical, etc. Some questions stimulate more for research, such as , I—"how do we miniaturise or minify X" or—"how do we magnify X many times" or "what is the opposite of X", etc., where X is the proposed solution. As someone has put it, questions are the creative acts of intelligence, for they could be so designed, as to force a dramatic shift of perspective.

To summarise the principles that underlie creative thinking techniques, they are:

1. Structure the problem so that it is well-understood.
2. Separate the phase of idea production from idea evaluation. Do not evaluate or criticise ideas—whether of one's own or another's during the time they are being articulated.
3. Ideate copiously. Churn out a large number of ideas, both, because this heightens the possibility of hitting upon some really good ones, and also, to let one idea lead to another and to still another, and so on, like a chain-reaction.
4. Create constructive psychological strain by continuously enticing the person to go from the familiar to the unfamiliar terrain and back to the familiar, such as by coming up with analogies, metaphors, and empathic statements.
5. Force wide shifts of perspective by asking such questions as—"What could be the opposite of the current solution?", or "How could we magnify or minify the solution?", or "Is there a radically different way of looking at the problem?"
6. Having generated a large number of ideas or solutions, identify the ones with the greatest potential by some sort of an assessment and selection procedure, such as experts picking out the three most promising ideas.

The creative person I pioneers, seeks to do new or novel things, in novel ways. These are intrinsically risky activities that often invite a good deal of criticism or opposition from those wedded to the status-quo. Hence, the creative person needs a good deal of courage, independence, and ability to take risks. Failures in such novel activities may be frequent. Therefore, persistence and self-confidence are needed. In doing something creative, one needs to be very open to ideas and one must seek a good deal of information. Thus, the creative person must be inquisitive. Finally, creation requires a high degree of psychological complexity—ability to visualise a new order of things, ability to intuit or grasp the basics, a capacity to be moved by higher emotions, the endless search for the elusively aesthetic or true or good.

3

New Public Management
Emerging Concerns

RAMESH K. ARORA

Ever since the discipline of public administration was given an identity more than hundred years ago, there has been a constant confluence of management science and public administration. The impact of F.W. Taylor was evident in the writings of L.D. White and W.F. Willoughby; French scholar Henry Fayol built bridges between management and public administration; Chester Barnard was the prime motivator of Herbert Simon; the contemporary management super-guru, Peter Drucker has perspicaciously analysed government bureaucracies from a managerial angle; the fusion theory of Chris Argyris has been tested in the context of American federal government; and, today the burgeoning world of management science has its penetrating effect on the intellectual development of public administration. This convergence appears as a natural consequence of the integrated development of the discipline since the core of public administration has always been its external political context as well as its internal organisational (read managerial) dynamics. What is internal to a public administrative system is its process of management and what is external to it is its political (hinging also on socio-economic) environment in which it functions. It is universally accepted that most maxims, principles, guidelines and dictums of efficiency, economy and effectiveness have emanated from the writings of management thinkers and that they have been adopted and adapted by the scholars of public administration in their distinctive intellectual ambience. Both management and public administration are applied sciences. Hence, leaving aside their individual contexts of control and accountability, there is no drastic differentiation between the two as far as their cardinal goals and roles are concerned.

Current Paradigm

Currently, if there is one 'paradigm' in the discipline of public administration, it is perhaps 'New Public Management' (NPM).[1] This paradigm of NPM emerged on the heels of the movements of re-inventing government (1992) and good governance (1992). The sub-title of the book *Re-inventing Government* is *How the Entrepreneurial Spirit is Transforming the Public Sector.* If we closely examine this sub-title of book by David Osborne and Ted Gaebler, it would be evident that both these scholars were 'describing' what was already evident on the administrative scene. Hence, they were not essentially prescriptive but primarily descriptive while highlighting the presence of entrepreneurial governments. Truly, the movement of managerialising the government had started even before this monumental volume was published. Writings of these and other scholars had already appeared in 1980s (and even earlier) which highlighted the need for adopting in an effective manner sound management practices in government systems. One is reminded of what was happening about nine decades ago when Taft Committee was appointed to transplant Taylorism into the government system. Little wonder, certain scholars have branded NPM as neo-Taylorism. Even if we avoid a debate on a neologism like 'neo-Taylorism', it must be contended that public administrative organisations have liberally borrowed models and modes from their more vibrant sister discipline—management.

A historical perspective would reveal that bureaucracies throughout the world have rarely responded effectively to environmental challenges on their own. They have generally lagged behind the times. In 1968 itself, when Dwight Waldo was organising the first Minnowbrook Conference, Peter Drucker had come out with his perceptive volume, *The Age of Discontinuity,* which made a prescient analysis of the incompetence of bureaucratic government. One can even see this exasperation with straitjacketed bureaucratic system in tile writings of Harold Laski, Warren Bennis, Robert Reich, Tom Peters and Alvin Toffler and others.

And it is ironical that remedies to bureaucratic ailments have been offered more by scholars of management than by the wise men of public administration. But, what goes to the credit of public administration scholars is their alacrity and competence to imbibe and incorporate the pertinent and the precious from any other discipline and mould it as per their own intrinsic agenda and ambience. NPM is only one such manifestation of this resilience of public administration.

Essential Premises

The OECD believes that through NPM, public sector is being made more managerial. The introduction of a more contractual, participative and discretionary style of relationship between levels of hierarchy, between control agency and operating units, and between producing units, be they public or private. Further, the OECD avers that most countries are following two broad avenues to improve production and delivery of goods in services in public organisations. These two avenues are:

1. Raise the production performance of public organisations (to) improve the management of human resources including staff, development, recruitment of qualified talent and pay-for-performance; involve staff more in decision-making and management; relax administrative controls while imposing strict performance targets; use information technology; improve feedback from clients and stress service quality; bring supply and demand decisions together (e.g., through charging users).[2]
2. Make greater use of the private sector (to) promote a dependable, efficient, competitive and open public procurement system for contracting out production of publicly provided goods and services and contracting in intermediate goods and services; and, end monopoly or other protection for suppliers.[3]

In sum, the OECD view on NPM involves the following aspects of administrative management:

- Improving human resource including performance pay.
- Participation of staff in the various stages of decision-making, relaxing control and regulations, yet prescribing and ensuring the achievement of performance targets.
- Using information technology to an optimum level in order to make MIS more effective and enrich policy and decisional systems.
- Providing efficient services to clients and treating them as customers and even as members of the organisation.
- Prescribing user charges for services in order to make the customers as more integral part of the public sector management.
- Contracting out services as a part of the privatisation plan.
- Deregulation of monopolies and de-concentration of economic power among various organisations.

There has been a plethora of literature of NPM and one finds in the myriad writings certain common concerns and foci. Briefly, the most common attributes of NPM are:

- Focus on outputs, with greater stress on results rather than procedures.
- Strengthening professional management.
- Ensuring high standards and measures of performance.
- Greater emphasis on output controls.
- Increasing de-centralisation of business decisional power.
- Greater accent in the public sector on adoption of private sector style of management practices, discipline and parsimony.
- Ensuring accountability, progressive leadership and greater understanding between political leadership and the public.
- Added responsibility of managers for results.
- Gradual decrease in the size of government.

Over the years, there has been one important shift in the thinking of NPM. In the early stages of entrepreneurial government, there was stress on de-governmentalisation and privatisation which was sometimes called downsizing or rightsizing. The government was expected to be lean and mean but now once again, it has been recognised that the imperatives and inevitability of government's role and responsibility as a crucial facet of national life cannot be undermined. For developing countries particularly, the role of government in engineering socio-economic change and bringing about goal-directed progressive multidimensional development is likely to remain supreme. Therefore, the contemporary emphasis is not on less government but on *better* government. This is where the value of sound managerial practices has permeated the field of public administration.

Continuity of a Tradition

A question arises as to why the scholars of public administration have not resisted the 'onslaught' of a NPM on their discipline. Perhaps it is primarily because of the fact that howsoever new-fangled NPM might appear to be, it has its organic linkages with 'old' public administration. Accordingly, one can surmise that traditional administrative and managerial theories which emphasised efficiency, effectiveness and economy have assumed a new form as integral components of NPM. The difference, of course lies in the goals of the administrative systems in two divergent settings, but then NPM is not so much concerned with the goals of public administration, as with the strategies to achieve them. In this context, it ought to be appreciated that while the foremost concern of New Public Administration (NPA) has been with the goals, values and the spirit of public administration, NPM, on the other hand, is principally interested in the structure and style of public administration. There are certain elements of NPM that are perceivable in NPA and vice versa. Essentially, both are complementary to each other.

As we move towards the future we are likely to witness two parallel administrative realities. The first, anchored in NPM, would be more germane to the milieu in developed nations where the government is emerging as a facilitator and moderator of goal-directed change. The other reality will be more reflective of the enterprise of change in developing nations where the government's responsibility and role in tackling poverty and backwardness will remain prominent and legitimate for many more years to come. In a country like India, the traditional public administration focusing on organisational restructuring and managerial efficiency will continue to be ensconced on a pedestal of time-tested authenticity. And, besides, the principal values and concerns of NPA as well as NPM would also continue to perennially re-energise the discipline as well as the profession of public administration. Thus, in the foreseeable future, public administration is destined to flourish in a poly-paradigmatic environment facilitating its multifaceted growth.[4]

Notes

1. See for a perceptive analysis of the theme, Hughes, *Public Management and Administration;* Halachami and Bouckaert (eds.), *The Enduring Challenges in Public Management.* For a comparative perspective, see Christopher Pollitt and Geert Bouckaert, *Public Management Reform: A Comparative Analysis* (New York: Oxford, 2000). Also see, L.K. Kaboolian, "The New Public Management: Challenging the Boundaries of Management vs. Administration Debate". *Public Administrative Review,* Vol. 58, No. 3 (1998), pp. 189–93; and D.G. Mathiasen, "The New Public Management and its Critics", *International Public Management Journal,* Vol. 2, No. 1 (1999), pp. 90–111.
2. Hughes, *Public Management and Administration,* p. 67.
3. Ibid., p. 68.
4. For a glimpse of the multifaceted character of public administration, see Bidyut Chakrabarty and Mohit Bhattacharya (eds.), *Public Administration: A Reader* (New Delhi: Oxford, 2003). Also see Ramesh K. Arora. (ed.), *Public Administration: Fresh Perspectives* (Jaipur: Aalekh, 2003).

4

Better Governance Through Accountability and Transparency

N. VITTAL

We, the Indians, are notorious for self-flagellation. We probably are very good at criticising ourselves for our failures and in the process not take sufficient credit for our achievements. As we are meeting at a time when elections are in the air, it is better to recall that one of our great achievements is that India has been a real functioning democracy ever since it became independent. This cannot be said of many other countries which became independent around the time when India became independent and led the movement of decolonisation at the end of the Second World War. Equally important is the fact that India has remained united as a nation when at the time of our independence we had 600 native states which in theory were independent as the British paramountcy had lapsed. Thanks to India's Bismark, Sardar Patel, who in a unique achievement in the history of India, united our country under one system of government. Again, we should thank Sardar Patel for having had the vision not to disband the civil service and other services built by the British in a fit of patriotic

Text of H.C. Mathur Memorial Lecture delivered on 16th August, 1999 at HCM RIPA, Jaipur.

zeal but consider how the same instruments of the Raj can be used for building a new India. We need today a very strong dose of Sardar Patel's sheer pragmatism, vision and the sixth sense to get result in tackling the problems of our country and improve the quality of governance.

We also have increased significantly the life expectancy and the level of literacy but when we compare ourselves—in these sectors with other countries, our achievements are not significant. On the technology front, we have had very notable successes in the areas of atomic energy, space and missile technology but when it comes to general development of technology, especially technologies which are used in civilian life, we have nothing much to show.

So, in the fifty years since independence, we have shown at least certain core competencies as a nation. One is the capacity to run a democratic society. The second is to hold on as a nation in spite of differences in language, religion, etc. The third is a capacity to master technology. Perhaps, the most dramatic example of our mastering a technology as a nation was the green revolution in the area of agriculture.

While these are the positive developments, there are other areas where we are lagging as a nation. Three indices will suffice. We are still considered as a developing country. According to the UNDP's Human Development Index (HDI), we rank 132 out of 175 countries. Even though our rank in the UNDP's HDI, 1999 is six places above the 1998 rank, we are still way below other nations in this aspect. When it comes to competitiveness on the global economic front, according to the World Competitiveness Index, we rank 50 out of 53 countries. We are consistently slipping behind in the last three years and I am afraid we may probably even hit the bottom if we do not correct ourselves. Thirdly, when it comes to corruption, we are one of the most corrupt countries in the world. We are ranked 66 out of 85 in the Corruption Perception Index by the German NGO, Transparency International, which arranges nations in the order of perception of corruption in the country.

These three indices have a direct bearing on governance. If we are able to govern ourselves better, the quality of life of our people will be better and hence our performance measured by the

HDI will be much better. If our governance is better in the economic sphere, we should be more competitive and occupy a higher rank in the World Competitive Index. If our governance was better, we would be a less corrupt country because better governance also leads perhaps to a better sense of values and better moral standards in the society in general. Of course, one can raise a question whether it is better morals in a society which lead to better governance or vice versa? Corruption can be need-based or greed-based. Better governance can at least help to check need-based corruption. Better governance can check greed-based corruption also because punishment for the corrupt will be very effective and prompt in a better-governed country.

The word 'govern' according to the Concise Oxford Dictionary, means "rule with authority" or "conduct the policy, actions and affairs of the state either despotically or constitutionally". In the Indian context, having adopted the democratic form of government, the question of despotism does not arise at all but for the temporary aberration of the 1975–77 emergency period. As Churchill pointed out, democracy may be the worst form of government except when you consider all other alternatives for governance. In the context of our country, how has our democracy worked? Are we governing ourselves effectively?

The Indian democracy has developed certain special features. Universal adult suffrage was introduced even though the literacy levels were low. But, in successive elections, the voters have proved that they have an innate sense of wisdom. Hardly 25 per cent of the sitting MPs are re-elected. Today, the anti-incumbency factor has been conventional wisdom. Democracy gives an opportunity to "throw the rascals out". This our voters seem to be doing.

Under the Constitution of India, we have the executive, the judiciary and the legislature as the three major arms for governance. Each has to play its role and if anyone of these agencies is not able to perform, then there is a danger of the others emerging into the vacuum so created. For instance, judicial activism, we have seen in recent times, can be attributed to the failure of the executive and legislature. Between the executive and the legislature, we find that the roles of the politicians representing the legislature and bureaucrats representing executive have undergone dramatic changes over the period of fifty years. These was a concept many years back that the policy-making will be the responsibility of the political leadership and implementation will be that of the bureaucracy. But, over the years, the situation has almost been reversed with the politicians taking direct interest in day-to-day administration like postings, transfers and so on and the bureaucracy hopefully left with the task of working out policy potions.

We have to understand the dynamics of governance before we explore what could be done for better governance and how accountability and transparency can help in the process. The first principle of governance is that in a modern society there should be the rule of law and not the rule of the ruler. It was in the times of monarchy that the concept of *l'etat cest moi* (The state, I am the state) was so tellingly articulated by the French Sun King (Roi Soli), Louis the Fifteenth. This underlined the principle that the king was the law. In many of our Indian states that was the position even though some states like Baroda, Mysore and Travancore might have had enlightened rulers who tried to introduce the rule of law. Although in the Indian ethos the ruler is supposed to maintain the *dharma,* in practice the ruler was virtually a dictator.

The British brought the concept of rule of law and once they settled down, being a colonial power, they were able to set up processes by which justice could be administered. We inherited this system and over the years as B.K. Mehra, ICS (Retd.) pointed out in a talk in the India International Centre a few years ago that we seem to be going back to our old ethos of the rule of the ruler instead of the rule of the law. According to Jawaharlal Nehru, when an MP or MLA is elected he thinks that for the period of his tenure as a legislator, in his area and constituency, what he says must be the law. This tendency has been further accentuated by the fact that the bureaucracy also has gone along. Perhaps, the emergency of Indira Gandhi in 1975–77 did a lot to bring in this new concept of commitment of the bureaucracy not to the Constitution but to the party in power. The career-oriented approach of the services has also created a situation where the civil servants find that it helps them to hitch their wagon to a rising star politician. As a result, today, we find in many states that the civil servants have come to be identified with certain political leaders and their fortunes rise and fall in tandem with the rise and fall in the fortunes of their political masters. This is perhaps one of the major factors that has contributed to the deterioration of the quality of governance.

After all what do we mean by quality of governance? We mean that the rule of law must be observed. The rule of law means that every citizen will be treated equally. Article 14 of the Indian Constitution talks about equality before law and equal protection before the law. This principle must be observed in letter and spirit. The first step to ensure better governance therefore would be to have the concept of the rule of law restored. The second step is to ensure that bureaucracy is de-politicised.

We may begin with the issue of rule of law. The rule of law will be maintained if the judiciary is able to effectively perform and ensure that the laws are implemented. In fact, though, it is the function of the legislature to legislate the law and the executive to implement the law, many a time the judiciary has to intervene because the executive has been failing in its duty. We had in the late 1990s the spectacle of the politicians being involved in scams and the courts taking an active part and going to the extent of even directing the CBI and monitoring the progress of the investigations. This perhaps is a temporary phase in the governance of our country because the judicial activism becomes necessary only when the legislature and executive fail.

There are, however, certain aspects of the way our courts perform which raises issue about the effectiveness about the rule of law. One fact is that our court proceedings are enormously time consuming and there is a huge backlog of nearly three crore cases in our courts. The average time taken for decision may be from 10–20 years. For example, the CBI has got prosecutions going on from 2 to 35 years. Incidentally, the investigations by CBI also range from 2 to 12 years. So, one important feature of our judiciary, which is an important aspect in maintenance of law and order and which is very vital for governance, is the enormous delay in our legal system.

Attempts have been made in the past to resolve this issue using concepts like Lok Adalat etc., and also to strengthen the judiciary in terms of manpower. Nevertheless, I think, a stage has come when we will have to think in terms of managerial approach to judicial reform. If we look upon the judicial process in the context of good governance as a system for delivering quick punishments for those who are guilty, then we will have to see whether the managerial concepts of effectiveness and efficiency can be brought in the courts. In implementing a project, we have the concept of the Programme Evaluation Review Technique (PERT) or the Critical Path Method (CPM). Why cannot we apply a similar concept to our courts? We can first find out what are the critical delays that are taking place and then take appropriate corrective action to overcome these delays. Another managerial concept that can be adopted is the ABC analysis. While 'A' type cases which are major and significant may take a longer time, the 'B' and 'C' type cases can be disposed of quickly. It is true that we have summary trials but the need for bringing in such a concept is urgent and acute. We must also try the concept of Business Processing Reengineering (BPR) in judiciary. The basic principle of BPR is that if we were to design the organisation today, will we follow the current practice? We must redesign our system and procedures on this basis. In short, a managerial approach to judicial reform may go a long way in improving the efficiency of the judicial system which is very vital for good governance.

We then come to the next major factor which goes against good governance in our country. This is the prevailing culture of corruption. As Central Vigilance Commissioner (CVC), I am directly concerned with this aspect. I think corruption can be tackled and I would like to share my perceptions with you. There are people who believe that corruption cannot be controlled. It is an old disease. As Indira Gandhi once said, corruption is a global phenomenon. I would begin by inviting your attention to the global action against corruption.

One country, which tackled this problem, was Hong Kong where the Independent Commission Against Corruption (ICAC) was set up in 1974 after a notorious reputation developed by the Hong Kong Police and other departments. Something drastic was to be done to reduce corruption. Apparently, the ICAC was able to systematically bring down corruption by taking all stakeholders into confidence and discussing with them to initiate a number of processes to check corruption. There was also a strike by the Hong

Kong Police against the ICAC and a series of measures were taken to bring down corruption. We have seen, Lee Kwan Yew, single-mindedly making Singapore one the cleanest governments in the world. In Italy, the magistrates, who were empowered, were able to take on the mafia and tried to reduce corruption. In France also, the Italian experience has been repeated. It is true that some of the magistrates had to pay the ultimate price of their lives in Italy. But, the fact is that these countries had made efforts to bring down corruption. In a different context, in New York, where the crime was rampant, Rudi Giuliani came up with the concept of zero tolerance and brought down the level of crime substantially. The point to note, therefore, is that corruption can be fought and corruption can be eliminated. What we need first is a determined mind-set.

In India, we find corruption everywhere. The books—Shiv Vishwanathan's *The Foul Play* and S.S. Gill's *The Pathology of Corruption*—dramatically lists and describes various cases of corruption which have been seen in the last 50 years and our pathetic stage today. The important point brought out, for example, in Gill's book is that corruption is all-pervading. We have corruption among the bureaucrats, among the business community, among the political community and even the NGOs. In fact, I would suggest that today the five major players in corruption are the *neta, babu, lala, jhola* and *dada*—the corrupt politician, the corrupt bureaucrat, the corrupt businessman, the corrupt NGO and the criminal. Criminalisation of politics can also be directly traced to the corruption, which flourishes because of the need for ever increasing funds for political purposes in the country.

As CVC, I have a direct responsibility to see that at least corruption is eliminated so far as public servants are concerned in the Government of India. Ministries, departments, organisations like public sector undertakings and banks, and organisations of the Government of India should be freed of corruption. Is this possible?

I think this is possible and for achieving this we have to have a clear idea about the dynamics of corruption, why corruption flourishes and how it can be tackled? Corruption flourishes in our system because of five basic reasons. These are:

1. Scarcity of goods and services;
2. Red-tape and complicated rules and procedures;
3. Lack of transparency in decision-making;
4. Legal cushions of safety we have built for the corrupt people under the very healthy principle that everybody is innocent till proved guilty; and
5. Tribalism or *biradari* among the corrupts which protect each other. We say "thick as thieves" and not "thick as honest people".

As CVC, I am adopting a three-point plan to check corruption and hopefully one day eliminate it. The first is simplification of rules and procedures. Corruption is like malaria. One can deal with malaria by giving medicine to those who are affected by this or prevent the breeding of mosquitoes. Many of our rules and procedures breed corruption. I have, therefore, issued orders trying to check and simplify the procedures. One example is my insistence that all banks must computerise at least 70 per cent of their operations by January 1, 2001. We know that the Harshad Mehta scam took place because in the Public Debt Office of the Reserve Bank of India, there was no computerisation and that led to the scam. Like locking the stable door after the horse has fled, the Public Debt Office was computerised after the scam. Today, thousands of crores are lying unreconciled in our banking system. Why not go for computerisation directly? Incidentally, when I mean computerisation, my test is that if a customer goes to the bank with an outstation cheque, he should be able to get the amount credited to his account on the same day. If this is done, it means that automatically the systems are in place.

Today, one can go on cheating one bank after another. I have, therefore, directed that the names of all wilful defaulters must be informed by the banks to the Reserve Bank, which, in turn, must circulate the information among the nationalised banks. Our banking system is such that if you owe one lakh cf rupees to the bank, you are afraid of the bank. If you owe rupees ten crore, the bank is afraid of you. Our system is such that while industry becomes sick, the industrialist does not become sick. We have this excellent device of the Bureau of Industrial and Financial Reconstruction (BIFR) (also known as Bureau of Industrial Funeral Rites) so that when as industry becomes sick and it is referred to BIFR, the guilty industrialist can breathe easily because even the bank cannot recover his cost. Many of these sickness cases may be due to collusion. I have already requested the government to scrap the SICA and the BIFR. Such systematic elimination of the scope for corruption in our system is the first step.

The second step is empowering the public and bringing greater transparency. It is where that Rotary and other such organisations can play an important role if they want to tackle corruption. All the orders of CVC regarding checking corruption are in the public domain. They can be easily accessed through the website of CVC at http/cvc.nic.in. One such order I have issued is that there should be no post-tender negotiations except with lowest tenderer. Many industrialists have used this today to ensure that the corrupt practices, which used to flourish in the post-tender stage, are brought down substantially. Another order I have issued is that in every office there should be a board saying, "Don't pay bribe. If anybody asks for bribe, you can complain to the CVO, CVC, etc." When I suggested this, my office people said that just like under NO SMOKING sign, people smoke, under NO PARKING sign, people park vehicles, under NO BRIBES sign, people will take bribes. But, by putting this idea into effect, what we will be doing in effect is that we will be educating all the public who come to every small office of the Government of India and other organisations like banks and public sector undertakings that there is a way out if they do not want to pay bribe. Out of the 10,000 people who come to an office, at least one person may turn out to be a person who would like to take on the system and fight corruption. He has an ally in the CVC.

The third important part of my strategy is effective punishment. It is here that we have miles to go. Punishment of the guilty is possible under two circumstances, one is through departmental inquiry and another is through prosecution. So far as departmental inquiries are concerned, I found that there are no time limits for the inquiries. There have been classic cases where an inquiry officer was appointed after five years and he took two years, and by the time the inquiry was completed, the public servant retired. I am forcing to see that in all the government organisations retired honest people are employed to conduct the departmental inquiries so that the inquiry is completed within six months. This means that at least the public servant will know that the punishment will be quick. On the other hand, when it comes to prosecution, we have really miles to go because the courts are extremely slow. I am monitoring at least the cases which are handled by the CBI under the Prevention of Corruption Act. As of now, nearly 3,000 and odd are pending and many are pending from two years to ten years. If punishment is so slow, how are we going to bring the corrupt to book and then elimination of corruption will always remain in India a myth and not a reality.

In this context, therefore, I have taken another initiative. Corruption flourishes because it is a low-risk, high-profit activity. I have suggested to the government that the ill-gotten property of the corrupt must be confiscated. Justice Jeevan Reddy, Chairman, Law Commission agreed with me and has drafted an Act, called the Corrupt Public Servants (Forfeiture of Property) Act. If this Act is enacted, then the CVC will have powers at least to ensure that the corrupts do not enjoy the benefits of their corrupt practices. But, the law is yet to be enacted. I do not know when this will take place. In the meanwhile, I learnt that there is another Act, called the Benami Transaction Prohibition Act. This can be effectively used. Even the Act was passed in 1988, which provides that the *benami* property can be confiscated, there is no procedure prescribed so far to confiscate the property. I have requested the government to empower the CVC and prescribe the procedure. Eleven years are nearing and we are still waiting for the government to act.

It is, therefore, possible by adopting these strategies to tackle corruption by public servants, but what about the political corruption? Here, the following options are possible: While we can tackle, to some extent, the problem of public servants in the area of corruption, what about political corruption? The way our elections are conducted and the role of the money power and muscle power in elections, how are we going to tackle this issue? The Supreme Court judgment in the JMM case has declared that both the MPs and MLAs are public servants. We must build the public opinion in this country so that the MPs and MLAs, as public servants, are also required to give their annual property returns to the Speaker of the Lok Sabha or the Chairman of the Rajya Sabha, as the case may be. If they happened to have *benami* property, then it should also be liable for confiscation, if government would come out with a procedure for confiscation of *benami* property after a delay of more than eleven years.

We must also be able to initiate action to check the very process by which political leaders are able to realise large amounts of money. This comes in the form of various decisions in government starting with, of course transfers, contracts, clearance of projects and so on. In this process, the political leaders will not be able to get the financial benefits unless they have also the collusion of the corrupt public servants. There are, of course, exceptions where the political leaders could still make money even without the collusion of the public servants. I was told that there was a minister in one of the departments of the Government of India who insisted that only honest people must handle all tender cases. All the tender files will have to be submitted to him. He can then indulge in post-tender negotiations while taking final decision. In such cases, even though the record will show that a correct decision has been taken. If the files are deleted at the minister's level, the ready excuse is that minister unlike a public servant has many responsibilities and cannot be expected to clear files fast. There would have been kickbacks, which will escape notice. Thanks to globalisation, the salting of money and ill-gotten wealth in foreign bank accounts and countries abroad is also easier.

A healthy development is that OECD countries came up with an anti-bribery convention. The US Vice-President, Al Gore, took an initiative in February 1999 to call a meeting of 89 countries to talk about fighting corruption globally. While global public opinion may be slowly growing against corruption, what we have to tackle is corruption within the country.

The CBI, with the revised position of the CVC, is today in a position to take independent action. A corrupt politician, whether in power or not, is as much unable for criminal action under the Prevention of Corruption Act as any other citizen. It should be, therefore, possible to use the CBI to bring the corrupt politicians to book. But then, as I mentioned earlier, there are many areas in which we have to initiate action. First, to beef up the CBI's strength; second, to see how the investigation procedures can be speeded up; and third, of course, is to see how the prosecution processes can be improved and speeded up so that the delay in every stage of prosecution is removed. The main point to note is that if public opinion is in favour of bringing the corrupt politicians to book, there is a method today by which is possible to achieve this objective.

What about the *jhola,* the *dada* and the *lala?* Once we are able to check at least the *babu* and the *neta,* perhaps there will be a salutary effect and these sectors can be brought under control. In other words, I want to seriously put before you the proposition that we can eliminate the corruption in the country. It is a question of mind-set. If you are determined we can do it. Today, in our country, corruption is accepted cynically and with a defeatist attitude the people have become apathetic. I want to change this apathy and acceptance into an anger and action.

We then come to the third important aspect for moving towards good governance and this is the instrument of accountability. After all, in the ultimate analysis, good governance depends upon the willingness of people in positions of power to take responsibility and discharge them. As I see it, accountability means that the public servants who are entrusted with certain responsibilities must be able to respond to them and perform effectively. If the public servants do not perform effectively, they should also be suitably punished. Accountability in our system for better governance can be built in by ensuring that rewards and punishments are quick. Unfortunately, in our system, while rewards are also rare, punishment rarely takes place. As we have seen in the case of corruption, the really big fish always escape. The percentage of conviction in our country is 6. Hence, in prosecutions, there is a 95 per cent chance of escape. Further, the assurance of sense of security under Article 311 and buttressed further by the various rulings of CATs and the courts have created a system in which it is very difficult to punish anyone for inefficiency or failing in duty. It is only very rarely when a major train accident like the recent one at Gaisal takes place that we find that some action is initiated but even here one cannot be sure whether there will be any long-term improvement. We have, therefore, to look at the systems and ensure that the accountability is built into the system.

Our audit is generally post-facto and PACs come much later. Therefore, there is no deterrent effect generally of these also. We should devise methods by which the accountability can be enforced. A culture of accountability will develop if we can change the mind-set of the people. During the emergency, at least, there was a sense of fear and simple things like government servants coming to office on time were noticed. Railway wagons, which were in short supply, were suddenly available. The challenge before us is how to bring in this culture of accountability without the negative consequences of the emergency type situation.

It is here that transparency comes in. After all a person is accountable either because of his inner convictions and culture or because of the external pressure of the system. The external pressure in the system for public servants to perform can be built in if we provide for greater transparency. We should be able to bring in a Freedom of Information Act so that the citizen who is the customer of the government organisation is in a position to have access to information that he needs. Further, there must be an open commitment given by the departments about the performance of the services. The Citizen's Charter is a good concept and we have to put it into effective practice. If Citizen's Charter is able to fix time limits, then at least we can ensure that the government departments will be able to give the requisite services within the specified time limits.

Use of information technology perhaps can go a long way in building a culture of accountability. The great advantage of information technology is that it helps the processing of massive data and also provides for easy and random access. In fact, many of the delays in our government system which in turn lead to a sense of lethargy and lack of commitment can be overcome if we are able to use intelligently, information technology right across the government functions. The accessibility of public to information will also become easier with greater application of information technology in government.

We should tackle the issue of accountability both in terms of business process reengineering by reducing the time taken for processing cases, applying information technology to provide the requisite backbone for speedy communications and have clear guidelines about punishment in the event of failure to deliver. The cushions of safety in procedures which we have built for inefficiency and corruption must be gone into and once these steps are taken, the level of accountability in government should automatically improve.

Another reason for lack of accountability is that in course of time many organisations forget their basic objectives. Even though organisations are set up with certain objectives, in course of time the objectives get lost and totally different considerations prevail. For instance, education should focus on removal of illiteracy and educating the students. But, in many educational administrations, we will find that the considerations about the convenience of the teachers and their union problems will dominate. Similarly, in our judicial system, the convenience of the lawyers probably will take precedence over that of even dispensing with justice because the enormous delay that takes place in adjournments is for the convenience of the lawyers. Many government departments ultimately look as if that the objective of the department is for the benefit of the government servant's. When it comes to public sector undertakings, especially sick undertakings, it appears that the sick undertakings have to continue because the jobs of the employees have to be protected. This sort of reversal of priorities is one of the important reasons why there is no sense of accountability when we examine it in the context of better governance.

As we look to the future, we find that we are also moving from the era of highly interventionist governments to an era where the government's function, especially in the economic sector, will be more that of an umpire rather than an active participant. Law and order, education, public health and infrastructure are likely to be the key areas where the government will have to focus in the future. So, the issues relating to governance through better accountability and the accountability ensured by transparency should focus on these sectors.

I have placed before you some ideas about how we can move towards better governance and the means of achieving this objective. I am sure, an informed and intelligent debate on these issues will help us to forge appropriate strategies to achieve the objective of better governance.

5

Administrator as Manager

I.C. SRIVASTAVA

In the wake of globalisation and the predominance of market economy all over the world, coupled with economic liberalisation, the concept and content of governance has undergone a sea change. With the collapse of iron-curtain of Russia, democracy as a system of government has come to stay and dominate the polity of nations. Besides, it is now an accepted principle that good governance is inseparable from democracy and human rights including human dignity, justice, equity and participation. People-centred governance, relying on community-based institutions and envisaging consultation with NGOs/voluntary bodies, seeks to ensure participation of people at the grass roots level in self-governance institutions. Therefore, people-centred governance is not only the felt-need of the times but the participation of people themselves in the process of governance has also become an essential ingredient in the delivery of services. While government refers to the machinery and institutional arrangements required for the exercise of state's powers for protecting and serving the internal and external interests of community, governance implies the process as well as results of appropriate decisions taken for the benefit of society at large.

Public administration, which was earlier power-centric, bureau (desk) oriented and bound by rules and precedents, is slowly moving towards 'managerialism', i.e., the practices of management being adopted towards making good governance a reality. However, the quality of human resources remains the most significant determinant of the quality of performance by a government. The rationale of this change has been necessitated by the transformation in the government-citizen relationship which is no longer a 'donor-recipient' or provider-dominated. Instead, it has become client or citizen focused which would call for consultation with and participation of people as well as employees for an organisation in the bottom-up approach thereby ensuring transparency, accountability and responsiveness in the process of governance.

In these tumultuous times, administrators engaged in general and area administration or others required to administer welfare and development programmes and schemes are, therefore, called upon to become good managers. Management, in the simplest terms, is defined as "getting this done through men and material". Thus, in the broadest terms, the administering of government policies and programmes calls for development of managerial skills on the part of budding civil servants who will shape into good public administrators. In this context, the British legacy of the institutional arrangements of district administration with the predominant role of Collector, as chief coordinator and representative of government, has survived and delivered goods in the post-independence period in the face of floods, famines, wars, riots, etc., besides bringing about necessary coordination in planning and implementation of various developmental schemes. However, civil services no longer provide a steel frame of the elitist ICS and other allied services of pre-independence period and the morale of the civil servants is at a low ebb in the wake of increasing political interference, communal clashes and rapid changes brought about by revolution in communication and information technology. A good administrator has, therefore, to lead from the front and perform the onerous tasks of providing necessary coordination and convergence in delivery of public services in the face of numerous political and social pressures.

This paper seeks to provide a frame of mind and attitude for an upcoming administrator who, now, has to wear the mantle of a manager. In the first instance, the manager has to be conscious and conscientious at the same time. In his new role as manager he has to be conscious not only about his job chart but should also be aware of the management concepts and practices including time management, need of the hour and changes in day-to-day administrative situation. Being conscientious implies that he should be able to distinguish between right and wrong in a given situation besides setting an example of intellectual honesty as well as personal integrity in public dealings. Hopefully, the institutional training imbibed by him will stand him in good stead in this regard.

First and foremost, a good administrator has to develop a commitment to rule of law including rules, regulations and procedures which would help him in adopting the principle of fairness, equity and justice. The commitment to rule of law should be distinguished from commitment to the unwarranted dictates of ruling or any other political party or powers that be, for that matter. The period of emergency during 1975–77 brought into focus this distinction when overzealous officials overstepped the limits of their power and authority and threw to winds the rule of law in many cases at the behest of the then ruling political elite. In a parliamentary democracy, an administrator, more often termed as bureaucrat, has to remain neutral all the time in public eye as far as ideology and policies of various political parties as reflected in their manifestos or otherwise are concerned, except for the policies as legislated by the parliament or assembly or approved by central and state council of ministers which are required to be implemented and administered in programmes in the spirit of following the rule of law. Briefly, an administrator has to perform his duties as a member of what Ramsay Muir, one of the British Prime Ministers, called I 'anonymous empire', i.e., the monolith large bureaucracy. A good administrator, as manager, will, therefore, have to lead his team by display of qualities of administrative leadership including discipline, punctuality, team spirit in office along with objectivity and neutrality in his dealing with various sections of people and political parties including ruling party and others.

An administrative leader has the innate strength to own up responsibility for his decisions and thus would necessarily avoid 'buckmanship', i.e., passing on the buck or responsibility. By his exemplary conduct, positive attitude and responsiveness to public needs he will certainly practise both transparency and accountability. Being performance-oriented, he would be able to set an example for both flexibility and sensitivity in developing work environment and would also instil a sense of confidence in members of his team by following the principle:

We cannot continue doing
What we have always done.
Tomorrow cannot be just more of yesterday
We need flexibility and pragmatism,
As much as innovation
But the stress must invariably be on action.*

A good administrator as manager should, first of all, concentrate in transforming the dull, shabby and disorderly work environment in government office or organisation. With the institutional arrangement of appointing a regular caretaker or an officer of the week by rotation, he would ensure that good quality drinking water is provided, bathrooms do not stink and building is maintained properly by disposing of useless articles, equipment, files and records.

A good manager should motivate the staff by delegating the work design to the groups of workers in his office. They should be made to feel responsible for their work output by inculcating in them a sense of belongingness with encouragement for proper participation in functioning at all levels. Such a manager would also lend a helping hand in solving some of the genuine personal problems of the staff as an integral part of his work style and management policy.

As for the interface with members of public, Citizens' Charter which ensures delivery of concerned public service in a time-frame according to well-laid out principles of right to information, accessibility to public office and accountability of the concerned staff should come handy to a good administrative head. The Citizens' Charters have now come into focus and have assumed importance as instruments of good governance for they seek to lay down standards and norms of work. They call for openness and transparency in conduct of officials besides ensuring right to information for clients and concerned citizens in obtaining copies of public documents and giving value for money

*Cited in 'Management Techniques for Inculcating Aesthetic Sense', by S. Rajneesh, published in *Management in Government,* October-December, 2001.

to the affected, concerned and harassed members of the public. Briefly, Citizens' Charters aim at transforming and modernising public services as part of good governance. Therefore, a public administrator has to act as sheet anchor for his office in rendering of services in conformity to the provisions of Citizens' Charter.

As human resources management is the key factor for the success of any management or administration, a good administrator has to motivate and inspire his colleagues and subordinates towards rendering of quality services by:

1. Periodical inspection of his own office and field offices and setting both a model example of inspection note for his colleagues to follow in inspecting their own respective wings or subordinate offices/cells;
2. Holding weekly meetings of senior officers and subordinates with a view to monitoring necessary information and for coordinating their work with a focus on the goals and objectives of the organisation;
3. Coordinating in periodical meetings with other offices with a view to bring about convergence in field services like health, education, agriculture extension and women's development etc. Public representatives should also be invited for better interaction and long lasting solutions in such meetings;
4. Evolving proper Management Information System (MIS) by installing equipment of information technology and by computerisation of office for which there is no dearth of funds in government departments/corporations;
5. Purposeful touring of the area and field offices under his control unlike a tourist and more like a motivated leader who can bring about visible changes and progress by interaction with subordinates and public representatives in taking steady strides towards good governance;
6. Strengthening Panchayat Raj Institutions (PRIs), especially panchayats, with a view to bring together functionaries of field agencies at a common platform for better coordination and convergence in schemes like Integrated Child Development Scheme being implemented through Anganbari, health sub-centres, primary health centres, dispensaries and schools both formal and non-formal running under various schemes. Panchayat, as a coordinating mechanism for village-level field functionaries, should, therefore, receive priority attention of an administrator; and

7. Encouraging NGOs and voluntary bodies to develop an associate relationship with government officials and workers, and for this purpose, an administrator should set up forum for regular interface and interaction between government institutions and NGOs so that misgivings are removed and working relationship is established on a sustainable basis towards achievement of short-term and long-term goals of governance.

Finally, a good administrator cannot and should not wait for political will to be generated for providing necessary tools to his team for the delivery of public services. We have waited too long for political will to be embodied in various measures towards bringing about administrative reforms. A good administrator has to generate his own team and determined willpower to bring about changes in his work environment. Of course, he will also need to cultivate qualities of politeness, patience and perseverance before he embarks upon the task of motivating his colleagues. His personal example would certainly prove better than any precept or any preaching on his part.

In conclusion, an administrator should reach 'development at doorsteps' for the benefit of common man by applying Gandhiji's 'talisman test' which is as follows:

> I will give you a talisman. Whenever you are in doubt or when the self becomes too much with you, apply the following test: Recall the face of the poorest and the weakest man whom you may have seen, and ask yourself if the step you contemplate is going to be of any use to him. Will he gain anything by it? Will it restore him to a control over his own life and destiny? In other words, will it lead to Swaraj for the hungry and spiritually starving millions? Then you will find your doubts and your self melting away.

An administrator will find his work self-satisfying if he makes the above test the touchstone of his own work and performance which will be followed by members of his team in almost all situations and circumstances.

6

Management in Government

B.R. VIRMANI

The present system of public administration in India was developed by the British as a colonial power. The top administrators were British, joined by a few Indians of the elitist background. Although, after independence, many changes have been brought about, these have not been markedly successful in improving the socio-economic standard of the bulk of the people, which is the basic objective of any government administration. Impact studies of the development programmes show that the enduring benefits for the people have not been achieved to the extent desirable through efficient management of the government systems. This may be due to the tremendous gaps between the real needs/expectations of the people and the capacity of the government administration to gear its resources and administrative set-up to meet such needs of the public.

The present management principles, as operating in the Indian context, go back to the 19th Century after the War of 1857. At that time, British administration realised that it may not be very prudent, from the point of view of the British Empire, to trust the colonial people occupying government positions. Therefore, the government formulated very rigid rules and regulations for every aspect of administration, so that very little discretionary power was left with the lower level functionaries in the government set-up. The management by rules became the principle of public administration. The whole principle of formulation of rules was based on the mistrust of the natives. Even after independence, though the British have left, it was considered more convenient by our own government to continue with the same set of rules, regulations and approach. Rules became the ends rather than the means to achieve public good. In addition, the problem became more complex due to a democratic political set-up, the attitude of the bureaucrats, the expectations of the people, the present necessity to industrialise the country quickly and to improve the living standard of the masses. It is in this context that this paper discusses some of the concepts, issues and problems of management in government.

Administrators and People

Senior administrators in India are very largely a product of bourgeois upbringing, attitudes and beliefs which set them apart from the rest of the people. There is a hiatus between them and the real world of the people they are expected to serve. Even though there may be an awareness of the gap and also a desire to bridge it, one usually adjusts to reality in ways least threatening to one's self-esteem. The role of the bureaucrats in India is too vital to let them develop or drift the way they like. A deliberate effort needs to be made in the government administration and in the minds of the bureaucrats to create empathy with the people, the circumstances that surround them along with appropriate skills to deliver the goods.

The administrator needs to be influenced to adopt a more responsive attitude towards the clientele so that they can fashion or promote policies to serve their felt-needs and also take administrative measures, more appropriate to the responsibilities they are expected to discharge. For instance, if a Rs 2,500 crore plan to buy aeroplanes to augment Indian Airlines fleet can be approved, and the one requiring Rs 20 crore for manufacturing bus chassis is disapproved, there is a question of social priority which needs to be appreciated. Similarly, administrators regularly support projects to add highways, widen roads, build expensive flyovers and generally facilitate the movement of private car traffic in city. Scarcely, any thought is given to improve traffic arrangements so as to facilitate bus-operation, cyclists' and pedestrian movement, although only a tiny minority of the people in the city can afford to travel in cars.

Even the introduction of the auto-rickshaw system in a city like Calcutta or Bombay which provides a middle-ground between the cheap bus service and the expensive taxi, evokes hostility from the administrators; although it serves the needs of the middle-class, Similarly, most of the land reform measures have been unsuccessful because of the impression some administrators have that smaller holdings tend to affect agricultural production adversely. While this may be true, if the holdings are fragmented beyond a point, it is not generally true, as is proved from the Japanese experience. Much of this is the result of ignorance of the economic conditions of the people.

Partly, these problems arise from the kind of training given to the administrators during the initial years. The National Academies which train the administrators still emphasise on some of the elitist values which alienate the administrators from the larger public. Though, they are given theoretical lessons in socio-economic life and problems of the country, the attitudinal change cannot be brought about by merely explaining things in a class-room or short-term visits to rural areas or to different parts of the country. The programme must be of longitudinal type, where the civil servants would get an opportunity to go into the field, study the problems and take up action-research projects, so that they are aware of the real situations in which government has to operate.

Political Set-up

A charge is often levelled that the government management system cannot function effectively because of the political interference and the various pressure groups, which prevent them from taking decisions which are in the interest of the public good. The administrators should be alive to the political environment—to legislators and pressure groups, and also with the ways in which they function. An understanding of the political context and the forces that operate in it can help the administrator to employ them for the achievement of the social objectives. What appear to be constraints, can be intelligently turned into resources.

This suggestion may seem impractical and beyond the limits of conventional behaviour, but to dismiss it outright is perhaps to take a passive posture towards public interest. The administrator should not consider the environment around him as necessarily obstructive. As long as social objectives are paramount, employing forces to serve them should be considered good judgement and good work.

In addition to the question of accountability to one's superior, the Parliament or being on the right side of the audit, there is even a greater need for accountability to public interest. To feel satisfied in having exhausted all possibilities of action and therefore, having done one's duty, without achieving the objective is not enough. One must also ask oneself whether all the possibilities that could have helped achieve results have been explored. This is not to suggest that rules must be disregarded. Rather, there is often a wide degree of freedom to act within the spirit of the rules.

Often, the government administrators feel that old values of the civil servants like honesty and integrity have been under the onslaught of new political forces. The imperative of political power makes public leaders directly interfere with the system of implementation (administration), which was generally left untouched by them in the past. With the result, the bureaucrats are forced to compromise and while the brave resist the best they can, most are passing through a sandwich period of severe conflict and erosion of values. Therefore, there is a need to train and equip the administrator in the methods of coping with such environment while performing their jobs; and to preserve the good men and women before they get thoroughly demoralised. Though it is true that there is a necessity of upholding the image of the government functionaries as guardians of public interest, one wonders what their role should be vis-à-vis the public leaders, who too are guardians of public interest.

This raises the issue of the boundary of transaction between government bureaucrats and the elected leaders. In such a predicament, we run into difficulties and the only possible answer is to leave the administrator to discover for himself. The only thing one can do is to bring into line the various models and alternatives, which may sharpen their capacity to grasp and discriminate between the factors involved in a situation concerning his relationship with public leaders.

This further raises the issue of accountability. To whom is the administrator accountable? Theoretically, to the public, but the public is too remote. Or, is he accountable to his immediate boss? Moreover, who is going to decide public interest—the public leaders or the administrators? Thus, one does tread on uncertain ground, for which the rules of the game cannot be easily defined, and therefore, must be left to the better judgement of the game players themselves. The main point is that accountability is not necessarily or merely to the boss. There is something more involved in it, which is the interest of the public, even though it may be remote. Instances are not lacking where government administrators have been able to boost their career by manipulating politicians and environment to their advantage without public interest being kept in view.

Therefore, on the issue of political interference in government administration, there could be two views: one view is that the administrators can use the politicians, if the result orientation and the public cause is clear to them, just as they use these politicians to boost their own career; while the other view could be that it may be a difficult and even undesirable practice; It may be argued from the administrators' angle that their job is to bring out the facts before the politicians and if the politicians do not agree, the government administrators have to carry out the orders. Therefore, the focus on the part of the government administrators should not be how to manipulate politicians, but how to bring about coordination between the politicians and the administrators. The administrators should not become politicians themselves. The government administrators must also understand the problems of politicians and then see how best they can develop understanding with them, keeping in view the public good as the primary objective of both.

Personnel Policies

The government organisations being enormous in size, the major task any administrator faces is to keep the workforce motivated and to deal with their day-to-day personnel problems.

Some of the problem areas and constraints affecting personnel policies in government are:

1. Excessive reliance on rules and procedures;
2. Constraints imposed by the political set-up like delays and indecision;

3. Inefficient and ill-equipped staff due to constraints on recruitment, promotion and transfer policies (e.g., reservations of jobs, sons of the soil theory, etc.);
4. Development of multidimensional skills in public services because of frequent transfers from one function to another;
5. Disincentive to accept delegation due to public and parliamentary accountability;
6. Dependence on security of job, income, career and seniority;
7. Surplus staffing; and
8. Above all, the employees' expectation that their satisfaction is the primary objective of the government organisations; all others are secondary objectives.

In the Indian context, some sort of a paternalistic approach in motivating the employee will continue to play a role. The employees still want to be dependent on their superior and their organisation for personal security. In this context, it may be worth mentioning that MBO approach or independent goal setting exercise (borrowed from western philosophy of management) may not be very realistic in all situations in India.

There is a need to reorient manpower planning in government based on result orientation. Once the organisational objectives and expected results are clear, then one can do the organisational requirement planning, workforce skill planning and forecasting the manpower requirements, including manpower planning for special policy programmes such as for Scheduled Castes, Scheduled Tribes, backward regions, etc.

Employee Relations

There has been a tremendous growth of government employee organisations (trade unions) more or less on the pattern of industrial undertakings. Some of the reasons for such growth are:

1. Inability of an individual employee in a large bureaucracy to be heard by his employers, unless he speaks in a collective voice;
2. Growing sentiment in the clerical labour force that a concerted, organised action is needed to increase their earning power and protect their rights;

3. Encouragement of the collective bargaining principle by government as well as employee organisations which is normally used in industrial sector;
4. Awareness among trade union leaders that public services could be a vast potential area for their organised efforts; and
5. The most important is the attitude of many public administrators rooted in the traditional concept of the prerogatives of the administrators' sovereign authority and distrust of economic, political and social objectives of the employee organisations.

On one hand, the administrators deny that all the personnel related issues are joint prerogatives, as they consider them to be exclusive managerial rights of the administrators. On the other hand, they are giving up all these prerogatives, one by one, as a result of pressure from the employee organisations. Therefore, the only structure used to make exclusive employer prerogatives into joint prerogatives is that of conflict, based on principles of collective bargaining. The government administrators have to realise that the idea of exclusive prerogatives has to be gradually given up and a different institutional structure based on participative management be developed; where, almost all the personnel issues are to be treated as joint prerogatives, which are to be resolved without recourse to conflict.

Collective Bargaining

At times, the government employees may hold public welfare as a hostage to their demands. For instance, what might be the impact of a strike by all employees of Defence, Police or Posts and Telegraphs? Although, collective bargaining can take place in such a setting, the fundamental issues involved are not identical to those presented by collective bargaining in industrial sphere and some modifications of industrial practices are therefore needed.

Even in the industrial sector, there may be a moderating influence, i.e., by disruption; the organisation may close down. But in public services, this influence is not there because of public funding. It is in this context that in government services one has to evolve an institutional structure of cooperation based on participation rather than conflict and collective bargaining, so that the matters could be jointly resolved without holding the public to ransom.

Result Orientation

Many government administrators are not motivated to encourage any productivity improvement effort, because most of them do not understand what productivity is within the governmental context. As already mentioned, there are problems of environmental influences, like executive interference, legislature, constituencies, rules and procedures, which reduce the flexibility of an administrator's action. The major approach in government administration in India is on streamlining of the procedures, clearance of files and following rules. However, very rarely, the result of the efforts has been kept in view. The government administration is not for the sake of administration, but for the sake of producing results and increasing productivity for public good. Therefore, all the managerial policies in government have to be ultimately viewed in the context of productivity of employees and their result-orientation rather than devising of various systems and procedures for their own sake.

The government administrators rarely emphasise upon productivity improvement as a major administrative theme. Any effort made in this direction should be in line with result-oriented administrative theme of economy of efforts and creative conservation. Simply stated, the purpose of productivity-effort is to get improved results out of allocated resources.

Creating Empathy

The role of administrators in contemporary Indian society is too vital to let them develop or drift the way they like. A deliberate effort needs to be made through training, to create empathy with people, the circumstances that surround them and to instil in them the confidence in their ability, backed with appropriate skill to deliver the goods. Apart from attitudinal and motivational changes, a sense of commitment to their achievement is also needed and an attitude of mind has to be created which develops its own methods or techniques in response to the alternatives available in a situation.

Unless one is committed to public good, one will neither explore alternatives, nor exert oneself beyond the routine. Therefore, to develop the concept of productivity and result-orientation, the following suggestions may be of help:

1. Pursuit of most critical aspects which can affect realisation of the objectives; and
2. Delegation nearer the point at which the common public approaches the administrator for relief. This will involve appropriate controls to ensure that power is not misused and also the follow-up of the action.

Most of the administrators are career-oriented rather than result-oriented. In fact, so far as result-orientation and work are concerned, they develop a lot of cynicism during the early years of their career. The result is that they lose a sense of mission and concern themselves primarily with those aspects which can boost their career. This necessitates an intensive realistic initial attitudinal training during the first ten to fifteen years of their career so that cynicism does not develop in them.

It may also be kept in view that it is not only youngsters whose attitudes need to be changed but the top most functionaries like secretaries and even ministers need attitudinal change as they are often considered to be the stumbling blocks in the achievement of results, though changing the attitudes of an older age group may be a difficult task.

Training and Development

Till recently, development of government administrators through training was not given the importance it deserved. One possible reason could be that the benefits of training were not clear to the administrators. Training was often treated as a punishment, or in certain cases was based on the principle of "sparability". It was only during the past 4–5 years that increasing attention has been paid to the training of government administrators. It was even made obligatory by the Department of Personnel and Training that every government administrator should at attend least one or two training programmes in a year. Normally, training needs are identified at the central level by the Department of Training and then the persons are selected and directed to attend the training programmes. In certain cases, at the central level, the trainees were asked to give their preferences out of a choice of 2–3 institutions. Such selection methods were perceived by many officers as arbitrary, ad hoc and not in line with the needs of their jobs (Virmani, 1989). In some cases, the training programme was not related to their immediate job, nor to the one which they are likely to hold in the near foreseeable future, with the result that such "forced training" evoked a negative response and hostility towards training (for details, see, Virmani, "Management Training and Development: An Evaluation Approach", Hyderabad: Administrative Staff College of India, 1989).

There was also a feeling that because of the recent emphasis by the government on training, training has become an end in itself. Since the training needs identification has become the responsibility of a centralised agency; therefore, the individual departments themselves have abdicated their responsibility of developing their personnel. They have also got the belief that identifying the training needs and conducting training programmes is totally the responsibility of the training department or the training institution and they have no role to play in this. Also, no importance is given to planned on-the-job training where the immediate superiors can play a major role in developing their subordinates (Virmani, 1989).

In government, there is hardly any formal follow-up or evaluation of training with regard to transfer of learning to the job, except that at the end of the training programme the trainees are normally asked to give their views about the training. Recently, government had asked some experts to undertake a formal evaluation of a few courses conducted specifically for government administrators, but this evaluation was again confined to asking the participants—how did they like the course—but not about its contribution to the improvement in their performance. In fact, one very senior officer connected with the training function said that the government administrator—is a cog in the wheel and to expect any improvement in his performance through training is expecting too much. Similar was the view of one of the persons who did the evaluation of some of the government programmes (Virmani, 1989). If this is so, then one needs to question—what for are we training the officers and spending huge sums of public money? Certain criteria have to be evolved for measuring the transfer of learning to ensure that the training is need-based, realistic and results in change. The government has already declared to completely review their training strategy for government administrators. While reviewing the strategy, government may like to consider if there is a relationship between training and work performance; also that the placement after training is related to the training received; and the training serves the long term goals. Therefore, there should be a systematic attempt at identification of training needs, designing suitable programmes and linking the training with the job situation, with appropriate control measures to ensure that the learning is transferred to the job. In this connection, there may be a need to re-orient the annual employee appraisal system for identifying the strengths and weaknesses of the employees for developmental purposes rather than purely for promotions. There have to be proper methods of career planning and training, especially when seniority may continue to play a dominant role in promotion policies in government for some time to come.

Motivation and Reward

Another major issue is the motivation and reward system for government administrators. Many a time, they are supposed to implement the policies made at the political or top level and defend them as "Just and right" to maintain their authority, though in reality they personally disagree with them. This clash of their own values and the policies they implement (though with no commitment to them) could be tolerated up to a limit, but if pushed too much, may result in indifference to work, frustration with the job and lack of commitment to the public good.

Instances are not lacking where many of the middle level government administrators hate to do what they are doing, but still they have no choice. The result is that they are completely demotivated, frustrated and start hating their organisation. If the top and middle level functionaries are demotivated and have no commitment to what they are doing, then one cannot expect them to motivate their juniors to develop any commitment for the job.

Such a problem is more evident at the middle management level in the government. This is a serious problem and has no ready-made solution. To some extent, the adverse impact can be minimised by allowing a free debate among various levels of employees to express their views on policy issues. This will again mean developing an institutional structure of participative management at all levels. The indirect benefit of such discussions within the government functionaries and officers at all levels can also result in checking the abuse of power, both by the top level government functionaries as well as politicians.

So far as the reward system is concerned, theoretically, one can say that achievement of results in itself can be a reward, as in government it is very difficult to increase salaries or give extra monetary incentives. However, it will be too much to expect that the government servants will work only—for social good and that itself should become a reward.

This may be an idealistic concept because in most cases they also work for the family and themselves and one cannot lose sight of this aspect. The examples of wife and family members corrupting the civil servants are not lacking in government administration. Therefore, there is a need for in-depth study and evolving some in-built reward and incentive systems, linked directly to the result-orientation and public good and not necessarily to clearance of files on time. The focus has to be on how much real public good was achieved after clearance of files.

To conclude it can be stated that there is a need to make a systematic effort to understand the predominant attitudes and lifestyles of the government administrators; the way they tend to structure their work-environment; the work-strategy they adopt; as well as their perception of the scope of administrative action, limitations and sense of responsibility to public good (and, of course, which public?) and then possibly a well-thought out effort be made to streamline the system of management in government. Some of the problems and suggestions highlighted in this paper may be of help in reorienting management concepts in government administration.

7

Managerial Excellence for Effectiveness

N.K. KULSHRESTHA

Efficiency, effectiveness and excellence have become by words of modern management literature. They are not mere slogans but reflect a system, an approach, a managerial lifestyle and perhaps a living law for organisations. However, to realise excellence and to apply excellence to gauge organisational performance is a formidable challenge.

Excellence is conceptualised in various ways by various authorities in management literature. By and large, excellent organisations are forward-looking, highly innovative and foresee change with a view to taming it. They are excellent because they make exceptional efforts. Externally, their strategy is directed towards strategic thinking up to the bottom line of the organisation. Such thinking concerns, environmental challenges (threats and opportunities) and the mission of the organisation, to be measured by profitability, growth in terms of input-output and resources, market share, value addedness, consumerism, social welfare, community welfare, and finally a productive organisation that generates employment, national income, capital formation and thus opportunities for rich and varied life to the citizens. Excellence guarantees better quality of life everywhere. Internally, organisational excellence reflects employee-satisfaction, enthusiasm and loyal attitudes, innovation and creativity along with institutionalised mechanisms, balance between formalism and informalism—but with more formalism in culture and informalism in hierarchy. The design of excellent organisations permits failure in order to encourage experimentation and exploit new ideas, inventions, innovations and perhaps, it is never resting on the laurels. Such organisations are imbued with a culture of basic organisational personality, where every one from the top to the bottom thinks of success, achievement, commitment, work performance and derives spiritual satisfaction out of organisational work. There is horizontal/vertical loyalty amongst people with perhaps a fellow feeling, a sense of belonging together. The concept of quality is a pivot of an organisation's mission. There is a searching inquisitiveness where constraints are looked at as opportunities by analysis, new notions, new actions described and identified constantly rather than harping on past transactions. The organisation values arguments more highly than serenity of pearls of wisdom spread from elsewhere and perhaps, encourages attitudes and experimentation to contradict the prevalent beliefs, myths or mysticism in corporate culture. Usually, models of excellence are created by an organisation through its outstanding products and services. Such an excellence is ascribed to individuals, who because of the unique skills which they have, the organisation permeates excellence. Individuals by their problem-solving style along with their innovative future-oriented dialogue pass on such excellence to the organisation. These individuals provide a leading edge of new trends and ideas on which a developing organisation always thrives to act.

Earlier observations of excellence emphasised on strategic-planning, which was a device adopted by an organisation to tame a turbulent environment—socio-economic, political, demographic and technological. A strategy is after all an organisation's reaction to changes in the environmental perspective through constant adjustments. An organisation faced with change must shape environment or otherwise be reshaped by it, if it wants to attain its objectives and mission. This task was done by corporate planners in the name of corporate planning, strategic planning and management by objectives.

The logistics of achievement, the mission of corporate planning was reflected by operational plans and action plans reviewed periodically at different levels of an organisation. This requires re-designing of organisational structure. Hence, the concept of excellence demanded that to realise the strategy, structural re-designing has to be done, so as to produce excellent results for the organisation. This approach had highlighted the significance of corporate planning/strategic planning, but at the same time created frustration in the middle and bottom line executives, who had no role to design its destiny and as such a corporation could hardly achieve excellence. Hence, the concept of entrepreneur was developed, where doers' were also planners and all levels in the organisation were enlightened to think strategically. So entrepreneurship-spirit was pushed downward instead of keeping it as a reservoir at the top.

Areas of Excellence

Researches in America have established that "any intelligent approach to organising had to encompass and treat as interdependent, at least seven variables: structure, strategy, people/staff, management system (style), procedure guiding concepts (system), shared values (i.e., culture) in the present and hoped for organisational strengths or skills".

The afore-mentioned parameters are christened as Mckinsey's 7-S Framework of Happyatom organising for excellence in the company. Such a multi-variable framework of parameters of excellence in organisations has also been propounded by Harold Leavitt, as Leavitt's Diamond which propagates the task, structure, people, information, control and environment as key aspects of excellence.

Approaches and Parameters of Excellence

Thomas J. Peters and Waterman, in their book, *In Search of Excellence*, have highlighted the following eight attributes of excellence by analysing the most effective American companies:

1. *A Bias for Action:* It calls for a restless organisation that counters tendency towards conformity and inertia and encourages problem-solving groups to bring action-orientation. Such devices are adopted as they make the organisation future-oriented and deploy right resources, matching each problem. Excellent corporation takes an idea and makes metal out of it. The standard operating procedure usually is, 'Do it, Fix it, Try it or Ready, Aim and Fire'.
2. *Close to Customers:* This requires services to the customers, listening to them intently, regularly and providing them matchless, outstanding, unparalleled quality and reliability in service.
3. *Autonomy and Entrepreneurship:* Excellent companies are innovative companies which are big, but act as small at the same time, by encouraging entrepreneurial spirit among the people through autonomy. The idea is to develop a band of product champions or bureaucracy beaters, who are crazy for productivity, invention and innovation.
4. *Productivity Through People:* The philosophy is to boost to the maximum, productivity of an average man.
5. *Hands on Being Value Driven:* Focus on achievements of the basic premises of the organisation.
6. *Stick to Knitting:* Stay close to business that is known.
7. *Simple Form and Lean Staff:* Preferably a matrix-organisational structure is required.
8. *Simultaneously Loose Tight Property:* The organisation is centralised so far as the core value is concerned, but decentralised and autonomous so as to develop entrepreneurial spirit.

According to another exponent of excellence, Crack R. Hickman and Silva, it is a direct outcome of strategic thinking-cum-planning, its proper blend with organisational culture and new age attitudinal skills on the part of management. Corporate leaders need now to adopt new attitudes, skills and abilities, so as to face new challenges and new situations that characterise the present New Age. They have to apply the following six essential skills for managerial excellence on the basic foundation of strategy and structure in an organisation:

1. *Creative Insight:* Asking right questions for developing a superior strategy.
2. *Sensitivity:* To bind the people in a culture where they are fully motivated to achieve goals and form a foundation for excellence.
3. *Vision:* Creating a future which is shaped through organisational introspection and clear understanding of business environment.
4. *Versatility:* To invent and anticipate change by pursuing organisational interest beyond organisation's orbit.
5. Focus: Implementing change.
6. *Patience:* To plan in the long run and commit to the long-term perspective of the enterprise.

These indices need to be applied in varying mix in all organisations.

There are three deadly attitudes that check the development of New Age outlook, like excessive short-term orientation, shallow thinking, concentration on daily crisis and quick-fix type cheap solutions which provide temporary relief to agonising problems.

Excellence is generated through the use of strategic thinking, culture-building and application of these six skills through the following four common stages:

1. Start on original strategy and culture.
2. Growth through holding strategy and culture together.
3. Crisis through radical strategy and culture.
4. Evolution through fine tuning of strategy and culture.

It is only then that an excellent organisation lives, thrives, and meets the challenges posed by a changing environment.

8

Inventory Management and Control Techniques

GIRISH K. SRIVASTAVA

Inventory is an important item not only in an organisation where accounts are maintained on commercial principles but in other government departments also which render service to the public. Proper inventory control affects the efficiency and effectiveness of the government activities.

Huge amounts are invested in inventories. Due to lack of knowledge of modern techniques of inventory control, the inventories are not properly utilised and the government has to bear loss caused due to theft, pilferage, obsolescence, surpluses, inadequate supply, delay in execution of works, improper maintenance, etc.

It is, therefore, necessary that government departments should design their inventory control system in a form best suitable to their specific requirements so that scarce resources of the government are utilised efficiently to ensure that works/services are executed/rendered in an efficient and economical manner and unnecessary blocking of funds is avoided.

There are several techniques of inventory control. Some of the important techniques which may be applied in government departments are discussed as under:

Month's Consumption Analysis for Head of Departments/Controlling Officers

Month's consumption analysis is useful for the top management/heads of departments. It is calculated in terms of "month's consumption" basis rather than in absolute figures. It will help them in knowing average consumption of inventory and assist them in setting periodical target/stock limit for inventories.

Inventory Classification

In government departments, a number of items are kept in stores for various purposes. Such items are not of equal importance. It is difficult to have control over each of them. At the same time, a department is expected to have adequate knowledge of items in stores for better supervision and control. To achieve this objective, inventories need to be classified into groups on the basis of their use, consumption, value, lead time, etc. Government departments may adopt any classification given below as may be considered suitable to them:

ABC Classification

The classification is based on the principle of 'Vital Few' and 'Trivial Many'. It means department should pay high degree of attention on Vital Few, which significantly affect the funds placed at its disposal. In departments, certain items are used in small quantity but they involve high value, while certain items are used in huge quantity involving low value. There are other items which are neither used in large quantity nor in small quantity and may be termed as of medium importance. The items may, therefore, be classified on the following basis as may be convenient to the department, e.g.,

Itemwise category	*Percentage of consumed items*	*Percentage of rupee value*
A	Small (10)	High (70)
B	Medium (20)	Medium (20)
C	High (70)	Least (10)

The above classification will help department in deciding the extent of supervision and control over those items which are considered critical to the requirements and are of high value, requiring constant watch on their stock position at a given time and thus prompt the department to have better planning in advance for their purchases, etc.

FSN (Fast, Slow and Non-moving) Classification

The classification is based on the frequency of issues of the items. In the departments, the frequency of issue/consumption of certain items may be considered fast moving. Such items will need constant control and monitoring regarding their stock position, etc. The classification will help the department to keep close supervision over fast moving items, their replenishment, etc., at the proper time and at the same time help them in arranging action for timely transfer, disposal, etc., of non-moving item.

HML (High, Medium and Low) Classification

The classification would involve an analysis on the basis of cost per item. Inventories may be classified on the basis of High Cost, Medium Cost and Low Cost. Although need to exercise control over medium cost and low cost is there, but this classification will give focus for keeping control over consumption of high cost items and to decide the frequency of physical verification of inventories to have proper control.

VED (Vital, Essential and Desirable) Classification

The classification is based on the 'vitality' of an item and its effect on services or production. Such type of classification is useful in management of spare parts inventory or in hospital administration where the drugs and other items can be classified on the basis of their vitality of use. The departments should keep watch over selected vital items to ensure their uninterrupted supply and availability in stores and thus efficient functioning of the department is ensured.

SDE (Scarce, Difficult and Easily)/GCLF (Government Controlled, Local and Foreign) Classification

The classification is based on the availability of items which are scare/short supply/government controlled items or to be imported from other countries. The items are procured and stored irrespective of their value, volume and frequency of issues to avoid the critical situation of failure of services or production. Seasonal and off-seasonal items should also be viewed in the same context. Items which are easily available in local markets are thus not to be stored in large quantity. This would need planning in advance keeping in view that longer lead time would be necessary for those items which are to be imported or procured from government sources.

Ordering System: EOQ Approach

Placing order of items involves two important aspects, one regarding its quantity at a given time and the other is the periodicity. In this, two costs, viz., ordering costs or acquiring cost of the purchase section and inventory carrying cost of store section are to be considered. Ordering cost is reduced with the increase in size of order while inventory carrying cost goes up with the increase in size of order. While placing an order it is necessary to examine the size of order where the above cost would be minimum. This size of order decided at a given time would be 'Economic Order of Quantity' (EOQ). If the department places an order more than this size or less, it will not be an economical order of the department.

Reduction of Lead Time

The procurement time is lead time. It is the time taken in making requisition for an item and in invitation of tenders, receipt, inspection and final lodging in store. The lead time is of two types, viz., Internal Lead Time (ILT) and External Lead Time (ELI). The internal lead time is often more due to lack of advance planning as per requirements of the department and, therefore, needs attention at higher level to arrange initiation of the process of procurement well-in-time so as to ensure constant availability of items in the store. ELT is the time taken for making supplies by the supplier which is beyond control but efforts should be made to monitor and reduce it.

Inventory Level

Another important aspect of inventory control is the level at which inventories are required to be kept at a time to ensure proper working of the department. The inventory level should not be too much or too low. This would avoid chances of being surplus, obsolescence and consequently blocking of funds and avoid stock out situation. The following levels are explained for the information of the departmental authorities who may adopt any one or all of them as convenient to them:

1. Minimum Level or Safety Level
2. Re-order Level or Replenishment Level
3. Maximum Level

Minimum Level

The level indicates the lowest quantity of stock to be kept at a particular time to ensure proper functioning of the department. The level is worked out on the basis of month's average consumption and average lead time involved in procuring the items. Analyses like VED analysis for vital items, SDE analysis for scarce items and GOLF analysis for government controlled local and foreign items as explained above are useful to ensure adequate safety stock all the time to avoid running out of stock.

Re-order Level

This is the level at which the department should place an order for fresh supply of inventories. The level can be worked out as under:

Re-order Level = Safety Stock Level
+ Maximum Lead Time Consumption

Maximum Level

This is the level at which the department is required to keep maximum quantity of inventory at a time to avoid surplus stock, chances of obsolescence and consequent losses thereon. The level can be worked out as under:

Maximum Level = Order Quantity + Safety Stock

The levels explained above should be reviewed periodically and revised, if necessary.

Inventory Records

Proper records of inventories are necessary for effective inventory control, formulation of policy and taking decisions for purchases, fixing limits, etc. The records should provide information regarding consumption pattern, lead time, progressive consumption, and balances of items. Bin cards are an effective tool of inventory control. Bin cards should be prepared for each item of inventories and kept with the items or hung on bins or racks in the store rooms. They provide ready information about the description of material, specification, location, receipts, issues, and the balances in stock and helps physical verification and provide counter check with Stores Ledgers.

Inventory Reporting System

An effective inventory control system would need proper information and reporting system. The decision-making process depends upon timely, accurate, adequate, relevant information. The following reports are given for adoption:

Special Reports

The following information will keep the higher officers informed about the level of inventories, etc., and help them in taking important decisions.

1. Budget allocation for purchases.
2. Total investment in existing inventories.
3. Planning for acquisition-determination of methods of inventory control relevant to department.
4. Purchases position.
5. Position of physical verification.
6. Inventory losses due to
   (i) obsolescence,
   (ii) deterioration,
   (iii) damages, and
   (iv) theft/losses etc.
7. List of non-moving items on yearly basis.
8. Supplier's performance and dependability.
9. Alternate suppliers and their price patterns.

Routine Reports

The following reports are used for routine decisions and should be prescribed monthly, quarterly or half yearly as may be considered necessary:

1. Likely stock out items—Quarterly basis.
2. Pending purchases orders—Quarterly basis.
3. Inventory turnover rates—Monthly basis.
4. Excess stock item—Quarterly basis.
5. Inventory carrying cost—Yearly basis.

Standardisation, Variety Reduction and Codification

Standardisation

Standardisation is a potential tool to eliminate unnecessary varieties of inventories and thereby affect cost improvement and savings on inventories. In case of non-standardised items, there may be chances of non-availability of spare parts in the market after a period of time. It is necessary for the department to standardise items to the extent possible within the purchase rules. This will help them in finding out established suppliers and save time to locate them and ensure timely supplies.

Variety Reduction

Variety reduction is another important aspect of inventory control. It would help in reducing variety in stores which would ultimately affect the cost of inventory of spares and other items. The lesser the items to be controlled, the easier and more effective will be the inventory control process. It would also help in reducing unnecessary paper work and savings in establishment. The technique would benefit government departments to eliminate keeping unnecessary types, grades, shapes and sizes of items and specifying fewer items to serve the same purpose of a lower cost.

Codification and Computerisation

Another important aspect of inventory control is codification. It implies assigning of symbol-numeric or alphabetic for each classified item to ensure proper maintenance of stores and to facilitate computerisation of inventory control. It would avoid ambiguity, vagueness and confusion in naming any item. The departments would benefit in the form of time saving, easy identification of item, easy store operation, improved record keeping, maintenance of secrecy, and adoption of computers in inventory control process. This will also help them in designing better information system.

9

Developing Management Competence

HANS C. BLAISE

"Government has ceased to be merely the keeper of the peace, the arbiter of disputes, and the provider of common services. For better or worse, government has directly and indirectly become a principal innovator, a major determiner of social and economic priorities, the guide as well as the guardian of social values, the capitalist and entrepreneur or subsidiser and guarantor of most new enterprises of great scale".[1]

In the decade of the 70's management[2] competence could well prove to be one of the most critical of the scarce resources in developing countries. More progress has been made in the area of development planning competence than is true for the ability to implement development projects. The technological and professional knowledge and skills in fields ranging from family planning and education to agriculture and industry have developed faster than the management competence necessary to design and carry out action programme. Although the shortage of personnel with management skills is found in both the public and the private sector, it is in the public sector that this shortage is particularly acute. A recent meeting of economic planners of the ECAFE region was only one of the many occasions where reference was made to the "implementation gap", to the inadequacy of translating plan targets into effective means of carrying out development programmes and projects. At the meeting, the lack of administrative capability was cited as a major obstacle to target achievement.[3]

It can hardly be suggested that the field of public administration has been a neglected area in the development efforts of most countries. Schools of public administration, government training institutes and centres have mushroomed in the developing countries over the past two decades. Hundreds of foreign experts have assisted developing country governments in their administrative reform efforts.[4] Yet, the results of the government reform and modernisation efforts are on the whole disappointing, the actual contributions of most of the schools of public administration to the improvement of performance in the public sector has at best been marginal, and government agencies continue to have a severe shortage of management personnel capable of guiding development programmes and projects to their effective completion. The government services of most countries still have a long way to go to develop the capability required to perform the innovative and entrepreneurial role referred to in the above quote from Frederick Mosher.

It will be suggested here that there is a need to re-examine the concerns of public administration as a professional field. To make a more viable and significant contribution to the development efforts, more attention must be devoted to public administration research, training and consultation to the actual management problems, processes and techniques of substantive government programmes. "in plain language, the focus of action in development administration must be upon actual development programmes".[5] I do not want to go into the somewhat sterile argument about the difference between public administration and development administration here. I do want to suggest, however, that scholars and practitioners of public administration need to focus much more on the management of concrete programmes in agriculture, education, family planning and other critical development areas than has been the case in the past, although the ideas expressed here are primarily based on my observations in South-east Asia, many of the points made will apply to other parts of the world as well.

Administration as an End-in-itself

On the surface, the statement that administration is a means to an end sounds like stating the obvious. One's immediate reaction to this statement would almost certainly be that obviously administration is a set of functions, processes, and techniques for the accomplishment of the objectives and targets of an organisation. Yet, if we look at the reality of the concerns, the research and writings, the teaching and professional activities of those who are considered professionals in the field of public administration, then we frequently find that their focus is on administration per se, without any direct relationship to substantive action programmes. When we examine the curricula of public administration schools and training institutes, we find that the teaching is almost entirely devoted to administrative functions (e.g., personnel management, financial administration), to administrative procedures and techniques (office management, O&M) and to an understanding of the administrative culture (the bureaucracy, organisation behaviour, the political system, etc.). More recently, the analysis of the policy making process has become an additional popular area. By far the majority of the education and training programmes devote little attention to the integration and application of the administrative functions and techniques to the management of actual substantive operating programmes. To a certain extent, therefore, it can be said that the emphasis in education and training on the means, and that the means-ends relationship that is only evident in the examination of the application of the administrative function and techniques to concrete action systems receives little attention. One might say that public administration research and teaching suffers from 'horizontalism' from an excess of concern with the internal elements of administrative structure, processes, and techniques and a lack of emphasis on the vertical dimension of the management and operation of social and economic programme areas.

Not only at public administration education centres but also in professional practice, public administration specialists have concerned themselves more with administrative forms and practices than with the application of knowledge about administration to government action programmes. A clear example of this can be found in the foreign technical assistance programmes of the UN, of AID, and of foundations. Ten years ago, Weidner pointed out in an article that—very little interest has been shown in functional ministries by the administration experts attached to foreign assistance projects".[6] Eight years later, Esman and Montgomery stated that—the public administration groups in AID have had only minor influence on the important administrative component ... of substantive projects (in education, public works, health and similar fields).[7] The emphasis of the public administration specialists has been on broad administrative reform and on the introduction of new technologies like personnel classification systems, PPBS, and the like. Seldom have they been focused on the analysis, design and guidance of the administrative structures, processes and techniques that would further the implementation of the department programmes in a given programme area.

A well-known phenomenon in bureaucratic organisations is "goal displacement", which occurs when "adherence to the rules, originally conceived as a means, becomes transformed into an end-in-itself".[8] The public administration literature is full of examples of this tendency among cautious government officials who by dogmatic compliance with the established norms and rules protect themselves and their position, even while in the process they block attempts at innovation and may severely hamper the pursuit of the targets and objectives of their organisation.[9] It would appear, however, that the very scholars and professional experts in public administration who have analysed and bemoaned the "goal displacement" tendencies in the public bureaucracy have themselves contributed and continue to contribute to this evil.

The displacement of goals does not only take place when the bureaucratic norms and rules, the proscriptions in the General Orders become more important than the values and purposes for which an organisation was created. It can equally result from a narrow focus on functions and techniques in administration, divorced from the reality context of specific organisation and programmes. Weidner has said that "public administration has glorified the means and forgotten the ends. Good administration and good human relations have become ends in themselves, quite apart from the achievement of other values that they may or may not facilitate".[10] In other words, "goal displacement" is not only expressed in the rigid adherence to rules by the officials of organisations, it can also be found in the functional and technological focus of the public administration experts.

A factor that has contributed to the concern of public administrators with the internal functions and processes is the perception of the role of the public servant. The idea that the public servant's primary if not exclusive concern is with the implementation of programmes, with faithfully carrying out the policy decisions of their political masters frequently still prevails. In the 1967 edition of their famous textbook, Pfiffner and Presthus still define public administration as "the coordination of individual and group efforts to carry out public policy. *It is mainly occupied with the routine work of government*" (emphasis added).[11] The same idea I have often heard expressed in university lecture halls and at conferences in developing countries.

The practicing higher civil servants are fully aware of the influence they can and do exert on both policy and programme decisions of government. Decisions on basic objectives and the final decisions on policy and programme matters may not be theirs. Political leaders could not function, however, without the strategic planning by career civil servants of economic and social programmes that will further basic objectives, without their creative and systematic analysis of action alternatives, and without their calculation of probable consequences of action alternatives.

The clear separation of policy and administration is a myth and the concept of public administration as being primarily concerned with the routine work of government a dysfunction orientation. It is both more realistic and more positive to recognise that the public administrator has an entrepreneurial and managerial role in government, albeit that he is bounded by the policy determination and decision-making powers that are vested in his political superiors. The creative, entrepreneurial and decision-making role of the public administrator as a manager warrants more attention than it has had in the past. This is particularly important with regard to the planning and management of economic and social development programmes.

As stated earlier, public administration experts have not shown much interest in the management and administration problems involved in the operation of substantive development programmes. Very little research has been conducted on the administrative aspects of programmes in fields like agriculture, health, education, etc.[12] Given the lack of attention paid to programme administration and the lack of demonstrated capability of public administrators in solving the concrete management problems faced by officials responsible for carrying out action programmes in these substantive fields, it is not surprising that "those of us who have a vested interest in public administration technical assistance have not been able to convince those who exercise "real bureaucratic" power that we have a valid body of knowledge which is useful in the development process".[13] In theory, it is certainly true that "a highly skilled specialist in some profession is not ipso facto a good administrator".[14] It is, however, up to the public administration specialist to demonstrate that he is capable of making a unique and relevant contribution to the functioning of an organisation in a given field. He must be able to show in practice that his contribution will help the man who is responsible for getting results in his programme area, and who may not himself have any specialised knowledge about administration.

By far the majority of organisations, departments and agencies are headed by people whose professional preparation has been in a field other than administration. They may be lawyers or doctors, engineers or educators. It would be unrealistic to aspire to having all management and administrative positions become the exclusive domain of those who are professionally trained for such positions. Apart from, or even more than, functioning in a management capacity as such, the management specialist can render staff assistance and consultative services to the managers and administrators who are responsible for organisations, departments and management.

Clearly, the management professional must have a demonstrable substantive competence, a unique body of knowledge that the de facto manager is convinced will help him to solve the problems he faces. If the head of an agricultural extension service, of a family planning organisation, or of an economic planning department fails to call upon the services of a public administration specialist, then this is not necessarily because these executives are too proud or that they fail to recognise the needs of their organisation. Even executives who have called on the advice of lawyers, economists, and statisticians may not call on management and administration specialists to assist them in the analysis of their management problems. And, if they call on such an expert, it is more likely to seek advice on a limited technical problem like record keeping or personnel practices. Could it be that the public administration profession has thus far failed to show that it has the capability to contribute to concrete problems of programme management?

Programme Management

Both expertise and recognition can be gained if the public administration fraternity would systematically focus its attention on programme management. By programme management I mean the planning, design and operation of action systems for the pursuit of specified objectives. It involves the making of allocative decisions or choice among alternative structures and processes of action. This, in turn, requires the systematic collection and analysis of pertinent data for decision-making. In programme management, the administrator continues to be concerned with functional areas like personnel management and financial administration, but he will analyse and apply his knowledge about administrative functions, as well as his knowledge about administrative techniques, about organisation behaviour, etc., to the problem at hand of achieving results in family planning organisations, in public works programmes, in crop diversification programmes and the like, "The problem in development administration" as Weidner states, "is to get results, not how to conform to a predetermined set of criteria of rationality".[15] Public administrators may have been overly concerned with "across-the-board changes", with drastic changes in personnel practices of the entire civil service, with the reorganisation of whole ministries if not the entire government.[16] Their contribution to economic and social development may be more effective if they concentrate their efforts on "a few large or otherwise important projects or programmes and concentrate on improving administration to the extent required to facilitate the preparation, execution and operation of these projects and programmes".[17]

Any development programme or project requires the coordination of many resources. Physical resources must be available at the proper time and place. Alternative allocations among programme elements must be considered to determine the optimum combination to achieve the desired results. The activities of many specialists and professionals need to be coordinated. An effective communication system must be set up both to guide action and to provide the data necessary for planning, monitoring and evaluation. All of this must take place not in an abstract world of administrative rationality, but in the real world of specific programmes with specified goals and objectives as the desired end state.

The question may legitimately be asked whether the engineer is not better prepared to decide on the management and resource allocation decisions of a highway construction programme than someone whose professional preparation is in administration. Or, it may be asked whether the physician is not better qualified to make decisions regarding a family planning programme than is a management specialist. The answer to this can be given in three parts:

1. There is an increasingly extensive, complex and precise body of knowledge about the elements, methods and techniques of analysis and decision-making relevant to the structuring of an action system designed to pursue social and economic objectives. The management professional has acquired this specialised knowledge and is able to make a unique complementary contribution to the technical and professional considerations that guide the choices and decisions made by engineers, physicians and other professionals in their work.
2. The programmatic considerations going into the planning and execution within any given substantive area are not limited to the professional elements for which the engineer, the agronomist, the physician or educator have been trained. Any action programme requires the coordination and reconciliation of professional inputs provided by people with a

variety of professional skills and backgrounds. Thus, the family planning organisation manager has to integrate and reconcile the contributions to the programme made by communications and promotion specialists with those of physicians' operating clinics. The highway programme manager must relate the legal and financial aspects of land acquisition to the construction requirements. The professional manager, if he is well prepared, is qualified to guide the analysis of these multiple professional contributions, to determine the manner in which the various inputs and activities can be coordinated over time to optimise resource allocation and target achievement.

3. Frequently, development projects are not an end-in-themselves, they are means to an end. To the highway engineer, the target or end-product of a road construction project is likely to be the physical construction of the road. To the development planner, however, the construction of that road is an improvement in the means of communication, providing access to the market for farm products, stimulating the geographic distribution of industrial production or whatever the ultimate objective may be. Programme management in terms of development administration, contrary to the more intermediate concerns of the highway engineer, involves analysis and action design of any project in the context of the larger system and the ultimate rather than the intermediate objective. Thereby, the development administrator engaged in programme management will provide not only the internal management and coordination guidance for the execution of programme and projects, but also link the programmes and projects to related programmes and activities, to a system of interdependent projects that, in their complementarity, lead to the desired results.

The "Integrationist" Administrator

The above are three significant areas in which public administration, through a focus on programme management, can make a more significant contribution than it has made to the development process in the past. What is called for in development administration is what Bertram Gross has called "integrating generalists".[18] Gross referred to that breed of administrators as people who "are looked to for skills not only in communication and compromise, but in the integration of divergent interests. they are expected to understand the organisation's broad environment as well as, or even more than, its internal workings they are expected to know enough about the relevant techniques to enable them to understand, evaluate, and coordinate the activities of many specialists and professionals".[19] The term "integrating generalist", which Gross uses to distinguish the now administrator from the traditional "gentleman generalist",[20] is somewhat misleading. Gross is certainly not using the term "generalist" in the sense of an erudite person with a broad, general liberal arts education. An example of what he means by "generalist" is given in a recent UN publication, prepared by him and a number of his colleagues. In that publication, it is stated that "the development administrator requires a thorough working knowledge of his own society in all its principal dimensions" and continues to list no less than sixteen of those "dimensions", ranging from agriculture and business to labour, natural resources, religion, science and technology.[21]

It is unquestionably true that the complexity of the development process as such, the scientific and technological advances made in health, agriculture, engineering, etc., as well as the technological advances in field of management itself are rapidly changing the character and the knowledge requirements of managers. The professional managers of the 70's need to develop the skill to discern the administrative elements and requirements in substantive programme areas with the professional and technological content of which he is at best vaguely familiar. He must have the ability to design the most appropriate interaction among dissimilar professional fields, each with their own requirements, preferences and priorities. He must be master of the analytical methods and tools that will make it possible to construct an effective action system. He must be able to analyse, guide and design the interdependencies of his own project or programme with those operating in the environment. Using the term in a somewhat different manner from the way it is used today, one might say that the manager of development programmes needs to be a systems analyst and systems manager.

Professional Education

At the time, particularly in the developing countries, there is neither the systematic knowledge available, nor are there the training programmes needed for the kind of management specialists referred to. There is an urgent need for scholars and researchers in administration to analyse the management and administration dimensions of substantive action programmes. Although management specialists correctly hold that the functions and processes of administrative analysis, decision-making and design do not vary fundamentally from one area of activity to another, there are yet technological and action requirement differences between, for instance, an agricultural extension service and a public works department. Only a series of analyses of action programmes in the respective specialised fields will provide the management specialists with the insights and the substantive knowledge required to render effective services to the different professional areas.

With regard to education and training, considerably more emphasis will need to be placed on the development of the ability to apply the functions, methods and technology of administration to substantive programme areas than is presently the case. For one, this means the teaching of programme and project management, both with regard to training in programme management for development fields of particular importance, and as a general approach to the analysis and design of administrative action required in the planning and execution of development programmes. This teaching needs to be related to actual cases and situations. It must be a practical approach, exposing the students to both case analyses and exercises in the application of analytical methods, in decision-making, in organisation design, in the design of management information and reporting systems, etc. Programme management should be taught as the integrating entity in which the various elements, functions and techniques of administration are brought together in an action system.

The management education and training to be provided is necessarily of different levels. It is not enough to think only in terms of the university level programmes that offer courses leading to a degree in public administration. In reality, the schools, institutes and departments of public administration in all countries supply only a small percentage of the management personnel in the public sector. The development of management competence needs to be carried out through three kinds of programmes: (a) within university level programmes in public administration, (b) in connection with in service government training programmes for management personnel, and (c) as part of the education and training programmes for professionals in fields like public health, education, public works, agricultural services and other government programme areas in which substantive programme specialists tend to assume management responsibilities.

It is up to the faculty members at the schools and institutes of public administration to develop and demonstrate their competence in programme management. Thereby, the schools of public administration and their staff members will be in a better position to prepare the managers and management specialists of the future. As schools and through their graduates they will also serve as a resource for management training personnel for in-service training programme and for developing the management competence of substantive programme specialists.

Management Technology

As a corollary to the emphasis on programme management, in fact, as an indispensable part thereof public administrators need to develop their competence in handling the analytical and decision-making techniques available to modern management. Even those who favour the introduction of sophisticated management technologies have argued that its introduction into the developing countries must be done with great care because "implicit in these technologies are attitudes toward the value of time, the integrity of objective data, the quality of interpersonal and intergroup relationships".[22] There is a great deal of truth in this statement by Esman and Montogomery. The same, however, applies to many of the modernisations that have been introduced into the developing world, from the modern factory to the birth control pill. In actual fact, there has also been a noticeable reluctance on the part of schools of public administration in the US to introduce modern management technology into their education programmes. The schools of business administration are the centres where modern management techniques have been developed and where they have become an important ingredient in the education programme.

My personal observation of management education and practices in Asia indicates that management technology is increasingly applied to business management, but is still rare in public administration. In each of the six Asian developing countries with which I am most familiar, one or more of the schools of business administration teach systems analysis and related subject matter in analysis and decision-making. In not one of those countries do the schools of public administration count a specialist in modern management technology among their faculty members. In a way this is not surprising. The major schools of public administration in all these six countries were established with the technical assistance of similar schools in the US. As far as I have been able to ascertain, only one of six US technical assistance projects at schools of public administration with which I am familiar in Asia had one technical assistance team member for a two year period with specialised knowledge in management science. Moreover, most of the programmes of the schools of public administration that were responsible for rendering the technical assistance did not themselves have any courses in management technology at the time the assistance was rendered.

Analytical techniques, including quantitative analysis, are an indispensable tool of programme management. This does not mean just offering a course in statistics or mathematics. The quantitative methods and techniques are only tools. They must be taught in such a way and to the extent that they are necessary and useful to the manager. A mere course or two in statistics, without the simultaneous use of this analytical tool in other courses does not serve much purpose. Similarly, systems analysis and computer utilisation are only tools and techniques. They are only useful and significant as they are applied to real-life situations. A danger arises when sophisticated technology becomes an end-in-itself. And here we are back to what was said earlier in this paper about administrative form, functions and techniques being ends-in-themselves. "Goal displacement" can just as readily be found in the gadgetry of modern management technology as it can be found in rules and regulations. This, however, does not negate the usefulness of either administrative rules and regulations or management technology.

Conclusion

The extent to which the development aspirations of nations are reached and plan targets are accomplished depends largely on the management capability and entrepreneurship found in government departments and semi-government organisations. "For better or worse"—as Mosher puts it—government is the principal innovator, major determiner of priorities, capitalist and entrepreneur in the development process. Yet, as Hahn-Benn Lee and Abelardo Samonte state in the introduction to Administrative Reforms in Asia, "in this era of change, the discipline and practice of public administration in Asia has not been marked by imagination and adaptability ... "it suffered from narrow image of being only an instrument for the maintenance of the existing system of law and order" ... and "public administration has been too often divorced from the change in the larger society within which it operates".[23] Unquestionably, this same statement could be made for other parts of the world as well.

There is no simple prescription that would lead to a more dynamic, entrepreneurial, responsive and responsible government bureaucracy. Attitudes, habits, and patterns formed over generations, and frequently being remnants of a colonial era and a society in which government had a much more delimited role, are not changed easily. In the preceding pages, only one possible and partial approach to the improvement of management within government has been suggested, namely a focus on and development of competence in programme management. I have suggested that the emphasis on programme management may hold more promise for administrative improvements in general and for the planning execution of development programme in particular than continuing attempts at fundamental, government-wide reforms. The approach is partial because programme management itself is constrained by the conditions and rules that govern the larger system of which a public sector programme is a part. Nevertheless, improved management competence will enhance the administrative planning and execution of development programmes in key areas and the analysis of the programme management requirements will help highlight the specific weaknesses in the larger system that hamper effective programme execution.

It has not been the intention to imply that all public administration education should be directed toward programme management. Certainly there continues to be a need to prepare functional specialists in personnel and financial administration etc. Similarly, policy analysis and the other current concerns of public administration remain important. I suggest, however, that there has thus far been a lack of emphasis on strategic decision-making and on the management requirements of substantive programme areas in the study and teaching of public administration. Adding this dimension to the concerns of the field of public administration will be a significant addition to the capability of public administration as a professional field and, thereby, contribute to the effectiveness of government operations.

In the foregoing, I have argued that the public administration professionals must sharpen their tools of analysis and demonstrate more clearly the contribution they can make to the design of action systems, to the allocation of resources within those systems, to the coordination of the activities and contributions of many different professionals engaged in action programmes, and to the linkage of programmes and organisations with the environment. Only by developing unique and distinct professional competence that are viewed by decision-makers and operating heads of organisations and programmes as contributing to the achievement of their objectives, will the public administration specialist be able to play a viable and possibly vital role in the development process.

Notes

1. Frederick C. Mosher, "The Public Service in the Temporary Society", *Public Administration Review,* Vol. XXI (January/February, 1971), pp. 48–49.
2. Both in usage and in the literature the terms, 'management' and 'administration' tend to be used interchangeably. There is, however, a difference in connotation. Management implies direction and the ability to influence and/or control the organisation and its

environment. Administration, derived from the Latin word *Ministrar* (to serve), implies a more passive role. In this article, an attempt has been made to use the term management consistently for references to strategic decision-making and administration for references to the technical and support functions in the operation of organisations.

3. United Nations, Information Service, Bangkok; Press Release No. G/153/71, December 10, 1971.
4. Milton J. Esman and John D. Montgomery, in "Systems Approaches to Technical Cooperation: The Role of Development Administration", *Public Administration Review,* Vol. XXIX (September/October 1969), state on p. 514 that public administration projects in the AID programme "have represented only seven per cent of technical cooperation expenditures in recent years". They add, however, that "it is impossible to estimate the undesignated public administration component of projects listed in education, public works, health, and similar substantive fields". According to the *Public Administration Newsletter,* United Nations, New York, Department of Economic and Social Affairs, Public Administration Division, No. 41 (September, 1971), p. 13, the UN's 1970 obligation for technical cooperation activities in public administration was $4, 172, 604.
5. United Nations, *Public Administration Newsletter,* No. 36 (January 1971), p. 9.
6. Edward W. Weidner, "Development Administration: A New Focus for Research", in Ferrel Heady and Sybil L. Stokes (eds.) *Papers in Comparative Public Administration,* (Ann Arbor, Michigan: Institute of Public Administration, The University of Michigan, 1962), p. 102.
7. Milton J. Esman and John D. Montgomery, op. cit., p. 514.
8. Robert K. Merton et al., (eds.) *Reader in Bureaucracy,* (New York : Free Press, 1952), p. 365.
9. See e.g., B.B. Schaffer, "The Deadlock in Development Administration", in Colin Leys (eds.), *Politics and Change in Developing Countries* (London: Cambridge University Press, 1969), p. 419; and Anders Richter, "The Existentialist Executive", *Public Administration Review,* Vol. XXX (July–August, 1970), p. 419.
10. Edward W. Weidner, op. cit., p. 103.
11. John M. Pfiffner and Robert Presthus, *Public Administration* (New York: The Ronald Press Company, 1967, 5th ed.), p. 7.
12. Edward W. Weidner, op. cit., p. 102.
13. Garth N. Jones, "Failure of Technical Assistance in Public Administration Abroad", *Journal of Comparative Administration*, Vol. 2 (May, 1970), p. 5.

14. George F. Gant, "A Note on Applications of Development Administration", *Public Policy*, Vol. XV (Cambridge, Mass: Harvard University Press, 1966), p. 205.
15. Edward W. Weidner, op. cit., p. 105.
16. Albert Waterston, *Development Planning: Lessons of Experience,* (Baltimore, Md.: The Johns Hopkins Press, 1965), p. 285.
17. Ibid.
18. Bertram R. Gross, "The Administration of Economic Development Planning: Principles and Fallacies", *Studies in Comparative International Development,* Vol. III, 5, 1967–68 (St. Louis, Mo.: Social Science Institute, Washington University), p. 92.
19. Ibid.
20. Ibid.
21. United Nations, *Appraising Administrative Capability for Development,* (New York: United Nations, ST/TAO/M/4–6, 1969), p. 49.
22. Milton J. Esman and John D. Montgomery, op. cit., p. 513. We want to note, however, that Esman and Montgomery basically appear to agree with the need for emphasis on programme management and management technology. They recommend a strengthening of American assistance in public administration by "(1) deemphasising projects which aim solely at transferring auxiliary administrative techniques; (2) linking administration and applying modern management concepts and methods directly to the planning, organising, and management of substantive action programmes; and (3) drawing more liberally on the expanding body of knowledge and research now available in development administration" (p. 514).
23. Hahn-Been Lee and Abelardo G. Samonte (eds.), *Administrative Reforms in Asia,* (Manila, the Philippines: Eastern, Regional Organization of Public Administration (EROPA), 1970), p. 1.

10

Managerial Effectiveness

Attitudinal Model

R.H. JOSHI

If we analyse conventional and large organisations which are not able to maintain their level of performance to keep the pace with the need of the time, we will notice, as one of the direct contributing causes, the inadequacy in qualitative and effective performance of the senior core-group of persons. On the other hand, a large number of good persons, having potential for growth and development are neither recognised nor given proper opportunity to develop. The criterion of awarding promotions without pre-promotion training for the relevant field has adversely affected the performance of the promotees when they are expected to equip themselves for shouldering higher responsibilities carrying variety of functions or activities. In several cases, it is observed that such persons, against the work pressure, have adopted wrong tactics to produce results, not confidently knowing proper course of action or approach. This is because the apprehension of failure or criticism is more dangerous than the failure or criticism itself. The cumulative effect of such working has produced improper image of such functionaries which would inadvertently affect their control span and authority. Good functionaries who have spent one or two decades in the organisations do possess required knowledge and skill but for advancing further beyond middle level will require one more input, that is, an 'attitudinal input'.

On the basis of my experience with several organisations for a long period of more than two decades, I have observed that a person possessing professional knowledge and reasonable skill is not accepted on long term. He is often misunderstood or mistaken for lack of required attitudinal inputs in him. Acquiring and practising attitudinal input is comparatively easy. They give quicker and positive results with long-term effect. I have developed a functional model with attitudinal inputs just before about five years. For about three years, different inputs of the model were discussed in training classes of different levels. Thus, the model has received quite an encouraging response all over. Since last two years, the model is used in training programmes for developing managerial effectiveness by practicing attitudinal inputs.

The model is expected to create a management culture with the efforts of middle/senior level executives, officers and managers on account of its following built-in characteristics:

- It is relatively easy to understand by officers from all disciplines.
- It lucidly pinpoints a success area of the executives, as also indicates the threat areas for them.
- It ensures self-improvement by developing a positive personality.
- It helps in creating better working climate in the process of inculcating a sense of willing working in the subordinates.
- It ensures decreasing the present rate of misunderstanding and unnecessary stress, tension and apprehensions.
- It helps creating a group of well-wishers and supporters on a long term (rather lifetime) basis.
- It is not very difficult to put in practice.

Since the model encourages and promotes effective and positive leadership quality and style with above built-in advantages therein, it is offered for practicing in any functional area. If the officers possess adequate job knowledge, as also reasonable skill for explaining jobs to their subordinates, the model will help tremendously in getting their work done besides benefiting them too in a great deal.

The need for developing this input is often realised for the senior level position in which incumbent, besides running his own office, has to essentially coordinate several functions or activities, create harmony and strengthen team spirit for timely accomplishment of tasks qualitatively. Leadership is a style pertaining to managerial area of functioning. Thus, there are no altogether different leadership needs or styles for management of technical functions. We have observed leadership quality and style of several administrative, professional and technical officers, occupying senior positions and after constantly observing for a long time their actions, style and net results of their performance, we could identify the essence of their success. We have also observed the functioning of other category of senior persons who have failed in their leadership role. In both success and failure 'attitudinal input' was a common contributing factor and its absence has resulted into failure. We have observed this for more than two decades.

The adoption of the model for regular and consistent practice will certainly contribute in strengthening the leadership quality to a great extent. It will not allow the officer to fail on the count of leadership needs.

The model presupposes following situations:

1. The expected group of participants have tried conventional ways of handling people/subordinates and peers but the results have not been satisfactory: The officers desirous of understanding the model may be assembled in a group of 30 to 40 in number. The session takes a reasonable time between 2–3 hours to explain the strategies with appropriate illustrations or discussing a case study. The model is designed to develop 'acceptance'. Nothing works well until 'acceptance' is created, retained and strengthened. Following strategies of the model will help in that direction. These strategies are of two kinds: (a) prescriptive, and (b) restrictive. Their use will require determination that the officer should do something and should not do something to become an acceptable leader/manager or officer as the case may be.

2. Possessing a flair and having preparedness for improving the present standard of working: The model expects that the officer concerned should be keenly interested to improve the present standard of working in the organisation. Therefore, a pre-model strategy should be accepted for practising. This strategy suggests three basic parameters for initiating the process of improvement:

Parameters	*Action*
Efficiency	Doing things better
Effectiveness	Doing right thing
Excellence	Better doing

These inputs can be distinctly noticed only as an outcome of post operating analyses or assessments of the works carried out under a specific officer during a pertinent period of time. All activities which undergo the hands of the officer should be filtered through the above parameters so as to carry their effect. This should be the first commitment and the functional style of the officer should change accordingly.

Observation and Decision-making

It is the performance of the officer that forms impression on other persons interacting with him. It is, therefore, very much necessary that the officer remains a point of guidance for juniors and occasionally for peers as well. When letters at dak stage are pursued and instructions in margin are given, when a person is making presentation, seeking the opinion or decision of the officer or when the officer wants to give directions while at site visit, it is recommended to practise following the strategy before giving opinion, decision or direction.

Decision-making Process

0 Observation – 0 = E^2NT^2+A (for decision-making)

E^2 = Ears and Eyes

N = Nose

T^2 = Taste and Touch

A = Awareness

Action		Process
Physical observation	:	What is it?
Impression	:	Do I get it?
Understanding	:	Do I understand the point clearly (without prejudice or partially)—neither less nor more?
Need-based analyses	:	Why this has come to me? What should be done? (options) How much I (my office) can do? How about similar incidences in past? (learning from the past)
Conclusion	:	Considering a specific course of action.
Review	:	Periodical analysis of recent past decisions/opinions taken vis-à-vis developments and the resultant effects of such decisions/opinions on the decisions on hand and thus determine to divert marginally or otherwise and then come to a suitable viewpoint for decision, direction or opinion.
Decision	:	Finally prepare to act/or to do.

In the above exercise, what plays important role is awareness. Awareness is a basic competence which has to be stretched in appropriate direction in the decision-making process. The awareness (knowledge plus relevant experience) helps to successfully proceed in a process between observation and decision-making.

Test: The above exercise, when adopted and practised consistently, will produce positive results over a period of time. It will form positive image of the officer. It will fetch him 'respect'. Gradually, people around him will recognise him as a right man. His knowledge, method of decision-making and decisions/opinions will be honoured, being impartial and appropriate.

Use of 5 'Rs' Strategy for Positive Effect

After decisions are taken or opinion is firmed-up, it is necessary that the officer concerned practises following *modus operandi* for communicating, so that his decisions are well-supported and well-accepted for further actions.

Strategy	*Process*
Right man	Proper person to communicate.
Right time	Appropriate time to communicate.
Right purpose	Appropriate purpose to communicate.
Right place	Proper place to communicate.
Right way	Proper way to communicate.

This exercise helps to determine the mode and style of communicating on the basis of the fact as to where the officer stands in terms of situation at the time of communication, and to whom he is communicating? Therefore he should decide how should he communicate for the desired effect or output?

Test: Officer practising this exercise consistently will be honoured with 'regard' from the people interacting with him.

Healthy Interaction for Better Output

While the former two exercises were prescriptive, this exercise is restrictive in nature. It restricts the behavioural parameter of the officer while he is interacting or communicating with the resource person at 'P' or at 'A' and while in the process of directing or explaining to other resource person at 'C'. The exercise is drawn up in Figure 1.

At the bottom, appropriate behavioural parameters are recommended in respect of 'T', 'A' or 'C' as the case may be.

Every officer is expected to function in such a way that the determined targets or objects are accomplished through the coordinated efforts of the subordinates and thereby suitably calibrating their behavioural aspects. For this purpose, the subordinates may be classified into two behavioural boxes, viz., 'P' and 'N'. Following (Figure 2) are some of the commonly noticed behavioural outcomes which will help the superior officer to classify the individual subordinate into 'P' or 'N' box on the basis of consistent behavioural pattern of such subordinate.

The control span and positive performance in both the boxes are possible with proper approach as indicated in each box for a particular class of subordinates. A range of response is the success area of individual officer and a threat area is indicated in last

Figure 1

Healthy Interactions

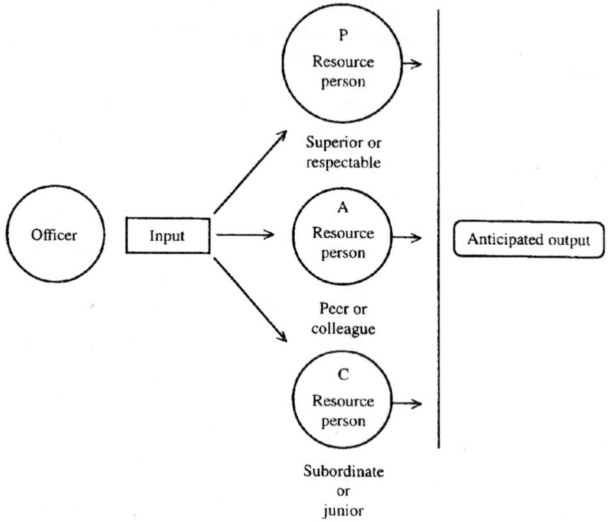

Factors Determining Mode

	P	A	C
Status →	1&2	5&6	7&9
Education →	1&3	4&6	7&8
Experience →	2&3	5&6	8&9
Age →	1&2	4&6	7&8

1. Submissive
2. Persuasive
3. Explaining
4. Friendly
5. Participative
6. Consulative
7. Authoritative
8. Democratic
9. Participative

Figure 2

Officer

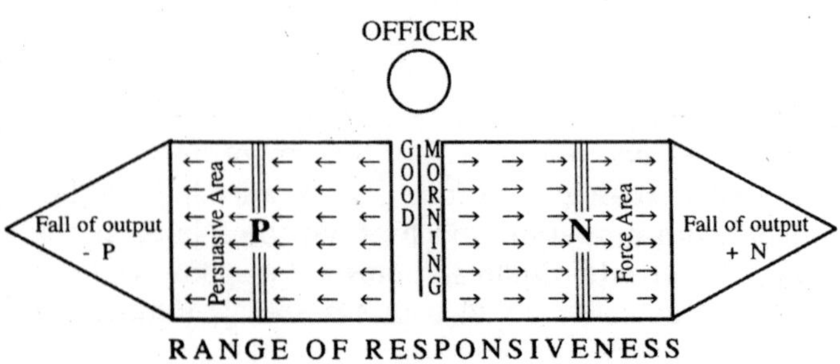

column of each box if appropriate attitudinal approach is not used.

Generally Noticed Characteristics

Generally quiet	Generally talkative
Obedient	Excessive obedient
Sober appearance	Assertive behaviour
Punctual	Non-punctual
Good at record/filing	Indifferent to record-keeping files
Service motive	Commercial motive
Inclination to maintain distance	Inclination to familiarity
Generally introvert with limited contacts	Extrovert with wider contacts
Restrictive to criticism	Inclination to loose talking
Uninquisitive to out-of-scope events	Inquisitive to know off the record or out of scope events
Cordial	Critical
Generally a table sticker	Inclination to loitering
Knowledgeable yet less talkative	Smart and argumentative
Patient	Generally impatient
Force + non-recognition = –P	Lack of required force + over reliability = +N

(the above observations are not for exceptions)

Figure 1 indicates the factors which determine the level of the person and accordingly the appropriate style is recommended for adopting as a tool to get the work done through the efforts of that other person at a specific level.

Figure 2 represents the behavioural group of members with which the officer concerned has to regularly interact for accomplishment of targets and thereby to decide the appropriate course of style in the specific situation as also to visualise the consequences in case of applying pressure beyond the 'range of responsiveness'. A person falling under positive behavioural box may function alright up to a certain limit, beyond which the torturing or frequent pressurising may lead to a situation wherein he will develop tendency to refrain from initiative and ultimately from regular working also. On the other hand, a person under negative behavioural box may also carry out assignment satisfactorily up to a certain limit beyond which he is likely to behave unpredictably and creating situation hazardous in nature producing tangible or intangible effect and even both at times. The exercise conveys that 'P' category needs a little push (with good touch) whereas 'N' category should be made to work with calculated force, applying the course of regular and occasionally close supervision and review at specified intervals.

Test: Consistent practice of this exercise will create a positive image of the officer in the minds of persons (superior, equal and junior or subordinate) interacting with him.

The image of the practising officer over a period of time will gradually be reciprocated in terms of 'liking'. Both 'P' and 'N' categories of subordinates will like to work with the officer. His superiors will not like to lose such officer to the extent possible. The colleague officers shall extend support to him.

Improve from and Eliminate the Adverse Image of the Past Behaviour

The essence of effective leadership lies in the ability of the officer to inculcate a desire for work in the subordinates or people working for him, thereby preparing them to willingly receive command for action. For creating the desire, the subjective person will have to be either motivated or otherwise suitably dealt with and place them in a situation that induces them take up the assignment willingly. This exercise will give good results comparatively faster but in a little long time if the past image of the officer is not positive among the concerned subject persons. The exercise is split into a group of directive words ranging from six words to a group of one word in the respective directive.

Six Words: I admit I made a mistake

The officer should remain introspective to look through his own deeds and actions and admit his mistake or lapse at the earliest. The sincere admittance of the mistake strengthens his esteem to help him refrain from the repetition of such mistakes thereafter. It is popularly said that a wise man is he who does not repeat the mistake.

Five Words: You did a good Job

Use of these five words motivates the person and generates in him a desire to do the job with his optimum capacity. In fact, subordinates would all the time strive to maintain high level of functional efficiency, if the above course is adopted and used whole-heartedly.

Four Words: What is your opinion

Use of these words excels the status of the officer in the eyes of subordinates. Through these words, the officer gives a fair chance to the subordinate for presenting his views. The subordinate shall, therefore, endeavour to present himself at his utmost capacity. This is an indirect way to improve the subordinate by pulling him upward towards his optimum functioning capacity.

Three Words: If you can

These three words have power in them to induct the busy subordinate to willingly take up more work to help the officer meet the challenges to cope up with additional work comparatively early as also in meeting the deadline in terms of time.

Two Words: Thank you

A right officer does not miss to use these words when a person does work quite satisfactorily. These words have a built-in power within them. Appropriate and timely use of these two words help strengthening a spirit of willing worker in the person or in the subordinate. He shall be willing to accept the subsequent job too in reciprocation of these words. What is important is that each of the above sentences should be uttered from within, exhibiting corresponding regards in the eyes with appropriate gestures. Incidentally, it is also important that the officer develops "I Less Eyes". In this context, even a look with thankful eyes shall work as powerful substitute for the verbal expression, i.e., literally uttering the words "Thank you".

One Word: We

The essence of 'acceptance' lies in repetitive use of the word 'We'. This one word has great power to help maintain team spirit as also recognise the colleagues/subordinates to the implied extent of their contribution for 'gain' or 'lose'.

Incidentally, it is worthwhile to indicate that unless grammatical needs so warrant, the officer should restrict the use of the word 'I' to the bare minimum. It is the excessive and unwarranted use of 'I' that creates undesirable consequences.

Test: Consistent exercise of this theory will create a positive image of the leader in the minds of people he is regularly interacting with. They will reciprocate such an approach of the officer by extending their 'love' towards him.

Thus, the use of above exercises in their true spirit shall fetch following four credits to the officer playing leadership role and trying to establish and strengthen his 'acceptance' for accomplishing determined work targets:

Respect

Regard

Like

Love

When people and subordinates 'accept' the officer with above four credit cards, there will be practically no apprehension left for him for inadequate cooperation and support.

Effective Functioning During Live Situation

Having understood the above strategies well, when the officer goes back to his work area, he will be processing following live situations:

I am OK – You are OK

I am OK – You are not OK

I am not OK – You are OK

I am not OK – You are not OK

For every officer to practice successful leadership role, it will be pertinent to remain at second situation. He cannot afford to go below that situation. It is a realistic situation. To maintain himself successfully in that situation, he shall have to use all the above exercises meticulously, consistently and willingly. If this is done, whatever work he does, he shall always have responding people working with him and working for him.

The training institutes are particularly requested to teach the above exercises to their officer-trainees, as a part of regular training programmes. This approach will help the institutions contribute in bringing about a good functional culture in times to come.

11

Improving Individual Effectiveness in Government

N. VITTAL

Productivity is very much in the news these days. Added to this, we have started emphasising quality also as one of the pre-requisites for development, especially industrial development. We are looking forward to the public sector enterprises to generate more resources by becoming more productivity oriented and quality conscious.

In a way, the entire progress of the country will depend upon the governmental systems, both at the Centre and in the States, becoming more productivity conscious and effective.

We have the Administrative Reforms Departments and circulars are issued from time to time about the need for improving efficiency. Commissions and advisory bodies are constituted for improving the administrative effectiveness. Can we claim that all these efforts have had an effective impact?

Whatever be the reform efforts, ultimately, effective improvements in government systems will come only from individual government servants. There has long been a tendency to advocate a theory that a government servant is a mere cog in the machine. The governmental system is huge, and especially since it operates within a framework of rules and regulations, the system becomes one where every individual is reduced to an automaton.

These approaches have de-emphasised the potential of the individual government servant to contribute and make the governmental system work more effectively. This write-up, therefore, is based on the assumption that every human being has a lot of potential and we will be able to improve the governmental system and gear the country towards the 21st century provided we look upon the individual government servant not in a limited way.

The improvement in governmental efficiency and the systems will come only if we allow the individual government servant to rise to his full creative potential. Here, the argument is not that we should move away from the framework of rules or make overnight radical changes in the system. Such a macro-approach is not going to give any results. In fact, one of the reasons for the limitations of the strategies adopted in the past for administrative improvement by having departments, commissions and advisory bodies is that the improvement and effectiveness becomes the concern of a limited number of people.

What is required is to develop a system by which the individual government servant will be able to make a contribution. Every individual government servant should realise that his human potential is not in any way restricted and in fact even while working within the parameters of rules and regulations, there is excellent scope for showing initiative and creativity at every level.

There is another myth that only if one is at a very high level in government, say, Secretary to the Government or a senior official or Head of a Department, one can influence changes. It is true that the higher a government servant is placed, the better may be his capacity to influence decisions. Nevertheless, even the junior-most government servant has within him the capacity to bring about healthy and productive changes.

Barriers to Initiative

An objective analysis of the governmental systems, both at the Centre and in the States, would show that there are three main factors that kill an individual's initiative. These are:

- The perception that rules and regulations are more important and any violation of the rules and regulations will invite very adverse consequences, not to speak of the perennial audit paragraphs and examination by the Public Accounts Committee and so on.
- The departmental culture which makes an individual not to look at the issues in a wider perspective but from the limited tunnel vision of the department.
- Jealousy of the peer group and sometimes even superiors against an individual government servant who turns out to be outstanding.

Looking at the Rules

Let us begin with the rules. It is generally forgotten that the rules are man-made. If the rules have to be very literally interpreted and implemented, then junior officers and even clerks can run the government. One senior colleague used to talk about the need for "idiotisation" of procedures. His approach was that as the general level of intelligence in large systems is bound to be low, we should devise procedures such that even idiots can run the show. While this can be a very telling way of setting up simple procedures, the adverse effect of this is that the system designed to be run by idiots, ultimately, is likely to have a certain amount of idiocy in itself.

The basic approach behind the rules and regulations is to ensure a degree of objectivity in treatment of people and issues so that the government systems not only function fairly but appear to be fair. While this is the basic spirit behind the rules, what happens is that as the system functions, when loop-holes are detected; to plug the loop-holes, rules are amended from time to time. As a result, in many governmental systems we find that the rules appear to have been designed on the basis that every government servant is potentially a dishonest person. The whole system and procedures reek of distrust.

It has been pointed out by many people that we should operate our system on trust, but in effect this has not been found to be so. And one cannot also think that any large scale or drastic change of rules and regulations in immediate future may be possible.

What is possible is for the individual government servant to retain his initiative and even though he operates within the confines of rules, to act in a manner which will bring better results. Specifically, one could suggest the following steps:

Amendment of Rules

Rules are framed at a particular point of time but as the situations change, there comes a need for amendment of the rules. How many of us take the initiative to move the appropriate authorities for amendment of the rules? Many of us often tend to remain satisfied by shrugging our shoulders and maintaining that solving of a problem is not possible because rules are rules and amendment of rules is not possible.

It is true that government appoints, from time to time, special committees and commissions for looking at rules, but this approach is generally not effective for the simple reason that implementation and formulation of the rules is a day-to-day operation. This is not subject to an on again off again approach. In fact, such a discontinuous approach or to borrow a phrase from Physics, the quantum approach, has probably led to a situation where at any given point of time in the governmental system, some rules are up-to-date and many are not. The dissonance between the need of the environment where the government department operates and the rules under which it operates, can be overcome only if every government servant is vigilant and instead of taking an attitude that he is impotent, considers that he is a partner in the entire exercise of good governance and continuously makes suggestions for modification of the rules, taking up the matter with powers that be.

Pro-active Approach to Rules

Many a time a pro-active approach to rules is desirable. Normally, amendment to rules takes place as a reaction to some development. One could go to the extent of suggesting that apart from waiting for problems to arise, it is always better to look at all our rules to see whether there is a need for amendment. Take, for example, the case of various rules and regulations relating to labour. In an area like, say, Boiler Maintenance, the rules of Boiler Regulations framed, are based on technologies that might have been probably prevalent in the 1920s or 1930s. With the technological improvement, a stage has come when one should make a distinction between modern chemical and petrochemical industries which require maintenance over a longer interval of time, than the standard boilers which were probably prevalent 30–40 years ago. Unfortunately, this fact is not appreciated. The point is that someone has to take an initiative within the government, to bring to the notice that the rules framed at a given technology level, have become out of date and as a result, modifications are called for.

Instant Effectiveness

Another standard excuse often heard is that each of us as government servant is so much busy with routine government work that we do not have the time for innovative thinking. There is also a perception that civil servants in general and IAS Officers in particular are birds of passage. As the transfers are uncertain, it is not possible for a person to settle down, learn the problems about a particular department and make improvements. Here, one would like every government servant to adopt the concept of instant approach to effectiveness.

Similarly, where it comes to the uncertainty of transfers, we can draw a parallel with the game of cricket. In cricket, one is never given a guarantee that one will always score a century. In fact, in every sport there is no guarantee that when you enter a game, you are going to win. It depends upon your skills and circumstances. While we enjoy the glorious uncertainties of cricket, why can not we also adopt the same approach for a moment and enjoy the glorious uncertainties of a governmental career?

Keeping in view the concept of instant effectiveness and the uncertainty of transfer, this author has evolved a method of working. On the first day of taking charge of any department or office, a questionnaire is issued to every officer concerned on the following lines:

1. What is the work that we should be doing but which we are not doing?
2. What is the work which we need not do but we are doing?
3. What is the paper work that can be eliminated?

4. What are your problems and what are your suggestions for improvement?
5. What is the source of corruption and how can we plug it?

A time limit of 30 days is given to the officers to respond. It has been generally found that about 20 per cent of the officers respond to such a questionnaire. Another 10 per cent may ask for time. This immediately helps separate the wheat from the chaff in the organisation. By going through the entire set of replies, one also gets a firm grip of the state of the particular department, at a particular point of time. More important, one finds a readymade programme of action to improve the organisation. Such an approach also gives a tremendous side benefit by way of improving the morale. Every government servant has got some spark of creativity in him and it only requires a little touch to be brought out.

Responsible Intransigence

One of the senior IAS officers, late S.S. Ghosh (who had been Secretary of Defence in the Government of India) used to say that there were situations when one would have to disobey the rules, which he called "responsible intransigence". This is not to advocate that we should disobey the Service Rules or Conduct Rules. However, in the public interest when there is a genuine case, one should be able to record detailed reasons and go beyond the rules. In fact, improvements in the government systems can come by officers taking initiative, acting and advising the government about the need for modification. It has been found that certain actions though not warranted under the rules, are supported by superiors if:

- it is clear that the bonafide are beyond doubt,
- detailed reasons are recorded, and
- especially, the officer taking decision does not personally stand to gain.

Departmental Culture

The second factor that tends to stifle the initiative of the individual government servant is the departmental culture. There is a tendency of tunnel vision, to look at every problem only in black and white. What happens in government that, because of the departmental approach most of the government servants spend their time in meetings establishing their departmental point of view. In the meetings, it becomes a matter of cleverness and skill in debating rather than looking at the issues jointly to find solutions. Many a time of course, the views of the presiding officer belonging to one particular department prevail.

Alternatively, it is a continuous game of wits. Late S.G. Barve, senior ICS Officer of the Maharashtra Cadre, used to observe that the better is the enemy of the good. In many government organisations, we find a situation that if someone comes up with a good solution to a problem, the superior officer often tries to find an even better solution. In the process, even the good suggestion is not implemented. For example, if someone suggests that in slums the quality of life can at least be partly improved by providing sites and services, there will be a suggestion to provide a more complete set of facilities including pucca houses. The cost of this will be much more. At the end of a prolonged debate, nothing will get done.

In this context, it is a welcome measure that the Government of India has started training programmes for IAS officers and other senior officers, respective of the years of service and also based on a vertical approach. Normally, as one grows older in service, there is a tendency to cling to seniority as the only justification for one's authority. Years are supposed to add intelligence and experience to one's ability. In reality, it may not be so. These training programmes, which have been organised over the last few years, have been helpful for many people to appreciate the other's point of view and come out of the departmental culture. More such exercises, done all through the government systems, will be helpful in developing a wider vision among government servants.

In addition to developing a wider perspective, one could suggest that every government servant should realise the need for a certain degree of impractical thinking. If we look at the development of mankind itself, breakthroughs in science or in other areas have come from people who have thought things which at one time were considered impractical. Man would not have landed on the moon if there had not been somebody thinking that it was possible to break off from gravity and go for inter-planetary travel. The very fact that the late Prime Minister Indira Gandhi could consider that it was possible to cover the entire nation within just one year with TV network, geared the government and the governmental system in 1984 to go out to put low power transmitters all over the country and achieve a remarkable coverage of TV network in the country. These are instances which show that if one starts thinking at any given stage that certain improvement is possible, even impractical thinking would be useful.

Edward De Bono, one of the excellent writers on the subject of thinking postulates the need for what is called the intermediate impossible. Beyond yes or no, there is a possibility 'PO' (possible operation). So, whenever we are faced with any particular problem we can adopt not merely logical thinking but also lateral thinking advocated by De Bono. We will find that there is opportunity for coming up with better solutions and improvements.

Peer Group Jealousies

The third factor that checks initiative in government is the jealousies of the peer group. One way of overcoming such a situation is to project every suggestion you make, as if it were that of your boss or of a peer. This practice of non-origination, which was advocated by Parkinson in his book *In laws and Outlaws* is found to be immensely useful in the organisational setting.

Walter Lippman said that diplomacy is the art of putting in other people's words what you want. The same technique may also be useful in selling of ideas and reducing potential jealousies.

Exposing individuals to properly designed training programmes in organisational behaviour may also help in spreading over the entire governmental system—a culture by which we could encourage merit.

In fact, all of us are familiar with the standard joke about how we as Indians tend to pull down each other. The story goes that when crabs were to be exported from India they were exported in cans without any lids. When someone asked why there were no lids, he was told that there was no need for lids, because they were after all Indian crabs; if any one tried to get out of the can, the others would pull it down!

Let us hope that some of the observations made in this article for increasing governmental effectiveness by encouraging individual initiative and bringing about a change in the perception and role of the individual government servants will help us come out of this 'Indian crab' situation.

Part II

Organisational Behaviour

12

Motivation

M.L. MEHTA

All executives are concerned with motivating their men to perform better, for it is central to their leadership role. While some do it by threat of punishment or offer of reward; others do it by persuasion and by taking employees along with them and then there are those who make no demand on their subordinates for fear of hostility or antagonism.

Motivation is a complex process of human interaction between two or more individuals in a given organisational environment. Human response is conditioned by beliefs, past experience, perceptions, social setting, institutional culture, nature of authority, reward system and other factors. No standard recipe exists for motivation. One has to find his own motivational leverage, depending on the nature, needs and conditioning of men to be motivated.

The importance of motivation arises from the fact that men play a crucial role in the efficiency of the administrative system. They are the most important variables and, therefore, their response determines the nature of the output.

An effort has been made here to present basic concepts and approaches to motivation.

Nature of Motivation

The term motivation is derived from the Latin word 'mover' which means 'to move'. The concept of motivation implies:

- The contemporary influence on the direction, vigour and persistence of actions ;
- How behaviour gets started, is energised, is sustained, is directed, is stopped and what kind of subjective reaction is present in the individual's mind, while all this is going on; and
- A set of independent or dependent variable relationships that explain the direction, amplitude and persistence of an individual's behaviour holding constant the effects of aptitude, skill and understanding of the task and the constraints operating in the environment.

Three common denominators of motivation pertain to:

1. What energises human behaviour?
2. What directs and channelises such behaviour?
3. How is this behaviour maintained or sustained?

Approaches to Motivation

Carrot and Stick Approach

This is the oldest approach to motivation and rests on the assumptions that people are basically lazy by nature; they despise work; are avaricious and fearful; they seek pleasure and avoid pain; and would work either for getting money or for fear of losing it. Implications of these assumptions are that for motivating men, pay them some money but not large enough to spoil them and that it would pay to keep them insecure. Both reward and punishment can be used in a judicious mix to motivate people to work. Problem areas in this approach relate to the following:

1. Fear helps only to some extent. Once people get accustomed to fear, threshold of fear has to be increased. A stage comes, when employee gets de-sensitised; refuses to get intimidated by fear and becomes rather demotivated.
2. Monetary incentives cannot be offered in the government, except for an occasional overtime. Once it becomes a habit,

people neglect their duties during office time, so that they can do the work after office hours and get overtime. They can ask for money even for performance of routine jobs.

3. People get suspicious of the incentive offered.
4. Frequent threats disturb organisational harmony and lead to conflicts.

Instinct Theory

Freud, James Mcdougall and other psychologists added two more factors of 'Instinct' and 'Unconscious Motivation' to the earlier factors of man seeking work for pleasure or avoiding it when it causes pain. It was suggested that irrational behaviour of an employee may be due to his instincts. Since there are a large number of instincts—some predictable and some unpredictable—it becomes difficult under this theory to work out motivational factors. Further, it is difficult to state categorically, whether instinctive behaviour is a learned behaviour or an involuntary instinct.

Drive Theory

According to Woodworth (1918), the drive is the reservoir of energy, which impels an individual to behave in a certain way towards or away from a goal. Canon (1939) introduced the concept of 'Homeostatic' to describe a state of disequilibrium which exists in a person whenever internal conditions deviate from their normal state. In the state of disequilibrium an individual is motivated by his internal drive to reduce the disequilibrium and to return to a normal state.

Inner State of Disequilibrium

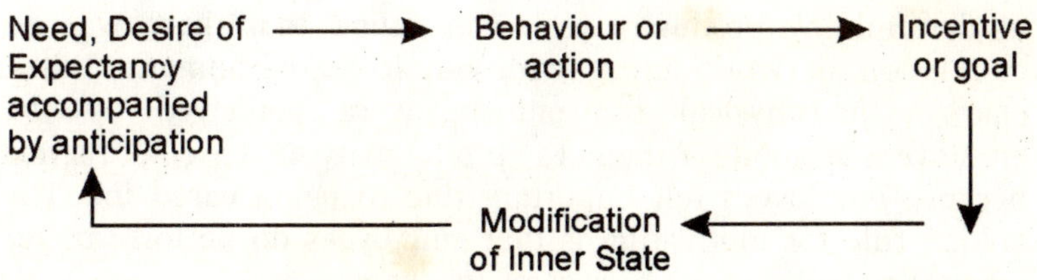

According to Hill (1943), the greater the extent of deprivation, greater is the intensity of achievement-effort to remove the deprivation.

Cognitive Theory

Major determinants of human behaviour under this approach are beliefs, expectations and anticipation concerning future events. Behaviour is considered as being purposeful, goal-directed and conscious. According to this approach, motivation is a function of expectancies (beliefs about causal effect of action and outcome) and valences (value placed on outcomes by an individual). Thus, if an individual places a high value on a particular outcome, he would work hard for getting that outcome. Under this approach, attitudinal orientation in values is necessary for greater motivation. Knowledge of value system of an employee would be helpful in deciding as to what motivates him.

Scientific Management Approach

Scientific Management Approach of F.W. Taylor and others emphasises standardisation of work procedures and systems for getting better work performance. This approach was based on experiments at Midvale Steel Company. According to this approach, the man is mechanistically-oriented and economically-motivated. One can get larger output by proper structuring of jobs and by providing suitable incentives or penalties for individual workers. This approach paid no attention to group feelings of workers.

Human Relations Approach

Elten Mayo's (1927–22) experiments at Hawthrone works of Western Electric Company disproved that employees were guided by economic considerations only and that wages alone are crucial in determining productivity. It was found that there was no co-relation of work-output with physical environment. When changes in physical environment were perceived by the employees as good for them, the productivity increased. This was because employees felt important due to being cared for. The golden rule for motivation is that employees do perform better when they feel that the boss cares for them.

Needs Theory

According to Mallow (1954), every one has a hierarchy of needs and he works for satisfying these needs. Five need-levels brought out by Mallow are as follows:

1. *Basic Physical Needs:* Food, clothing, shelter, sex, rest, etc.
2. *Safety or Security Needs:* Security from physical attack, job-security etc.
3. *Social Needs:* These are needs of association, i.e., belonging to a group.
4. *Esteem Needs:* These are felt needs for recognition, status, achievement etc. They are ego-needs related to one's feeling for one's own worth and importance.
5. *Self-Actualisation Needs:* These are higher order needs, relating to self-expression and developing the potential within individuals to the fullest.

According to Mallow, the lower order needs are activated first. When these are satisfied, next higher order needs are activated. There is a progression of need-satisfaction. However, it appears that different needs are active in some degree at all times. Satisfaction of lower order needs is a prime motive for work for those who are at low wage employment; while those at high wage employment level are better motivated by group pressure or by recognition or by self-satisfaction. Reward system does not motivate them as much.

Job Enrichment Theory

In the 50s, Frederick Herzberg (1959) and his team interviewed about 2000 accountants and engineers working in industrial firms in Pittusburg area to find as to when they felt enthusiastic or dissatisfied with their work. On the basis of these studies, Herzberg found that:

1. Work situations which people find most satisfying for performance, in order of priority, are those which provide for:
   - opportunity for achievement
   - recognition
   - challenge of work itself
   - genuine responsibility and scope for the individual
   - scope for advancement

   Herzberg called them 'Job Satisfiers' or 'Motivators'.

2. Work situations which people find most dissatisfying generally arise from unhelpful nature and inadequacy of the organisation relating to:
   - company policy and administration
   - supervision
   - salary, status and security
   - inter-personal relationships
   - working conditions

   Herzberg called them 'Job Dissatisfiers' or 'Hygiene-Factors'.

Reduction of job dissatisfiers does not have as much power in motivating employees as does an increase in job-satisfiers. According to Herzberg, major job-satisfiers like achievement, recognition, responsibility and advancement are connected with the task itself and hence they are better motivators. They enrich the job content and thereby increase the job-interest of employees. Job satisfiers are non-monetary in nature and are intrinsic to the job. Job-dissatisfiers like company policy, supervision and human relationships relate to job context or job environment and are extrinsic to the job. According to Herzberg, "the promise of money can move a man to work, but it cannot motivate him. Motivation means an inner desire to make an effort". According to him, motivational effort should be directed for getting improvements in job satisfiers without allowing job dissatisfiers to worsen.

Like Mallow's theory, Herzberg's theory also does not recognise individual differences arising out of personal, social and cultural factors. Further, there is only a semantic difference between effect of increase in job satisfiers or decrease in job dissatisfiers. Yet, Herzberg's work remains seminal. Problem areas in this approach relate to lack of opportunities for personal achievement in government; rigid promotion rules and status-quoism having high value.

McGregor's Theory X and Theory Y

According to McGregor (1960), supervisors motivate either by addressing to the lower order needs, or to the higher order needs, depending on their own perceptions of their employees' needs. If in the supervisor's view, people do better when they are properly paid and feel secure, he would appeal to lower needs. On the contrary, he would address to the higher order needs of recognition and self-actualisation, if he thought that employees are bothered about higher order needs. McGregor called the first approach as Theory X and the second as Theory Y. These theories are based on the following assumptions about human nature.

Theory X	*Theory Y*
1. Average person dislikes work and will avoid it if he can do so.	1. Work is natural to man, as is play and rest.
2. He needs to be coerced or induced to work by threat or reward or both.	2. A person can exercise self-control and may make efforts for achieving what he wants to achieve.
3. He needs to be told to perform the task, has little ambition	3. Average employee in an organisation seeks satisfaction in his work and wants to assume responsibility.
	4. Employees do have their share of talent and creativity. Tapping of their talent can help the organisation.

Theory X or Theory Y are ideal constructs. Use of Theory Y in motivation can lead to better results, as it is built on participation, trust and appreciation of role of employees in an organisation. Theory X treats employees as pawns in the hands of the supervisor to be dealt with in the way he thinks proper. This may lead to conflict, withdrawal, and disinterestedness on the part of employees.

McClelland's Need Theory

McClelland (1961) lists three categories of needs for individuals

1. Affiliation Needs
2. Achievement Needs
3. Power Needs

Those who have high achievement needs are self-confident and have high risk-taking capacity. Such persons are not motivated as much by incentives as by perceived challenges and the thrill of achievement. Those who have low achievement needs require monetary incentive to reinforce their view that they are doing well. Those with high affiliation needs would be more bothered with social relations on the job and would perform better in a non-competitive group-task.

Some General Comments

1. Subordinates try to live up to expectations of their superiors, provided these are genuine and realistic. Negative expectations lower performance. They hurt self-esteem of a person and he avoids picking up challenges.
2. Executives seem to be more effective in communicating low expectations than higher expectations.
3. Success thrives on itself. Once an employee does well and gets appreciated he would tend to do better thereafter.
4. Early years of an employee's career are important because during this phase he tries to imbibe job-attitudes.
5. Superior-subordinate relationship affects subordinate's behaviour. A subordinate does well when he has a supportive relationship with his boss because he feels important and worthwhile.
6. People accept friendly criticism meant for better performance if it is genuine and supported by proper evidence.
7. Subordinates try to seek superior's favour by better performance.
8. Many organisations have the capacity but do not perform well because the executives do not set high performance expectations for fear of criticism, antagonism, resistance and rejection. Instead, they prefer to play safe. They get obsessed with the means and overlook the end.
9. When people have no opportunity for satisfying their motivational needs they get pre-occupied with routine maintenance needs.
10. People bring varying patterns of needs and motives into work but their central aim is to achieve a sense of competence (Morse and Lorsch).
11. Look for strengths of your men rather than their faults.
12. People will make efforts to subvert organisational goals if the management fails to recognise their needs (Chris Argyris, 1964).
13. Do not be too quick to abandon those who are slow to understand.

Motivation is a complex process with interplay of personal, social and economic factors. It is the key to better man-management and, therefore, to better performance. Every executive must develop and strengthen his motivational strength with his subordinates as that is the key to his success. Motivation is the magic touch for good performance and maximising human resource potential.

13

Work Motivation

JAGDISH C. KUKAR

An effective manager must be able to get the best out of his people. Performance of employees doing the same job in any organisation will differ from person to person. These differences could be partly due to varying abilities or skills possessed by individual workers and partly due to their level of motivation. At any given point of time people vary in the extent to which they are willing to direct their energies towards the attainment of organisational objectives. People, thus, differ not only in their ability to do but also in their "will" to do or motivation. The motivation of people depends on the strength of their motives. Motives are sometimes defined as needs, wants, drives or impulses within the individual. In the study of motivation the two terms—motives and needs—are used interchangeably. Motivation is our speculation about some one else's purpose. In other words, motives are the 'whys' of human behaviour. As has been rightly said, motivation theory attempts to explain how behaviour gets started, is energised, is sustained, is directed, is stopped and what kind of subjective reaction is present in the organism. The problem of motivation is as old as organised activity itself. But it has only been during the last few decades that attempts have been made to apply the conceptual and methodological tools of the behavioural sciences, particularly psychology, to the relationship between man's motivation and his work as well as to the managerial issues involved in that relationship.

Approaches to Motivation

The traditional concept regarding the 'whys' of human behaviour at work has been that people work only for consideration of fear or for monetary rewards. This is also called 'carrot and stick approach'. In a democratic set up, no organisation can afford to use force for getting the work done from people. Further, recent researches have shown that for getting the best out of the people, monetary rewards are not sufficient. This approach may be relevant only in case of those people who are living in great deprivation. During the early part of this century, the 'scientific management school' put forward the 'concept of rational man' to explain the motivational process. According to this, man being rational would work for his economic betterment, if given a proper opportunity. However, Hawthorne studies conducted by Elton Mayo and others during the early thirties have shown that a worker is governed more by the 'logic of sentiment' rather than the 'logic of reason'. Thus, besides being rational, he is also a social being. A man joins an organisation not only for the satisfaction of his economic needs but also the social needs. Mayo studies led to the emergence of 'Human Relations Movement' and brought into prominence the view that workers and managers must first be understood as human beings. Human relations approach has, however, been criticised on the ground that it presents a too simplistic view of human nature, which in fact is very complex. This unidimensional approach to man's behaviour at work has been modified by the behavioural 'concept of complex man' who strives to satisfy various levels of his hierarchy of needs within an organisation. The relative pre-potency of these needs would depend on the interplay of various situational factors. According to the behavioural approach to motivation, an understanding of the dynamics of the employees' response to the work climate would enable a manager to effectively control and direct their behaviour in a meaningful manner so as to achieve greater productivity.

Motive Strength

As stated above, motives or needs determine our behaviour. All individuals have hundreds of needs and all of these needs compete for their behaviour. The need with the *greatest strength* at a particular point of time would be the most proponent motive which would determine behaviour. Further, two factors that affect need strength are *expectancy* and *availability*. Although these two concepts are interrelated, expectancy tends to affect motives, or needs, and availability tends to affect the perception of goals. Expectancy is the perceived probability of satisfying a particular need of an individual based on past experience. Availability reflects the perceived limitations of the environment. It is determined by how accessible the goals that can satisfy a given need are perceived by an individual. Employee motivation would thus depend on how they perceive the probability of satisfying a particular need as well as the availability of goals to satisfy such a need.

Mallow's Hierarchy of Needs

It has already been stated that behaviour of people at a particular moment is usually determined by their strongest need. According to Mallow, there seems to be a hierarchy into which human needs arrange themselves. This means basic human needs are organised into a hierarchy of relative pre-potency. In other words, once the basic needs of the individuals are reasonably satisfied, his higher level needs become motivators as has been illustrated below:

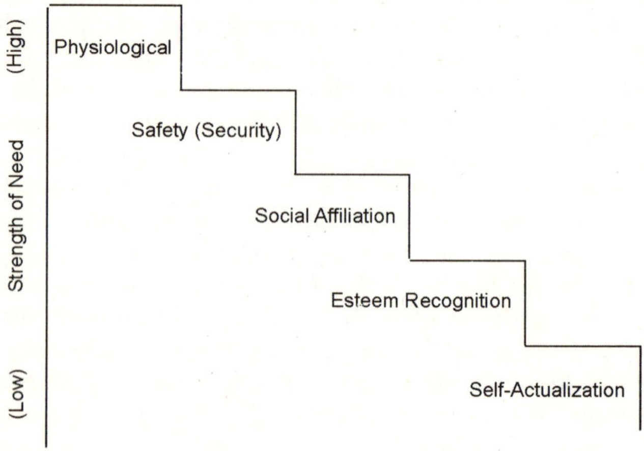

The Physiological Needs: The physiological needs are shown at the top of the hierarchy because they tend to have the highest strength until they are somewhat satisfied. These are basic human needs to sustain the life itself—food, clothing and shelter. If all the needs are unsatisfied, and the organism is then dominated by the physiological needs, all other needs may become simply non-existent or be pushed into the background. It is quite true that man lives by bread alone—when there is no bread. But what happens to man's motivation when there is plenty of bread and when these basic needs begin to be fulfilled. In such situations, in place of physiological needs, other higher level of needs emerge and these motivate and dominate behaviour of people. And when these needs are somewhat satisfied, other needs emerge and so on down the hierarchy. Thus, man is a perpetually wanting animal. However, satisfied needs decrease in strength and normally do not motivate individuals. An important implication of Mallow's hierarchy of needs is that gratification becomes as important a concept as deprivation in motivation theory for it releases the organism from the domination of relatively more physiological needs permitting thereby the emergence of other more social needs. A want that is satisfied is no longer a want. The organism is dominated and its behaviour organised only by unsatisfied needs.

The Safety Needs: If the physiological needs are relatively well satisfied, a new set of needs take their place which may be categorised roughly as the safety needs. All that has been said of the physiological needs is equally true, although in lesser degree, of these desires. These needs are essentially the need to be free of the fear of physical danger and deprivation of the basic physiological needs. In other words, this is a need for self-preservation and a concern for future as well. Will people be able to maintain their property and/or job so that they can provide food and shelter tomorrow and the next day. If an individual's safety or security is in danger, other things seem unimportant. Like the average child, an adult also usually prefers a safe, orderly, predictable, organised world which he can count on and in which unexpected, unmanageable, or other dangerous things do not happen. In the developed and affluent countries, people, by and large, have not to worry for such needs as a welfare and well-governed state takes care of all such needs. The peaceful, smoothly running affluent society ordinarily makes its members' feet safe enough and they no longer have any safety needs as active motivators. However, in less developed countries, people who are threatened about their survival will put up with almost any work condition in order to earn the money necessary for food and shelter. While human motivation to work is not entirely governed by survival needs, it does seem to be based strongly upon them.

Social or Affiliation Needs: If both physiological and the safety needs are fairly well satisfied, social or affiliation needs will become dominant. Since man is a social being, he has a need to belong and to be accepted by various groups. One cannot spend one's entire life in a job that satisfies only the basic needs. Most people seek something more from their job. Even infants deprived of some basic minimal level of human contact have stunted growth. When social needs become dominant, a person will strive for meaningful relations with others. Like the survival needs, the social needs do not just disappear from the scene once provided for. They continue to exert influences on individual's behaviour throughout their entire lives. However, unlike the survival needs, the social needs do not seem to demand immediate gratification, at least among most adults. Also, the social needs are expressed and satisfied in a greater number of ways than are the more basic survival needs.

The Esteem Needs: Another need which influences the behaviour of people in our society (with a few pathological exceptions) is the need or desire for a stable, genuine, high evaluation of themselves, for self-respect or self-esteem and for the esteem of others. By genuine self-esteem we mean which is based upon real capacity, achievement and respect from others. These needs are of two types. First, the desire for strength, for achievement, for adequacy, for confidence to face the world and for independence and freedom. Second, what we call desire for prestige and power. Prestige is something intangible, bestowed upon an individual by society. In case of some persons it is inherited. For example, the son of a big industrialist inherits instant prestige because of the family background. People seek prestige throughout their lives in various ways. Many tend to seek only the material symbols of status, while others strive for personal achievement or self-actualisation, which might command prestige in itself. People also tend to seek power for the satisfaction of their esteem need. The ability to induce or influence behaviour is power. Individuals who derive their influence from their personality and behaviour have personal power and those who are able to influence the behaviour of others because of their influence in the organisation have position power. Power motive is very dominant in individuals who feel somehow inadequate in winning the respect and recognition of others. Alfred Adler, a one-time colleague of Freud became very interested in this power motive and introduced two well-known concepts on this topic—inferiority complex and compensation.

The Need for Self-actualisation: The need for self-actualisation is a difficult need to pin down and identify. The emergence of this need depends upon prior satisfaction of the physiological, safety, love and esteem needs. Even if all these needs are satisfied, a person may still feel some void in his life unless he is doing what he is fit for. A musician must make music, an artist must paint, a poet must write, if he is to be ultimately happy. What a man can be, he must be. This need we may call self-actualisation need. We can expect fullest creativeness among such people. Since, in our society, basically satisfied people are the exception, we do not know much about self-actualisation either experimentally or clinically. A very few people attain this goal in their lives with the result there is no proper utilisation of human resource. This is a serious problem in the less developed countries where there is a tremendous underutilisation of human potential. As has been rightly said that the underdeveloped countries are under developed because the people have no opportunity to rise to their fullest stature and utilise their maximum potential.

Motivation—Hygiene Theory

The motivation hygiene theory resulted from a study conducted by Herzberg and his colleagues at the Physiological Service of Pittsburgh. The study involved extensive interview with some two hundred engineers and accountants from eleven industries in the Pittsburgh area. In the interviews, they were asked about what kinds of things on their job made them unhappy or dissatisfied and what things made them happy or satisfied. On the basis of this study, Herzberg concluded that people have two different categories of needs that are essentially independent of each other and affect behaviour in different ways. He found that when people felt dissatisfaction with their jobs, they were concerned about the environment in which they were working. On the other hand, where people felt good about their jobs, this was due to some intrinsic factors relating to the work itself. Herzberg called the first category of needs hygiene factors because they prevent job dissatisfaction. These factors are: organisational policies and administration, supervision, working conditions, inter-personal relations, money, status and security. Hygiene factors do not increase the worker output capacity, they only prevent losses in worker performance due to work restriction. These are, therefore, also called "maintenance factors". Satisfying factors which involve feelings of achievement, professional growth and recognition that one can experience in a job that offers challenge, are referred to as motivators. Herzberg used this term because these factors seem capable of having a positive effect on job satisfaction often resulting in an increase in the output capacity of the employee.

A relationship between the Mallow and Herzberg frameworks could also be established. The physiological, safety, social, and a part of the esteem needs are all hygiene factors. The esteem needs are divided because there are some distinct differences between status and recognition. Herzberg's views are also explained in terms of job enrichment, which means the deliberate upgrading of responsibility, scope and challenge in work.

Theory X and Theory Y

According to Douglas McGregor, supervisor's views about human nature would largely determine his approach towards motivating his subordinates. The traditional assumption of management about human motivation has been that most people prefer to be directed, are not interested in assuming responsibility, and want safety above all. This assumption is further strengthened by the belief that people are motivated by money, fringe benefits and the threat of punishment. This approach is called theory X which lays emphasis only on the lower order needs of the employees. Managers or administrators who accept theory X assumptions attempt to structure, control and closely supervise their subordinates. They feel that such a control is clearly appropriate for dealing with the employees, most of whom are unreliable, irresponsible and immature. However, McGregor drawing heavily on Mallow's hierarchy of needs, concluded that theory X assumptions about human nature, when universally applied, are often inaccurate. Management by control and direction may not succeed in motivating such people whose physiological and safety needs are reasonably satisfied and whose social, esteem and self-actualisation needs are becoming prominent. Management, therefore, requires a better understanding of human nature and motivation—and for this McGregor developed an alternative theory of human behaviour called theory Y. This theory assumes that people are not, by nature, lazy and unreliable. They can be basically self-directed and creative at work if properly motivated. According to theory Y, a supervisor while dealing with the employees should take into account higher order needs of recognition and self-actualisation in order to get the best out of them.

The Achievement Motive

Some people have an intense need to achieve. Others, perhaps the majority, do not seem to be concerned about achievement. Quite a large number of research studies have been conducted with a view to highlighting the role played by achievement motive in the lives of the people who were influenced by it. But the most intensive work in this area has been done by David C. McLelland and his associates at Harward University. The achievement-motivated person is likely to excel all others in his zeal to improve his performance when he is challenged to do so. He tries harder and demands more from himself in such situations. As a result of this, he accomplishes more. For example, college students who have a strong achievement drive will usually get better grades than equally bright students with weaker needs for achievement. Executives "on their way up" in their organisations are usually driven by stronger achievement needs than those who do not rise so quickly. The stronger the achievement drive, the greater the probability that the individual will demand more from himself.

Further, the most important way in which the achievement motive is related to managerial success is the individual's attitude toward risks. An achievement-oriented person prefers a moderate degree of risk precisely because his efforts, skills, and determination stand a reasonable chance of influencing the outcome. In such a case, the achievement will be personal and not just a lucky break or a foregone conclusion. This sort of aggressive realism is one of the main characteristics of a successful executive. However, such an executive will prefer activities whose feedback is prompt, precise, and unmistakable. Besides, the kind of feedback that is provided is also important. People with achievement needs will work harder when they are told precisely what is right and wrong about the way they are working. If they are merely told vaguely that they are doing "alright" or they being co-operative, pleasant, or else are "nice" but irrelevant will not effect their efforts at all. Achievement-motivated people might want task relevant feedback. Incidentally, quite the opposite is true of people who have stronger affiliation needs than achievement needs. They work harder when they are complemented for their attitude than when they are told about their efficiency. This means that for stimulating people to their greatest efficiency, it will help to know beforehand what their basic motives are. However, a really effective executive will not be predominantly achievement-motivated or affiliation-motivated but there would be a fairly strong but balanced blending of both.

Further, the man with a high degree of achievement drive is not necessarily more gifted in organisational ability than the next man, but his approach and attitudes enable him to make more effective use of his abilities than most other men make of theirs. He is practical, venturesome, and determined—a formidable combination which can achieve brilliant results with or without organisational capabilities. Also, in case of an achievement-motivated person, his personal likes and dislikes do not stand in the way of achieving a goal. This is, of course, quite different from the way the man with a strong affiliation motive would be expected to react. The achievement-oriented people would either not let friendship stand in the way of accomplishment or would not allow the two to come together.

Generally speaking, people with a high degree of achievement motivation are more persistent, realistic, and action-minded than people with other kinds of motivational patterns. But this does not necessarily make them more productive which would depend on whether the task requires some degree of personal initiative or creativity. If it does, the achievement-oriented person is very likely to excel others. But if it is a routine type of task, his performance may be very ordinary and uninspiring. Thus, those organisations which offer them challenging opportunities, grow faster and show better results. As a matter of fact, they are the backbone of most organisations. McLelland has even extended his analysis to countries where he related the presence of a large percentage of achievement-motivated individuals to the national economic growth. However, this does not mean that such people always make the best managers. Although they are highly task-oriented they sometimes lack the human skills and patience necessary for being effective managers of people who are competent but have a higher need for affiliation.

The Affiliation Motive

The achievement and affiliation motives are, of course different but by no means antithetical. It would be, therefore wrong to assume that achievement-motivated people are always more productive than affiliation-motivated people. The distinction depends on the nature of both the work and the feedback. Nevertheless, there is a general impression and a persistent bit of folklore in management that "nice guys finish last". However, if being a nice guy means having strong affiliation with other people, then there are innumerable circumstances where it has not handicapped those who had both strong drives for achievement and affiliation. Although, in comparison to the study to achievement motive, very little research work has been done for studying affiliation motive. But it can be said that while the significance of the achievement motive in organisations is quite obvious, in its own way, the affiliation motive is just as important.

Money Motive

According to Gellerman, the most important and the most subtle characteristic of money is its power as a symbol. Its most obvious symbolic power is its market value. It is what money can buy not money itself, that gives it value. However, its symbolic power is not limited to its market value. Since money has no intrinsic meaning of its own, it can symbolise almost any need an individual wants it to represent. In other words, money can mean whatever people want it to mean. That is why money can represent achievement, prestige, power or security. For people who have suffered deprivation, money represents a sort of shield against disaster, to them it symbolises love and security and is more reliable than people. But, somehow, it is a fact that for some people money is everything all the time, that for others money is everything some of the time but not all the time, and that for still others money means very little at any time. In a sense, man's attitude towards money reveals his hopes and fears, his follies and his grandeur. Like the psychologist's ink blots, money is essentially a neutral object which each man interprets in terms of his own backgrounds and circumstances.

On the basis of his extensive research, William F. White has found that money, the "old reliable" motivational tool, is not as "almighty" as it is supposed to be. Like Mayo, he found that instead of money it is the work group which determines the level of productivity and only very small minority among the workers usually respond to money incentive schemes.

Leader Behaviour and Motivating Environment

The effective use of human resources is the central problem of management and as such motivation is the basic task of leadership. Managers as leaders have an important role to play in creating a motivating and supportive environment in their organisations. They must provide appropriate leadership style keeping in view the need level of their employees so as to integrate the individual objectives with the organisational objective. This will help in releasing the energy and creativity that now seem to be suppressed in many apparently apathetic employees. It may be mentioned that organisations merely hire the time of the employees and not their enthusiasm, which means their physical presence can be ensured but not their whole-hearted involvement. Therefore, besides the tangible reward structure of salary etc., organisations must also offer various intangible rewards to their men so as to get the very best out of them. Some of these have been discussed in the following paragraphs.

Appreciation

Appreciation of a job that is well done acts as a strong motivator. All of us look for acceptance and appreciation regardless of our status in the society. Whether a person be the lowest functionary in an organisation or the top level executive, everybody wants to be reassured that what he is doing is something useful and commendable. Successful managers always make it a point to give credit to their subordinates and workers and this has a tremendous influence on their performance. Such employees would show a great deal of enthusiasm for their boss and their work. But one must be sincere and frank while praising. Success thrives on itself. Once an employee does well and gets appreciated, he would try to do better thereafter. A behavioural scientist will call it a process of behaviour modification and positive reinforcement. Skinner suggests that people perform better and draw more satisfaction on the job if they receive proper appreciation and praise for their good work. Managers, therefore, must build upon the strength of their subordinates. Even the mistakes should be pointed out in a manner that the worker accepts it as an objective feedback indicating that something is wrong which he should try to improve. They must avoid butting subordinates' "ego" by openly criticising or snubbing them. People accept friendly criticism meant for better performance if it is genuine and supported by proper evidence.

Recognition

A subordinate does well if he feels important and worthwhile. People want recognition as individual human beings. The manager should recognise the contributions made by his subordinates. Credit should be given to those who deserve. However, there are innumerable instances of such bosses who, instead of giving credit where it is due, themselves take the entire credit for the work done by the others in the organisation. These managers are, in fact, mainly responsible for the growing trend of alienation among the employees as they feel that whatever may be their efforts its credit will always be claimed by their boss. It is essential to give a feeling to the employees that they are useful for the organisation and their contribution would not go unnoticed. It may not be easy to raise the status of an employee but a manager can raise his stature through recognition. One's stature in an organisation may not have legal sanction but it is a powerful motivating factor as it satisfies the esteem need of a person. Recognition, therefore, sometimes works as a substitute for promotion.

High Expectations

Subordinates try to live up to the expectations of their superiors provided these are genuine and realistic while negative expectations bring down their performance. It is as though there were laws that cause a subordinate's performance to rise or fall to meet his manager's expectations. If an employee has a low self-esteem, he would avoid challenging assignments. The subordinates, more often than not, appear to do what they believe they are expected to do. It may be mentioned here that the powerful influence of one person's expectations on other's behaviour has long been recognised by physicians, behavioural scientists and teachers. According to J. Sterling Livingston, who had done similar studies, some managers always treat their subordinates in a way that leads to superior performance. But most managers unintentionally treat their subordinates in a way that leads to lower performance than they are capable of achieving. If we do not have much faith in the capacities of our subordinates, their productivity and efficiency will be low. But if we have faith in them, they will always rise to our expectations. This is very well expressed in Bernard Shaw's *Pygmalion* where Eliza Dorlittle says: "You see really and truly, apart from things, anyone can pickup (the dressing and the proper way of pronunciation and so on), the difference between a lady and flower girl is not how she behaves, but how she is treated."

Job Enrichment

Work itself is a strong motivator provided it is interesting and challenging. Sometimes, the work itself is dehumanising and degrading and the employee finds it meaningless and without a purpose. People want work that gives them a sense of satisfaction, a sense of accomplishment and a sense of creativity. There is a lot of dissatisfaction and discontentment in most parts of the world with the type of work one has to do in organisations. Even in the executive ranks, most of them feel that they are not really involved in policy-making and decision-making areas of their organisations despite their salaries and titles. Their higher order needs, thus, are not met on their jobs. The issue of participation at the executive level has become quite crucial as it has led to great deal of frustration and a sense of helplessness. Frederick Herzberg, while analysing the theme of job enrichment, observed that work could be made more meaningful through this approach as it leads to deliberate upgrading of responsibility, scope and challenge in work. It, thus, provides the kind of satisfaction that employees and executives look for in their jobs. Many large organisations like Sony in Japan, IBM in USA, VOLVO in Sweden and others have tried out this concept with success. Even at low levels in an organisation people can respond in responsible and productive ways to a work environment in which they are given an opportunity to grow and mature. People begin to satisfy their esteem and self-actualisation needs by participating in the planning, organising and controlling of their own tasks. According to the findings of a research study conducted in a Rajasthan State Government Department, people at higher levels are more satisfied in comparison to those at the junior management levels. This indicates that job at junior levels needs enrichment and should be made challenging so as to give the subordinates a sense of greater accomplishment and recognition.

Further, a challenging assignment or a job that challenges the employee is a very strong motivator. However, all people do not welcome challenges. It is only the dynamic go-getters who get bored with a job that provides no challenge. People want to climb mountains, become president or a prime minister of a country or chairman of a company because they are looking for a challenge. It is something to do for self-actualisation.

Senior-Subordinate Relationship

Numerous studies have shown that the nature of senior-subordinate relationship has an important bearing on the performance of both the seniors and subordinates. According to one of these studies conducted by Fleishman, people tend to manage as they are managed and also people emulate the behaviour of their superior. But these hierarchical relationships are subject to various internal and external environmental factors which determine their nature and mode of interaction. For instance, relationship between a boss and his subordinate will depend on how they perceive their role vis-à-vis each other and, often there may be perceptual distortions which may hinder a proper rapport between them. To overcome these barriers, the managers and the employees must have greater awareness of these perceptual problems which create an environment of mutual distrust and vitiate the organisational climate. However, the role of the manager is more critical in this regard. A good boss as a leader is a strong motivating factor. Under him, people feel greatly motivated and morale is very high. He builds upon their strengths and develops them for higher responsibilities through counselling. By trusting his subordinates, he gets their loyalty and trust. Besides, it is also necessary for a good leader to stand by his men both in success and failure. This requires moral courage and a sense of empathy. However. there are many bosses who would be quick to take all the credit and throw all the blame on the subordinates. A good leader takes responsibility when something goes wrong and be would give credit where it is due.

Communication Effectiveness

A corollary to senior-subordinate relationship is the issue of communication effectiveness. Managers must possess communication skills for motivating their men. Since the organisational goals are achieved through people they must be kept informed about the objectives, policies, procedures and practices of their organisations, However, communication is a complex phenomenon. It is not merely telling somebody what the goals are and how to achieve them. It is not even putting everything in writing through manuals. The purpose of communication is to influence the behaviour of the people. However, the response of the people would depend on their perception of the message. It is important to realise that the subordinates react to the totality of cues in a leader's behaviour and not just to those cues to which he wants them to respond. In effect, the leader is likely to communicate a great deal more than he intends. People are in the habit of reading between the lines. In other words, words have no meaning, people put meaning into words. As has been said, "the meaning of words is not in the words, it is in us." Mutual trust, personality and attitudinal factors, thus, largely determine the reaction of the people. The problem is further complicated in bureaucratic organisations because of greater emphasis on downward communication rather than on upward communication. According to Elton Mayo, upward communication provides the management with the necessary feedback and greater insight into the attitudes, grievances and aspirations of the employees. The communication from the subordinate to the superior is, therefore, essential for obtaining the involvement of the people. Bosses who are not accessible to their subordinates cannot motivate effectively. Channels of communications both upward and downward must, therefore, be kept open in organisations.

The Role of the Group

An individual has a strong urge to belong to a group and to be a part of a team. He would strive to live up to the norms and standards of his group. The famous Hawthorne studies had highlighted the role of informal groups with regard to behaviour and actions of the individuals. If the group as a whole is motivated, the performance level will go up and if the group restricts productions most workers will fall in line. There are very few individuals who could stand up against the group and have the courage to swim against the current. Every employee will like to gain recognition and acceptance from his group just as much as they would from management. The level of motivation in the group is, thus, a decisive factor in effectiveness. If a manager can obtain the commitment of the group as a whole for the organisational goals and higher level of productivity, the individual members would do their best to attain the standards set by the group. A successful manager can use this group consciousness in a positive manner so as to create a sense of work ethic among his men. One of his major leadership role is to ensure, so far as possible, to harmonise the official norms laid down by management and unofficial norms evolved by informal groups.

Managing versus Leading

In most of our organisations, we treat people like commodities. People cannot be managed in this manner. Inventories can be managed but people must be led. And when people are not being treated properly, they are not doing their best work. And when they are not doing their best work, the productivity will not improve whether in government, public or in the private sector. This is the core of the problem. The main issue is not technological or structural reforms in our organisations, it is how we treat our people. We can perhaps take a leaf from the Japanese style of management, where the philosophy is to treat every employee like a brother. All we have to have is a little leadership. Although we have some of the brightest and ablest of persons in our administrative and managerial cadres, who could have been incredible leaders, this resource is not largely being put to proper use. On the contrary, there seems to be a rat race among most of them for obtaining more and more benefits from their organisations in the form of perks, quick promotions and cushy jobs. They are more concerned with the powers of the post they are occupying rather than on what they are doing. Size of the office table is more important to them than the direction of the achievement curve. Needless to say, such executives who worry about themselves and look after their own interest, contribute very little for achieving the organisational goals. Instead, our top men should be the first to make the sacrifice and not the last. Under such leaders, employees will be highly motivated and would identify themselves with the organisational cause.

If we look at the present scenario in the government as well as in the corporate sector, we will find two types of managers at the top. Some of these are oriented towards power, status and material benefits and are more concerned with what they can get from the organisations. These managers could be called being type as they are more obsessed by the external trappings of their positions. While there are others who are doing type. They give more than what they receive from their organisations and are oriented towards creativity, integrity and legitimate authority. The doing type build organisations while the being type capture them. Employees show greater involvement in their work if they are led by the doing type. In case the being type are at the helm, the employees gradually get alienated from their organisations and they will have little sense of belonging. The successful functioning of any organisation will, therefore, depend on what type of managers reach at the top and how far they are capable of generating a motivating environment. Managers with a proper orientation would be able to make work a more satisfying experience for their employees.

According to the findings of social scientists, already mentioned in this article, human beings basically like working and would welcome challenging assignments provided they get congenial environment on the job. Organisations must throw up such leadership as would harness this untapped human potential. This would, however, require that the executives possess requisite skills to understand their own attitudes as well as the attitudes of people with whom they have to work. It is also important that managers must be willing to change their style of working, if it can help in improving the effectiveness of their subordinates. We know that it is easier to change one's own attitude than the attitude of others. In other words, they should concentrate more on improving their effectiveness in dealing with their subordinates than persuading employees to improve theirs. There is, thus, a greater need for a proper appreciation of the manager's role as a leader, a communicator and the captain of the team.

14

The Styles of Leadership

G.P. PILANIA

Leadership Process

Leadership is the process of influencing the activities of an individual or a group in efforts towards goal achievement in a given situation. In essence, leadership involves accomplishing goals with and through people. Therefore, a leader must be concerned about tasks and human relationships. These leadership concerns seem to be a reflection of two of the earliest schools of thought in organisational theory—scientific management and human relations.

The scientific management movement emphasised a concern for task (output), while the human relations movement stressed a concern for relationships (people).

Scientific Management Movement

Frederick Winslow Taylor: In the early 1900s, one of the most widely read theorists on administration was Frederick Winslow Taylor. The basis for his scientific management was technological in nature. It was felt that the best way to increase output was to improve the techniques or, methods used by workers. The main focus of a leader was on the needs of the organisation and not on the needs of the individual.

Human Relations Movement

Elton Mayo: In the 1920s and early 1930, the trend started by Taylor was to be replaced at centre stage by the human relations movement, initiated by Elton Mayo and his associates. These theorists argued that in addition to finding the best technological methods to improve output it was beneficial to management to look into human affairs. Contrary to scientific management theory, the main focus was on individual needs and not on the needs of the organisation.

Authoritarian-Democratic Leader Behaviour

Robert Tannenbaum and Warren H. Schmidt: It was felt that concern for task tends to be represented by authoritarian leader behaviour, while a concern for relationship is represented by democratic leader behaviour. The differences in the two styles of leader behaviour are based on the assumptions leaders make about the source of their power or authority and human nature.

The authoritarian style of leader behaviour is often based on assumption that the power of leaders is derived from the position they occupy and that people are innately lazy and unreliable (Theory X).

The democratic style of leader behaviour assumes that the power of leaders is granted by the group they are to lead and that people can be basically self-directed and creative at work, if properly motivated (Theory Y)

As a result, in the authoritarian style, all policies are determined by the leader and in the democratic style, policies are open for group discussion and decision-making.

A Continuum of Leader Behaviour

There are, of course a wide variety of styles of leader behaviour between these two extremes. Robert Tannenbaum and Warren H. Schmidt depicted a broad range of styles as a continuum, moving from authoritarian or boss-centred leader behaviour at one end, to democratic or subordinate-centred leader behaviour at the other end.

Douglas McGregor's Theory X and Theory Y

Assumptions about human nature:

Theory X	*Theory Y*
1. Work is inherently distasteful to most people.	1. Work is as natural as play, if the conditions are favourable.
2. Most people are not ambitious, have little desire for responsibility and prefer to be directed.	2. Self-control is often indispensable in achieving organisational goals.
3. Most people have little capacity for creativity in solving organisational problems.	3. The capacity for creativity in solving organisational problems is widely distributed in the population.
4. Motivation occurs only at the physiological and safety levels.	4. Motivation occurs at the social, esteem, and self-actualisation levels, as well as physiological and security levels.
5. Most people must be closely controlled and often coerced to achieve organisational objectives.	5. People can be self-directed and creative at work, when properly motivated.

Behaviour Patterns A and B

Chris Argyris recognised the difference between attitude and behaviour when he identified behaviour pattern-A usually associated with Theory X, and behaviour pattern-B associated with Theory Y. In pattern-A, individuals do not own up to feelings, are not open, reject experimenting and do not help others. Their behaviour tends to be characterised by close supervision and high degree of structure. In contrast, in pattern-B, their behaviour tends to be more supportive and facilitating.

Michigan Leadership Studies

The early studies of the Survey Research Centre at the University of Michigan identified two concepts which they called production-orientation and parallelled employee-orientation. These two orientations parallelled the authoritarian (task) and democratic (relationship) concepts of the leader-behaviour continuum.

Group Dynamics Studies

Dorwin Cartwright and Alvin Zander, summarising the findings of numerous studies at the Research Centre for Group Dynamics claim that group objectives fall into one of the two categories: (i) the achievement of some specific group goal, or (ii) the maintenance or strengthening of the group itself.

The Coch and French Study

Most early research on participation is connected with the Harwood Manufacturing Company. At the Marion, Virginia plant in the late 1940s, Lester Coch and John R.R. French conducted a study that examined the process of overcoming resistance to change.

Coch and French set up an experiment that tested the effects of degrees of participation on three work-groups:

1. Control group
2. Representative participation
3. Full participation

The control group (no participation) resisted change. When the change was first introduced, the representative participation group's productivity dropped even lower than that of the control group; but it quickly recovered to exceed the level of productivity before the change. The full participation group had by far the best record. Production soared and attitudes were positive. The study experimentally showed that participation did, in fact, has an impact on productivity, turnover and attitudes.

Ohio State Leadership Studies

The leadership studies initiated in 1945 by the Bureau of Business Research at Ohio State University narrowed the description of leader behaviour to two separate and distinct dimensions: Initiating Structure and Consideration. Initiating structure refers to the leader's behaviour in delineating the relationship between himself and his followers and in endeavouring to establish well-defined patterns of organisation. Consideration refers to the leader's behaviour indicative of friendship, mutual trust, respect and warmth towards his followers.

Managerial Grid

Robert R. Blake and Jane S. Mouton: In discussing the Ohio State, Michigan, and Group Dynamics leadership studies, we have been concentrating on two theoretical concepts—one emphasising task accomplishment and the other stressing the development of personal relationships. Robert R. Blake and Jane S. Mouton have popularised these concepts in their Managerial Grid. In the Managerial Grid, five different types of leadership, based on concern for production (task) and concern for people (relationship), are located in four quadrants similar to those identified by the Ohio State Studies.

The five leadership styles are described as follows:

1. Impoverished
2. Country Club
3. Task
4. Middle of the Road
5. Team

The Four Basic Leader Behaviour Quadrants

Paul Hersey and Kenneth H. Blanchard: In the leadership models developed by Paul Hersey and Kenneth H. Blanchard, at the Centre for Leadership Studies, the terms task behaviour and relationship behaviour are used to describe concepts similar to Initiating Structure and Consideration of the Ohio State studies.

The two types of behaviour, task-oriented and relationship-oriented, which are central to the concept of leadership style, are defined as follows:

Task Behaviour

The extent to which leaders are likely to organise and define the roles of the members of their group (followers); to explain what activities each is to do and when, where and how tasks are to be accomplished; characterised by endeavouring to establish well-defined patterns of organisation, channels of communication, and ways of getting jobs accomplished.

Relationship Behaviour

The extent to which leaders are likely to maintain personal relationship between themselves and members of their group (followers) by opening up channels of communication, providing socio-emotional support, 'psychological strokes', and facilitating behaviour.

The four quadrants which depict essentially different leadership styles are:

1. High task and low relationship
2. High task and high relationship
3. High relationship and low task
4. Low relationship and low task

The leadership style of an individual is the behaviour-pattern that the person exhibits when attempting to influence the activities of others as perceived by those others. A person's leadership style involves some combination of task behaviour and relationship behaviour.

The Tri-Dimensional Leader Effectiveness Model

William J. Reddin: In his 3-D Management Style Theory, William J. Reddin was the first to add an effectiveness dimension to the task concern and relationship concern dimensions of earlier attitudinal models, such as the Managerial Grid. Reddin felt that a useful theoretical model "must allow that a variety of styles may be effective or ineffective, depending on situation".

Effectiveness Dimension

By adding an effectiveness dimension to the Ohio State model, a three-dimensional model is created. This leader-effectiveness model attempts to integrate the concepts of leader style with situational demands of a specific environment. When the leader's style is appropriate to a given environment as measured by results, it is termed effective; when his style is inappropriate to a given environment, it is termed ineffective.

The difference between the effective and ineffective styles is often not the actual behaviour of the leader but the appropriateness of this behaviour to the environment in which it is used. In reality, the third dimension is the environment. It is the interaction of the basic style with the environment that results in a degree of effectiveness or ineffectiveness.

Effectiveness should be represented as a continuum. Any given style in a particular situation could fall somewhere on this continuum—from extremely effective to extremely ineffective. Effectiveness, therefore, is a matter of degree, and there could be an infinite number of faces on the effectiveness dimension. The Tri-Dimensional Leader Effectiveness Model is distinctive because it does not depict a single ideal leader behaviour style which is suggested as being appropriate in all situations.

An effective leader must be able to diagnose the demands of the environment and then either adapt his leadership style to fit these demands, or develop the means to change some, or all of the other variables. The concept of adaptive leader behaviour means that effective leaders are able to adapt their style of leader behaviour to the needs of their followers and the particular situation; and the more they adapt, the more effective they will tend to be. The leader "must be much like the musician, who changes his techniques and approaches to obtain the shadings of the total performance desired".

Two Types of Leadership Behaviour Orientation

1. Task-oriented or production-oriented.
2. People-oriented/employee-oriented or relationship-oriented.

Task-oriented Behaviour

1. Leader views his subordinates as "people to get the work done".
2. Leader is primarily concerned with achieving a high level of production.
3. Leader is responsible for initiating structure.
4. Leader supervises, organises and defines group activities and his relation to the group.

People-oriented Behaviour

1. Leader establishes a supportive personal relationship with his subordinates.
2. Leader takes a personal interest in subordinates.
3. Leader shows understanding when mistakes are made by subordinates.
4. Leader has consideration for his subordinates (consideration is a dimension of leader behaviour) which is indicative of warmth, friendship, mutual trust and respect. The satisfaction of subordinates is related to the consideration or employee orientation of their leaders.

Leadership Styles According to Behaviour-Orientation

Assuming that task and people are the two main dimensions of leadership behaviour; possible leadership styles could be variously labelled as follows:

	Task-Oriented	*People-Oriented*
1.	Boss-centred	Subordinate-centred
2.	Leader is the commander	Leader is the advisor
3.	Followers are subordinates	Followers are colleagues
4.	Close	Open
5.	Autocratic	Democratic
6.	Directive	Supportive
7.	Arbitrary	Consultative
8.	Authoritarian	Egalitarian
9.	Goal-achievement	Group-maintenance
	Initiating structure	Consideration (Refer The Ohio Leadership State Studies)
Production-centred	Employee-centred	(Refer Michigan University Studies)
Non-participative	Participative	(Refer Coch and French Study)
Theory-X	Theory-Y	(Refer Douglas McGregor)
Concern for production	Concern for people	(Refer Black and Mouton: Managerial Grid)

Human Dimensions that Influence Organisational Success

According to Rensis Likert, a well-known authority on management, there are five key human dimensions that strongly influence a firm's success:

1. Managerial leadership
2. Organisational climate
3. Group processes
4. Peer leadership
5. Subordinates' satisfaction

Managerial and peer leadership place importance on supporting, encouraging, and helping an individual to do the best possible job. Effective group processes refer to procedures that instil mutual trust, confidence, and teamwork among members of a work-group. Organisational climate (organisational personality) can contribute to organisational effectiveness, when it creates within employees the feeling that the company is concerned with their ideas, involvement and participation.

Interacting Components of an Organisational Setting

1. Leader
2. Superiors
3. Associates
4. Followers
5. Job Demands
6. Other Situational Variables
7. Organisation
8. External Environment

Leadership Style Reflected Through Different Processes of Decision-Making

The two leadership orientations can be broken down further into several different leadership styles. The four leadership styles identified by Rensis Likert, are useful in that they imply the amount of employee-participation or input into the decision-making process:

1. Exploitative autocrat,
2. Benevolent autocrat,
3. Participative,
4. Democratic.

The following decision making continuum of leadership behaviour shows the degree of shared leadership in a group:

1. Leader makes decision and announces it,
2. Leader 'sells' decision,
3. Leader presents ideas and invites questions,
4. Leader presents tentative decision subject to change,
5. Leader presents problem, gets suggestions, makes decision,
6. Leader defines the limits, asks the group to make decision, and
7. Leader permits subordinates to function within the limits, defined by a superior.

Best Style of Leadership

Some management writers have suggested a 'best' style of leadership.

Andrew W. Halpin, of the Original Ohio State Staff, seemed to conclude that the high consideration (relationships) and high initiating structure (task) style is theoretically the ideal, or 'best' leader behaviour, while the style low on both dimensions is the 'worst'.

Blake and Mouton, in their 'Managerial Grid', also imply that the most desirable leadership style is 'team management' (maximum concern for production and people) and the least desirable is 'impoverished management' (minimum concern for production and people).

Leadership Style should Vary with the Situation

While the Ohio State and the Managerial Grid people seem to suggest that there is a 'best' style of leadership; recent evidence from empirical studies clearly shows, that there is no single all-purpose normative style of leadership, which is universally successful.

Based on the definition of leadership process as a function of the leader, the followers, and other situational variables; the desire to have a single ideal type of leader behaviour seems unrealistic.

Good leaders recognise that each situation calls for a particular kind of action. Thus, it is possible for an individual to be autocratic in one situation and to be democratic in another. This is not necessarily indicative of leadership inconsistency. Being able, then, to adjust leadership style, while meeting the organisational and group goals to the greatest possible extent, will mark the presence of an individual, who could truly be said to be a "leader for all seasons," according to Grance & Milbourn.

Nearly all leaders have some blend of employee-orientation and task-orientation in their leadership styles. The assumption that employee-orientation and production-orientation were at opposite ends of a single continuum, has been found to be false by the empirical findings of the Ohio State Leadership studies.

15

Theories of Leadership
A Conceptual Overview

ASHA HINGAR

The need for effective leadership and motivational systems cannot be exaggerated in an organisational setting. A.M. Meerlo has emphasised that leadership stems from a man's desire to master his environment through group effort.[1] Leadership arises in the group where the members of the groups seek to satisfy their need through interaction. Leadership is one aspect of entire mechanism devised by the group for the fulfilment of its needs and goals. Through the device of role differentiation, groups make use of the various characteristics of the members to the advantage of all by assigning group tasks to those best qualified to perform them.

Research Efforts

A pioneering study in the field of leadership was conducted in the late 1930's by Ronald Lippitt and Ralph K. White with the assistance of Kurt Lewin.[2] The study was significant in the sense that it was the first serious attempt to analyse leadership through the use of scientific methodology. The analysis showed that different styles of leadership can have varying degrees of influences in the same groups.

The Ohio State Research Group identified consideration and initiation as two major functions of leadership.[3] Lester Coch and John French tried to testify the importance of participation in leadership.[4] Douglas McGregor also presented X and Y theories of leadership. Theory X represents the traditional and authoritarian type of management, while theory Y incorporates basic elements of human motivation, proper orientation and training.[5]

The Concept of Leadership

The concept of leadership has covered a wide variety of behaviours, many of which are unrelated with each other. In an unpublished review, V.J. Bentz has listed 130 definitions of leadership. These definitions were obtained through a review of literature published prior to 1949. Fred E. Fiedler has enumerated a dozen different definitions of leadership with varying connotations and degrees of emphasis. He has concluded that a leader is the individual in the group who directs and co-ordinates the group activities or who, in the absence of a designated leader, carries the primary responsibility for performing these functions in the group. Emphasis on coordination here seems to indicate that the task of leading is synonymous with managing.[6] But, essentially management is considered to be a much more broadly based function which also includes several activities other than leading.

Keith Davis has observed that "Leadership is the ability to persuade others to seek defined objectives enthusiastically. It is human factor which binds a group together and motivates it toward goals. Management activities such as planning, organising, and decision-making are dormant cocoons until the leader triggers the power of motivation in people and guides them toward goals".[7]

The above definition stresses the role of leadership in eliciting behavioural responses which are beyond routine. But Robert Tannenbaum and Fred Massarik have underscored the influence system in the total leadership structures. They have summed up the relationship between leadership and influence systems by stating that leadership is "interpersonal influence, exercised in situations and directed through the communication process, toward the attainment of a specified goal or goals. Leadership always involves attempts on the part of a leader (influencer) to affect (influence) the behaviour of a follower (influencee) or to follower in the situation".[8]

It may be pertinent to mention at this point that a definition of leadership should not be confined to one or two variables only but instead should incorporate all the crucial elements which collectively integrate themselves into the broader concept of leadership.

In social science literature, leadership is viewed with reference to three broad categories, viz., as the attribute of a position, as the characteristics of a person, and as a category of behaviour.[9]

This brief paper aims to examine whether all the three ingredients of leadership, viz., leader, situation and follower are included in a particular leadership theory or not.

Analysis is being attempted of the trait theories, socio-metric theory, situational theories, general interaction theories, and idiosyncrasy credit theory.

Trait Theories of Leadership

The scientific analysis of leadership initially started with the concentration on the leader himself. The question arises as to what makes a person leader? The earliest trait theorists emphasised that leaders are born not made. This "Great Man Theory" of leadership propounds that leadership traits are in-born, and generally cannot be acquired during one's lifetime. The Great Man Theory gave way to trait approach. But behavioural psychologists have observed through the use of scientific research methodology, that all traits are not completely inborn; some can also be acquired through learning and training. There upon, researchers began searching universal traits possessed by leaders. Numerous physical, mental and personality traits were researched between 1930's and 1950's. But the outcomes of these researches were not consistent. Only intelligence seems to hold some degree of commonality among the various lists of trait on the basis of numerous empirical researches.

According to H.C. Warren, leadership depends on attitudes and habits of dominance in certain individuals and submissive behaviour in others. In view of these limitations and the absence of any causal relationship, Keith Davis has highlighted four traits which appear to have an impact on successful organisation leadership. These factors are: (1) intelligence (2) social maturity

(3) inner motivation and achievement, and (4) human relations attitudes. That seems to be a reasonable blend of traits which might be found in successful leaders. And if good leadership is defined according to some consensual yardstick, these attributes gain significance. But a total reliance on the trait approach may not be a sound approach. Ben Solomon, who has suggested that certain specific qualities are obviously desirable in a leader but that more seems to be absolutely essential.

Trait theories of personality have certainly provided some insight into the traits of leaders, but in fact contain little analytical or productive value.[10]

Socio-metric Theory

A very large proportion of the research in leadership has made use of the socio-metric method. This technique was developed by Jacob Moreno,[11] while the first socio-metric study was made by Helen Jennings.[12] The approach provides an easily accessible and relatively objective means of assessing interpersonal attitudes within a group. The simple but important recognition that different choice criteria could be incorporated in the socio-metric question has led to very significant insights into the leadership of groups. The socio-metric method has also demonstrated that interpersonal designation of leaders varies in any group with the change in goals, tasks and internal structure of an organisation.

Situational Theories of Leadership

Limited success attained by focusing upon the leader in the theories of leadership led to a new perspective stressing an analysis of situational influences in leadership growth. Situational theorists emphasise that leadership roles, skills and behaviour considerably depend upon external and internal environmental situations. Leadership is a function of interaction[13] between personality and situation.

Since 1940's, several researchers have identified various situational variables which bear relevance to the conceptualisations on leadership. The general conclusion of such researchers is that depending on the situation, some leadership styles seem to be more effective than others. For example, Alan Filley and Robert House, in review of research literature on leadership found the following situational factors influencing leadership effectiveness.[14]

1. The history of the organisation, the age of the leader and his previous experience;
2. the community in which an organisation operates;
3. the work requirement of the group;
4. the psychological environment of the group which is going to be led;
5. the kind of job the leader holds;
6. the size of the group;
7. group member personalities; and
8. the time required and allowed for decision-making.

The list underscores the abundant impact of the situational factors on leadership. However, most of the variables enumerated in the above list have not been duly verified by further research. Nevertheless, their heuristic value remains.

General Interaction Theory

Basically, leadership under this conceptual scheme is a function of personality and social system in a dynamic interactional situation.

Some aspects of interaction theory have been systematically elaborated and investigated into by Fred Fiedler and his associates. Fiedler combines the trait and situational approaches to come up with an overall theory or at least a model, of leadership effectiveness.[15] To understand his model, it is necessary to have a resume of his research techniques and findings.

Fiedler chose to measure, as indicators of leadership effectiveness "assumed similarity between opposites" (ASO) and "esteem for the least preferred coworker" (LPC). ASO calculates the degree of similarity between the leaders' perception of his least and most preferred co-workers. LPC calculates the degree to which the leader favourably perceives his worst co-worker. The two measurements which can be used interchangeably, relate to leadership style in the following manner.

(1) The human relation-oriented leader who does not distinguish a great deal between the most and the least preferred co-worker which gives a relatively favourable description of the LPC. (2) The task-oriented leader sees a great difference between his most and least preferred coworkers (ASO) and gives very unfavourable description of the least preferred coworkers.

Fiedler's Contingency Model of Leadership

To test his hypothesis, Fiedler developed contingency model of leadership which contained the relationship between leadership style and the favourableness of the situation. This favourableness was described by Fiedler in terms of three propositions:

1. the leader-member relationships,
2. the degree of task structure, and
3. the leader's position power obtained through formal authority.[16]

Situations are favourable to the leader if all three of the above dimensions are high, and if these dimensions are low, situations become unfavourable to the leader. Fiedler observes that the favourableness of the combination with the leadership styles determines effectiveness.

Fiedler discovered that under very favourable and unfavourable situations, the task-oriented type of leader was not effective, and the situation was only moderately favourable, employee-oriented leader was most effective.[17]

The question arises why the task-oriented leader is successful in very favourable situations. Fiedler explains that in very favourable conditions in which leader has power and informal backing and a relatively well structured organisation, the group is ready to be directed for it expects to be told what to do.[18]

Fiedler's contingency model has so far stood the test of research but much more needs to be done. In general, Fiedler's contingency model suggests that the effectiveness of group performance can be affected by changing the leader's style and/or the situation in accordance with the described relationships.

Fiedler and Meuwese have also demonstrated that a leader's ability scores corelate highly with group performance only if the leader is socio-metrically accepted or liked.[19]

Hollander's Idosyncrasy Credit

It is noteworthy that both the trait and situational theories make a contribution to understand leadership behaviour. But they are only partial theories. They neglect or underemphasise the followers' role in leadership behaviour despite the fact that followers form the central part of leadership.

Probably the best word for the definition of leadership is "influence". The leader influences his followers but perhaps equally important is the fact that followers influence the leader. Edwin P. Hollander and James W. Julien use the concept of "exchange" to explain this leader-follower interaction process.[20] Situation, group, and leadership style can be integrated with an overall influence system of leadership.

Conclusion

The popular idea that leaders are born not made, highlights the importance of individual traits of leaders but ignores other equally relevant factors. The characteristics of social group which is going to be led is also an important variable in understanding situations. The presence of certain basic personality traits and behavioural characteristics is helpful but neither necessary nor sufficient for the success as a leader.

In conclusion, the most appropriate leadership technique is probably the one which recognises the importance of systematic interaction among style, group and situation. The administrator should attempt to adopt a style which is compatible with the needs and expectations of subordinates and is appropriate in the given situation. One should recognise that this style may vary from group to group or even from individual to individual and from situation to situation.

Notes

1. A.M. Meerlo, *Leider en geleide; bijdrage tot de* psychologie van bet leiderschap. *(Leader and Follower: A Contribution to the Psychology of Leadership)* (Mensch en Maarschappiji, 1934), pp. 196–210.
2. Ronald Lippitt, Ralph K. White and Kurt Lewin, "Patterns of Aggressive Behaviour in Experimentally Created Social Climates", *Journal of Social Psychology,* May, 1939, pp. 271–76.
3. Ralph M. Stogdill and Alvin E. Coons (eds.), *Leader Behaviour Its Description and Measurement* (Columbus, Ohio State University, Bureau of Business Research, 1957).
4. Lester Coch and John R.P. French, "Overcoming Resistance to Change", *Human Relations,* Vol. 1, No. 4, 1948, pp. 512–32.

5. Douglas McGregor, *The Human Side of Enterprise* (New York, McGraw Hill Book Company, 1967).
6. Fred E. Fielder, A *Theory of Leadership Effectiveness,* (New York, McGraw Hill Book Company, 1967).
7. Keith Davis, *Human Behaviour at Work,* 4th ed., (New York, McGraw Hill Book Company, 1972), pp. 103–04.
8. Robert Tennenbaum and Fred Massarik, "Leadership: A Frame of Reference", *Management Science,* October, 1957, p. 3.
9. Daniel Katz and Robert L. Khan, *The Social Psychology of Organization* (New York, Wiley, 1966).
10. L. Jacob Moreno, *Who shall Survive Foundations of Sociometry, Group Psychotherapy and Sociodrama Sociometry,* Monograph No. 29 (Beacon, New York, Beacon House, 1935).
11. On this point, see, "Leader Behaviour and Member Reaction in Three Social Climates" in Dorwin Cartwright and Alvin Zander (eds.) *Group Dynamics: Research and Theory.* (New York, Harper and Row, 1953), pp. 385–611,
12. Helen Jennings, *Sociometry of Leadership Based on Differentiation of Psycho-group and Sociogroup Sociometry,* Monograph No. 14 (Beacon, New York, Beacon House).
13. J.C. Wofford, "Managerial Behaviour, Situational Factors, Productivity and Morale", *Administrative Science,* Quarterly, March 1972, pp. 10–27.
14. Alan C. Filley and Robert J. House, *Managerial Process and Organizational Behaviour* (Gleenview, Scott, Foresman and Company 1969), p. 409.
15. Fred E. Fielder, *A Theory of Leadership Effectiveness* (New York, McGraw Hill Book Company, 1967),
16. Ibid., pp. 143–44.
17. Ibid., pp. 133–53.
18. Ibid., p. 147.
19. Fred E. Fiedler and Meuwese, W.A.T. "Leaders Contribution to Task Performance in Cohesive and Incohesive Groups", *Journal of Abnormal and Social Psychology,* 1967 pp. 86–87.
20. Edwin P. Hollander and James W. Julian, "Contemporary Trends in the Analysis of Leadership Process", *Psychological Bulletin,* May, 1969, p. 390.

16

Discussing Leadership

RAKESH HOOJA

There are those who believe that just as one only learns to dance by dancing, or can learn to swim only by actually swimming, one can only learn leading by actually leading. Others feel that leadership derives from the charisma that one possesses.

This brings me to the first of a set of questions that I want to set forth before this august audience at the beginning of this open discussion:

1. Are leaders born or made? To what extent can one make oneself a leader? And to what extent can leaders be trained or made into leaders by training and other external interventions?
2. Is the nature of leadership required in public sector/government bodies the same as is required in private entities, or in the not-for-profit NGOs—and what about political or social leadership within society or the

Being the remarks made at the open discussion on leadership organised by Jaipur Chapter of National HRD Network, IILM Academy of Higher Learning and Fortis Escorts Hospital at Jaipur on December 21, 2007, which the author was invited to moderate in his capacity as Director, HCM RIPA.

polity—does each of those categories require a different type of leadership? Surely, leaders in public/government sector organisations are constrained by jurisdictional norms, procedural systems and constitutional/statutory stipulations.

3. Can we suggest that effective organisations do not need to be dependant on great or even good leadership, and that it is the not-so-effective organisations that are in need of great leadership.
4. Is leadership only an art, or can we talk meaningfully of a science of leadership?
5. What is the best style (set of administrative or managerial behaviourisms and ways of doing things) to use for effective leadership? Can we rank different leadership styles in order of effectiveness?
6. Is leadership context-specific or can leadership attributes be universal? For example, would someone who is a good leader in the European context be equally so in Britain? Or, is what is required of a good leader in, say the USA, likely to be equally valid in the Indian cultural context?
7. In addition to country or cultural context, would the nature of problems or challenges facing a particular organisation or the specific situation being confronted by an organisation at a particular point of time, or even the type of organisation itself, and the type of followers available influence the different types of leadership attributes—may be leadership traits, may be leadership skills, may be leadership styles and behaviour—that are likely to prove successful? Does goal setting and goal getting have to be tailored according to the situation, the organisation, and the followers?

   For example, Kumble leading the Indian cricket team consisting of star players each with his ego and sense of experience and status as compared to Kumble leading the Karnataka team with young, not-so-established players who look up to Kumble. In one case facing international competition in ODIs or tests and in the other playing Ranaji Trophy matches. For the same task of captaining a cricket team, Kumble would need to employ different types of leadership in either situation.

8. Does a good leader also need to be a good administrator/manager or organiser?
9. Is it sufficient for a good leader that the entity he is leading functions like a well-oiled smoothly functioning mechanism? Or, is it necessary for a good leader to be continuously motivating the organisation to keep striving to reach out in new directions and to endeavour to reinvent itself through organisational change?
10. Are the characteristics of individual leadership similar to those required for organisational or institutional leadership?
11. To what extent does leadership, i.e., the quality of leadership actually make a difference?

Discussion Followed

Now, to turn to my concluding remarks at the end of today's fruitful discussion session.

Leaders need followers to work with them in facing situational challenges.

While leadership traits and leadership skills can reinforce each other, leadership styles differ and are dichotomous, and each leader adopts a particular type of leadership style.

Leadership styles may include those that are consensual or authoritarian, directional (i.e., based on giving directions) or delegative, inspirational, or motivational versus managerial and organisational. Each of these are dichotomous and a leader follows one or the other out of each of the dichotomous groups of styles.

Examples of leadership traits are self-confidence, decisiveness, flexibility, willingness to assume responsibility, resilience, innovativeness, ability to take hard decisions, willingness to take the initiative, ability to inspire others etc.

Examples of leadership skills may be communicational ability, social ability or social skills, team-building capabilities, ability to assess or evaluate others as individuals or as members of groups (this in fact may be more of a trait than a skill that can be acquired), analytic ability, technical ability (especially if a scientific establishment, or a hospital like Fortis, is to be provided leadership), ability to understand the environment in which the leader is to lead so that task-oriented behaviour, people-oriented behaviour and organisation-oriented behaviour can be evolved accordingly.

Skills can be taught or learnt, i.e., are fully acquired. Traits and styles, on the other hand, are partly what one is born with and partly what one acquires through experience—for these teaching/training is much less relevant.

Good leaders have the ability to ask the right questions and to provide the right answers—as has been said the measure of leadership is success.

Let me conclude by suggesting that if we have the right leader with appropriate styles, traits, skills etc., attributes, at the right place, at the right point of time, reacting to the right situation, then, the leader will succeed. If this combination does not exist, then, leadership would be found to be lacking.

17

The Decision Process in Administration

KAMLESH GUPTA

We all know that countless decisions are made by time and neglect. Some decisions are made by custom and tradition. Others are made in response to pressures, or to escape other current difficulties, or to emulate others, or for less certain reasons, both relevant and irrelevant. Many decisions are essentially negotiated. They involve so many people, agencies, and points of view that the process of getting assent to a course of action almost defies description, and the reasons are too hidden and complex to be traced. But in spite of much bad and much complex decision-making, it can be demonstrated that in many affairs, and especially in industry, we have moved a long way towards a more conscious deliberative appraisal of problems in an effort to improve results. It is this process that I wish to consider in some detail.

However, much they may be obscured or circumvented in practice, there are five general steps inherent in the process of rational decision-making. They are: (i) to identify the problem and understand it; (ii) to define or clarify the goals sought; (iii) to pose alternatives for the attainment of those goals; (iv) to analyse the anticipated consequences of each major alternative; and (v) to appraise the alternatives and choose. Let me elaborate.

Identify the Problem

Identifying the problem sounds like a simple task and sometimes it is; but most problems have to be discovered as well as defined. A plant breakdown presents a problem, but to anticipate and forestall a breakdown of operations calls for warning systems that notify in time to identify the problem and to take action. In business, elaborate reporting systems are established so that current activities may be compared with standards of satisfactory performance.

In the flow of events, the administrator has to be alert to know whether a problem is developing. An event occurs, perhaps outside the enterprise. Until its meaning is known, its import to the management cannot be diagnosed. Management must have an elaborate system of communication to detect and interpret such developments.

When we ask for the meaning of some event, the scholar is disposed to explain it by showing how it arose, what caused it, and why? But for the practical man, this is the smaller share of what he needs to know. He must know the future potentialities of the event, what it is likely to lead to. Since that usually cannot be forecast reliably, he wants to know the event's capabilities, what it could lead to and how, under what conditions. Thus, he wants past experience distilled to yield not just broad universal generalisation but also a great many special conclusions about how and why things behave as they do in different specified conditions. This will be of practical use to him.

For many years, the prevailing view in management was that if we got the facts, the solution would be indicated. It was supposed that if the facts were obtained and analysed, the cause of a problem would become evident; and by treating the cause, we would solve the problem. But few problems are resolved so simply.

In the first place, getting the facts is often a large investigation in itself. What are the facts and the dimensions of the problem of waste in a plant, or in a university, or in our foreign aid programme? To discover this calls for a major investigation. When the facts are known, the causes of the difficulty are usually not apparent and must be discovered, often by testing hypotheses and experimentation. And when the causes are found, the question still remains: Are they the strategic factors through the control of which, or modification of which a more favourable set of conditions can be created that will yield the results desired?

Thus, the cause of a problem may be morale of staff, and the remedy may be a wholly different system of mechanisation. My chief point, however, is that detecting, analysing, and understanding problems represents an elaborate and diverse process about which we know relatively little. We probably do it badly, but no one knows.

Define Goals

It is necessary next to define and clarify goals. The administered organisation ordinarily has fairly clear continuing purposes and goals. Yet these are never wholly given; they are administratively set and then are reaffirmed or neglected as time passes. The top administrators in-charge inevitably give import to this system of goals and values, emphasising some and de-emphasising others. Any change in leadership is watched for its effect on that vague but well-sensed system of purposes, goals, and values by which the participants are expected to operate.

Within an organisation, however, problems seldom come with solutions or clear goals attached. The decision maker must define the specific objective that will yield the larger goals of the enterprise without excessive cost or other disadvantages. Such goals are not final; they are instrumental. From above they are seen as but means to an end; from below they are purposes to be achieved. The structuring of instrumental goals is inherent in all administration.

All but a few of the most general goals that the administrator sets are instrumental goals to some more ultimate purpose. His task is therefore that of choosing systems of intermediate ends and means that meet acceptable standards of efficiency. Though the administrator does exercise value judgments in affirming or reshaping the purposes of the organisation and the standards it will follow, a great deal of this so-called goal-setting is basically an economic problem of finding and choosing the most economical course of action for the attainment of desired ends.

Discuss Alternatives

The posing of alternative courses of action for consideration is perhaps the most creative aspect of decision-making. But we must not overestimate the creativity actually shown. More ideas are in fact copied from other known experience than are generated de novo. A common practice is to discover what others do in similar situations and then do likewise or adapt such practices. Much effort is often expended on surveys to find out what practices are followed, while too little effort is ordinarily expended to discover which practices yield the best results; the latter involves the adoption of a standard, appraisal, and judgment. Simon has pointed out that alternatives are not given, they must be sought; and no administrator explores all alternatives, he explores at best only a few.

Now we may ask how the administrator decides to rule out some practices and to consider others. With an objective defined and various standards of ethical conduct established as policy, a quick appraisal will show that some alternatives will not serve the combination of ends desired. Others will be found to violate ethical or other policy criteria and hence are ruled out. Still others are too uncertain and undependable to warrant adoption. Some will seem promising; but to be effective, they would require changes that are undesirable. After considering a number of alternatives in a preliminary way, several may survive for more careful analysis and appraisal or better proposals must be thought of which deserve serious consideration.

Analyse Consequences

The fourth step is to analyse the consequences of each of the principal alternatives. At this point, the social scientist is inclined to revive his interest, for he believes that his science can predict consequences at least under specified conditions. The task soon proves formidable, however, for the social scientist cannot foretell the actual conditions that will prevail in the future. He finds it risky to assume them. Moreover, he finds that the administrator's problem is to foresee consequences under any of several possible conditions that may prevail. Here the social scientist is likely to retreat, insisting that since he cannot predict future conditions, he cannot reliably predict consequences. He cites an established dogma to this effect, and he believes it. He, therefore, insists that he should leave the whole matter to the administrator who, in his sloppy way, is expected to operate in the loose and unscientific manner required.

But I wonder if social scientists have really given this process the attention it deserves. The literature claims predictive powers for social science but none for social scientists in the real world. I wonder if the problem of prediction is properly represented. As I have observed, administrators do not predict the future; they postulate it, and ask how a given course of action will work and what results it will have under those postulated conditions. For example, by projection or extrapolation, they postulate a continuation of business about as it has been, using this or last year as a model for the future, or they assume a rate of growth or a recession in line with recent experience. But prudent administrators seldom risk a major decision on the basis of results expected under only one set of postulates. They also ask how this course of action will work if we have a war, or a depression, or a boom. They postulate a number of contingencies and consider the consequences under each. They may, and sometimes do, fail to postulate the most likely future or the future that is later realised but their several efforts are intended to come fairly close to any set of conditions that may emerge.

On this basis, the social scientist could be more effective in exercising his abilities in tracing out consequences under alternative models of prospective conditions. Strangely, he has seemed reluctant to do this. One difficulty is his preconception that he must come up with a judgement for one course of action as superior to all others when in fact there may be no such clear preference as between several alternatives serving slightly different objectives in contingent futures.

Some will argue that there remain for the social scientist even under a postulated future, insurmountable uncertainties rendering any statement of consequences too tentative for reliable choice. This indeed is a problem, and yet the administrator has ways of dealing with uncertainties. He does not insist on the impossible. He is accustomed to dealing with crude information having a wide margin of error. He is even accustomed to acting without information, if act he must. But he has devices of protection. He adopts measures that permit adjustment to change on what is now called the feedback principle. He operates with some slack that allows him flexibility for adjustment to unforeseen developments. He allows a margin of safety in his profit objectives; he keeps personnel for possible future use even when he may not need it currently; he builds up a cash account for uncertainties, reserves of space, personnel, sources of raw material, and a host of arrangements that permit adjustments on short notice. He keeps his policies flexible and adjustable. The administrator spends a good deal of his time reviewing contingencies and building precautions against them into his commitments and his operating system. Social scientists have made the problem seem more unmanageable than in fact it is, and this derives from our failure to look at the process carefully.

To return to the analysis of consequences for a moment, we may ask how the analyst applies scientific knowledge. He uses the concepts, skills and techniques of the scientist, of course. He may use scientist generalisations or established knowledge of relationships as major premises for deducing a priori conclusions. More often, he employs such general knowledge of experience to suggest hypothesis to be checked for consistency against other knowledge. But precisely how he uses the body of scientific knowledge available to him is again an unexplored region.

In spite of all that is assumed about the uses and applications of formal scientific knowledge (and here I refer mainly to the social sciences), the literature is strangely devoid of explanation of just what is meant by application and how it is done. We all apply such knowledge; but I suspect that if we examined how we do it, we would be astonished at how different the process is from what we assume it to be. And most of us would be surprised at how flimsy and inadequate our methods are. Our confidence in the results would surely be shaken. But I know of no way to improve this process until we understand what is done and wherein the defects are serious.

Appraisal and Choice

The appraisal of alternatives is the fifth stage in the process of decision-making that requires scrutiny. The several alternatives chosen for consideration are presumably selected because of their capacity to yield the results desired. But there are always incidental and secondary consequences to consider and moreover, some courses of action ordinarily yield the desired results more effectively than others. Hence, the several alternatives must be appraised.

The more promising alternatives at this stage have usually passed the test of scientific validity. On the basis of known causal relationships, they are expected to yield the results intended. They have also, as a rule, passed the test of ethical principle and established policy. They are acceptable on ethical and policy grounds. The final choice depends, then, on how well the alternatives serve the objectives of the enterprise or agency with regard to benefits and costs.

The consequences of several alternatives are accordingly compared with the results desired or considered acceptable. These results and requirements become the criteria, or norms, against which comparisons are made. At times, modifications will be made in the proposed courses of action to yield better results and to avoid undesired consequences.

The choice itself is an act of judgement; it amounts to a commitment if the decision is final, and it is therefore a judgement of high importance. But wherein does judgement enter?

In the earlier consideration of alternatives, a judgment is made that each alternative chosen for study will yield reasonably well the primary results desired and each alternative is judged and acceptable by the ethical and policy standards of the enterprise as administered. A judgement is also made as to the consequences to be expected from each chosen course of action under postulated conditions. In the final appraisal, a judgment is made as to how well the consequences approximate the desired objectives and which alternative offers the most favourable combination of results. Some of these judgements are reasonably objective; others are influenced more by personal value systems.

The choice of a course of action often is not final, but must be approved by others—by higher officials, by a board of directors, by other parties and so on. Here an explanation of the action proposed and the reasons for it are required, and often a defence of such proposals may be necessary. In my view, the most effective presentations to boards of directors come from officers who explain the problem, review the several actions that might be taken, offer a definite proposal and explain what results are expected from it and why it is a more prudent course to pursue than the others. The function of the board is not just to approve; it is also to test the analysis by inquiring about contingencies and consequences that may have been overlooked or improperly appraised. In the end, the board may approve the recommendation or modify it to achieve the overall purposes more effectively.

Conclusions

Let me review some of the major tasks in decision-making that deserve more study by social scientists.

A very great effort must go into the gathering and interpretation of information. This covers not only regular reporting but also special investigation of expected problems to find out what the facts are, what the situation means, what its import for the future is, and what the nature of the problem is in fact.

The setting of goals and the clarification of objectives, as I have suggested, are often tasks of posing alternative ends—means systems in which the ends are intermediate or instrumental to some more general purpose. No aspect of the decision-making process is less studied and less understood. The choice of instrumental goals that economically achieve a larger purpose is not the sort of value judgment that social scientists may justifiably rule out as beyond their province. Certainly, the expert can often indicate which ends-means systems are most economical on reasonably objective grounds.

The posing of alternatives often leads to more fact gathering, for it often calls for studies of what others have done in similar situations and what results were obtained. While the posing of alternatives affords opportunity for creativeness and social inventiveness, it also permits emulation and even slavish following of custom.

It is in the analysis of the consequences of one course of action or another that the social scientist has his greatest opportunity to draw on the body of scientific knowledge and skills in his field. But it would be an exaggeration to say that the art, at this stage, has reached a very high level of development. The native views of social scientists on the necessity of forecasting rather than of postulating is testimony of this.

The task of comparing alternatives and their consequences against some set of norms and requirements is often done in a slipshod way. Even the methods by which proper comparisons should be made for reliable results remain a subject about which little is known and less has been written.

In these areas are countless problems for research. The social sciences have important contributions to make if they will direct their attention to the neglected aspects of the decision-making process. But there is also an approach to problem analysis that needs development. Too often the social scientist seeks to play advocate rather than adviser, and this has added to his confusion about value judgments.

I can illustrate this point best perhaps by considering the role of the economic adviser. His task is not to decide for the administrator or the public what final action shall be taken. His primary task is to lay before administrator the best alternatives open—to show him their consequences, how well they will attain the stated or assumed objectives—and leave the matter for the administrator to resolve. If the adviser's recommendations are desired, they may be requested; and he should make clear the basis on which they are reached. It is not the function of the adviser to decide, so much as it is to lay a sound foundation for decision by others.

In these areas, there is ample room for systematic study of how we apply knowledge and how we can better use it.

18

Training for Organisational Development through Self-Development

ANITA

Training intervention is considered as one of the vitally important aspects of human resource development, and thereby, of organisational development. There has been a growing concern to find ways to assess the effectiveness of trainers, training programmes, and training institutions; in terms of gauging their lasting contribution to society.

Training for what?

Robert Lynd, an American sociologist, questioned the rationale behind the human pursuit of knowledge by giving the clarion call—"Knowledge for What?" In the same vein, it would be pertinent to call forth for the justification implicit in the training effort. Whither training? What price training? Or, training for what? Does training help in developing the self, the organisations and the human society at large? Can training help arrive at strategies for problem solving, both, at the individual and at organisational levels. Can training be the talisman to ward off the stress clouds threatening to engulf this turbulent world?

All these posers are byways of provoking an introspective stocktaking desirable at the level of trainers and training institutions. The enormous investment in terms of money, time, energy and manpower that goes into the training function—has it really demonstrated its value to the organisations and to the individual participants? The crux of the matter is whether training effort has been worthwhile as regards influencing the job performance of individuals, making them more sensitised, responsive and committed to serve, inspired with human ethos, with a view to achieve organisational and humanitarian goals.

Key Result Areas for Developing Trainers

A trainer should be able to LEAD:

L *Lead* the participants on through the process of self-introspection to creating a greater self-awareness for facilitating better inter-personal relationships capable of unfolding group synergy.

E Enhancing *enrichment of experience* and learnings derived therefrom; by taking the participants along the Kolb's Learning Cycle, viz.

Kolb's Experiential Learning Model
(From *Organizational Psychology and Experiential Approach* 1971, Prentice Hall. Inc., USA)

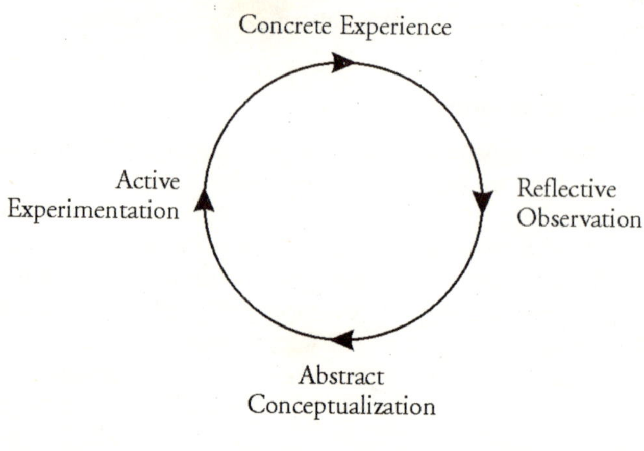

A *Anticipate needs and problems of* participants, as well as those of the organisations they serve; and design the training intervention to help effectively in answering these needs and problems by imbuing the participants with a heightened *Achievement Motive.*

D Dispel negatively-oriented or avoidance-centred motive strengths in the personality of participants and create in their *place—drive, dynamism* and the *doer zeal of dogged perseverance.*

Key Result Areas for Training Institutions

Training institutions should strive to CREATE a lasting impact towards individual, organisational and societal development, by way of:

C Being *Centres of Continued Learning* for individual trainees and *of Creativity* harnessing for their sponsoring organisations.

R Being *Resource Centres* for providing consultancy services for Organisational Development breakthroughs.

E *Enrich* the training exposure in terms of being capable of enhancing the knowledge, skills and attitudinal (KSA) aspects of the mental make-up of participants.

A Create a sense of *Advancement* and progress along the KSA parameters in the participants as also their organisation's own training impact assessment.

T Foster *Team-spirit,* group synergy, coordination, collaboration and cooperation as the watchwords of individual participants as well as of their sponsoring organisations.

E Enable internalisation of the *Ethos of Excellence* and enhancing the quality of work life both at the level of individuals as well as that of organisations.

Key Result Areas for Training Intervention

The rationale behind the training effort should be to EQUIP individuals and also organisations for:

E *Enhancing Effectiveness* at work by building on the strengths of individuals and enabling them to be result-oriented achievers.

Q *Quality of Work Life* should be promoted as a vitally important management function through innovating with both, job enlargement and job enrichment options to create a conducive motivational work environment.

U *Unleashing Latent Creative Potential* should be facilitated through training by bringing the participants to the threshold of self-exploration and discovery for knowing their own strengths, weaknesses and latent creativity, and highlighting ways or making manifest their latent creative potential to meet organisation and societal challenges.

I *Improving Interpersonal Relationships* in the organisational context, as also the individual's personal life-setting for enabling people to cultivate mutually helpful relationships and developing interpersonal competence for increasing organisational effectiveness in the long run.

P *Problems and People-Centred Approach* to training should help to bring about a widespread internalisation of a problems and people-centred work ethic, whereby, a professional commitment to organisational as well as social problems is ingrained in individuals as a mission of life, leading on to an empathetic, responsive, helping attitude towards people (organisational clients).

Toward a Unified Theory of Training for Organisational Development Through Self-Development

It would be pertinent to recapitulate at this juncture that with trainers taking the LEAD to EQUIP individuals and through them their organisations for greater effectiveness in tackling problems, people and priorities and with training institutions helping to CREATE the right climate for stimulating desirable change at the individual, organisational and societal levels; it would be worthwhile to synthesise a unified theory—a sort of guiding philosophy for trainers, training institutions and training activity for facilitating a symbiosis of individual and organisational interests. Answering to the resounding poser 'Training for what?', such a theory would propose the vocation of training practiced in the portals of training academies, by seasoned practitioners (the trainers), to be inspired with the ideal of making their professional pursuit, a SEARCH for:

S *Self-Actualisation:* A quest to be zealously pursued by individuals for realising/attaining the heights of their own creative potential, as well as to be internalised in the organisational work culture to provide sustainable avenues for job-enrichment, thereby, creating a motivating work-environment.

E *Enrichment of Job/Work Experience:* Skills to be developed to enable fulfilment of this objective both through individual innovations and creativity as well as organisational career development/HRD policies.

A *Achievement Motivation*: At both the levels, i.e., of individual work performance as well as organisational work ethic, a heightened drive for achievement motivation being the mainspring behind spreading a work culture of perseverance and commitment.

R *Recognition and Self-Worth:* To value this cardinal, time-tested principle of giving due recognition to the work and contribution of individuals working in the organisations, has been the hallmark of organisations excelling in their trade work area. This being a sure way to reinforce loyalty, commitment and zeal of individuals who make the organisations excel.

C *Creativity Training for Self-Excellence:* To unfold and harness the intrinsic but latent creative potential in individuals would make their sojourn through human life a more fulfilling and rewarding experience than all the material perquisites put together in their organisational careers. It would enable making their lives sublime with a deep aesthetic satisfaction, by providing to individual career pathing in organisations, not merely height and breadth, but also depth.

H *Human Resource Development:* This is the ultimate challenge to those in the vocation of training, keeping in mind the gigantic task in terms of sheer numbers of manpower of different levels to be provided access to and enriched through a meaningful training intervention. Not to speak of the woman power, that has largely remained invisible in proportion to their population, in the realm of being benefitted through training for skill-development. The challenge becomes graver still when one realises that if a scenario analysis of social inequalities is deepening due to differential access to avenues of education, training and therefrom, employment is undertaken, the threat looming large goads us to realise that there is no time to lose. Without urgent help, nearly a third of the world's population will be without access to basic skills by the year 2000. And if we are

> serious by our professed ideals of human rights—the most fundamental of them being the right to life and thereby, the right to livelihood and work—any slogan mongering in the name of 'equality', that much talked about ethereal ideology enshrined in prestigious tomes like the Constitutions of Nation States and the Universal Declaration of Human Rights, but fleeting as a caparicious utopia in the empirical human reality; we have to accept the dire need for promoting a *Training for All (for self-employment and self-development) Mission* to ensure a future of at least providing to human mortals the bare minimum for keeping their bodies and souls together. We have to turn the corner, as we turn the century; stop for a while to do some honest soul-searching and stop feigning ignorance of the reasons behind 'how the other half of the world dies?" The ultimate challenge before the training community—the HRD profession also then, is to bridge the learning gap and help build a more just and equal social order.

Another idea that HRD professionals may like to consider is to incorporate behavioural training as an HRD intervention at two major levels. Firstly, at the level of parents and teachers, who provide instrumental leadership in shaping the values and attitudes of children and teenagers. This by itself would be a major check on propagation of loser-scripts, unhealthy attitudes, and pathological or warped personalities, rendered to this irredeemable status through inadequate/inappropriate socialisation processes adopted by parents and teachers. Secondly, the most pertinent client group for being initiated in the realm of behavioural training is that of children and adolescents. The logic being to 'catch them young' for value shaping and personality-building. Such a systematic effort in value education is conspicuous by its absence in the currently prevailing HRD thrust, which aspires to be curative with limited success by catering to a clientele of organisational employees, who are already in the prime of their lives with deep-seated attitudinal biases and value predilections.

The HRD intervention should be meaningfully conceived to be more holistic by taking care of promotive, preventive as well as curative aspects of human and social development. Today's young entrants are the hope of the world of tomorrow!

19

Anatomy of Conflict and its Management

H.C. SUMAN

A conflict is a dispute of struggle in which each party expresses hostility towards the other party, or interferes, intentionally with the other's goal attainments. The conflict can also involve status, values, goals and strategies.

The conflict is a situation in which the interests of groups or individuals are perceived to be incongruous or in which there is a lack of adjustment between the individuals or groups and the job requirements or the circumstances in which it is performed. In conflict, unlike competition, opponents are primarily oriented towards each other rather than the objects they seek to attain. Indeed, achievement of the goal may be considered as secondary to the opponent's defeat.

In industrial terminology, the term 'conflict' usually refers to the divergent interests of management and labour.

The conflict easily breeds rather multiplies in group working and is an essential feature of human relations. It appears in variety of costumes, i.e., can be soft and gentle, can be harsh and direct, can be sneaky and may creep up on you gradually. This has almost as many faces, rather more than mythically perceived of that of Ravana—the ruler of Lanka. However, there is always one thing in common and that is the spark of opposition. This opposition can take the form of aggressive resistance. Or else, the resistance might be passive, but it is bound to be there. The conflict may be an organised or unorganised one. The former tends to be associated with high morale whereas the later one with low intensity.

Consequences of Conflicts

Generally, the conflict is regarded as an evil to be eliminated—whenever and wherever possible. It is assumed that conflict is an abnormal phenomenon with only negative outcome. But it is not true as it does not always have to be destructive. The behavioural scientists have since studied this myth in depth and found that certain level of conflict in any organisation, in general, and industrial organisation, in particular, is both inevitable and indeed desirable. It is both the cause and effect of change. As is said for stress that it is useful for the overall health of human beings, till it leads to the triggering impact, so is true for conflicts for the well-being of the given organisation. Where conflict or the possibility of conflict exists it is usually advantageous to secure its free expression so that the conflicting viewpoints may be fully explored and resolved or at least compromised. To quote: "In fact correctly guided conflict can be a value source of creativity and change. So it is best not to waste time trying to eliminate it. On the contrary, it is more productive to promote the right type of conflict and harness the outcomes for the organisation's benefits."

What the captain of the organisation has to do is to encourage productive conflict and reduce destructive conflict so as to foster the positive outcome of disagreements and minimise the more adverse effects. Notwithstanding, the conflict often being reflection of resistance by the opposite party to improvements/suggestions recommended by the other party can well be the source of motivation for both parties to seek innovative solutions that will resolve conflicts in mutually satisfactory ways.

Issues and Sources of Conflicts

Conflicts do arise from both *core* (value-based) *issues* and *motivational issues*. In every conflict, there is interplay between these two kinds of issues. Emotional conflict can be caused by people's deep-seated personal feelings about one another. Emotions tend to last longer and are harder to control. People in emotional conflict are never reasonable and often the neutral observer cannot see any reason why the conflict should exist at all. The issue of Babri Masjid is a classical example of a highly charged emotional conflict. In the existing society of divergent view and ideologies, at times *values* of life happen to be the root cause of conflict situations, which may on the surface appear to have other causes. Core issues are most often at the bese of the conflict (disagreement over goals) while emotional issues complicate the conflict. To address the conflict one must resolve the core issue first.

Sources of conflicts, inter alia, could synoptically be listed as under:

1. One major source of conflict in organisations is competition for scarce resources and those too subjective budgetary allocations and/or supplies of inputs, viz., people and support service etc.
2. Conflicts also arise from people having different viewpoints, especially divergent goals and beliefs etc.
3. Much of the conflict experienced does arise out of communication gap pertaining to one's wants, needs and values to others. When the communicator and communicate are operating on different wavelength, innocuously and/or deliberately, conflict is bound to emerge.

Repulsive and Strategic Outcomes of Conflicts

Following are the repulsive and strategic outcomes of conflicts:

1. One of the ways of reacting to conflict is flight, where one combatant leaves the battlefield to the victor. The second is to fight, where battle takes place and one party is defeated. But either of the situation is really no solution.
2. Another way is simply to avoid conflict by looking the other way or ignoring or denying that it does exist. It is obviously assumed either it will turn around or the conflict will disappear with the passage of time, believing that the time is the best healer of every problem. Although this can work

sometime but we run the risk of being seen as gutless as also it will seriously impair performance.

3. There is also a way of adopting 'accommodative attitude' when a person immediately gives in to another's demands. This response is termed as submission or appeasement. It is resorted to where maintaining a harmonious relationship is more important than getting one's way on any given issue. This approach is likely to have a snowballing effect, encouraging the other party, *inter alia,* to subsequently press for additional concessions. There has to be a limit of giving in, lest conflict(s) may endlessly go on intensifying.
4. The other repulsive outcome could be handling the conflict head on. It means standing firm and taking the role of a dictator and rejecting the views and beliefs of others. Every time this Sabre Rattling approach will drive the people to their shells keeping their ideas to themselves. Productivity can suffer and the damage can be difficult to repair. Using authority muscle to squash conflict is not the best prescription for gaining commitment.
5 The widely used strategy for managing conflict is that of compromise, i.e., give and take. Notwithstanding, the approach of compromise having considerable merit, if used too frequently, is not risk free and may be seen as a simple attempt to keep everyone happy instead of solving the problems. Compromise for the sake of compromise will defeat the whole purpose.
6. There is still another and perhaps the best way of addressing the conflict with a view to arriving at a settlement, namely, "Promoting a Collaborative Problem-Solving Culture" within the organisation. This collaborative approach aims for *win-win* rather than *win-lose* situations. People work together on problems rather than against one another in constant competition. It is an attempt to find a solution that satisfies the need of both the parties. Each party when starts understanding the conflict from the other party's point of view, it is not far away to discover that *needs* of the other party must be satisfied so as to arrive at a settlement of mutual interest. This requires an open exchange of information about facts involved, needs and feelings etc. Threats and punitive

actions are inconsistent with the creation of an atmosphere of trust and cooperation. To inculcate this sort of culture, the following are the prerequisites:

(i) To make communication open and constructive.
(ii) Avoid sneaky remarks behind people's backs.
(iii) To admit that a problem does exist and bring it into the open.
(iv) Catch conflict before it escalates, i.e., resolve the conflict constructively and at the earliest, as and when confronted.
(v) Ensure continual peer feedback as it helps in building strong relationships and sense of self-sufficiency.
(vi) Never judge a person until you stand in his place.

Process Of Conflict Resolution

The conflict could be addressed more objectively in the following manner:

1. Recognise the existence of the conflict, i.e., have courage to acknowledge that conflict does exist and take steps to resolve it. Timely steps to do so would enable you to mould conflict into an opportunity. This is obviously better than pretending its non-existence and keeping the things shut up so as avoid unpleasant scenes. If things are not opened up in time they grow in people's mind and then get blown up out of proportion.
2. Identify the real issues of the conflict. It is bit difficult but it has to be analysed what core issues are involved and how far the emotional part has crept in. In every complaint there is interplay between these two kinds of issues. Even if the main conflict is about how to do something, emotional issues such as danger of victimisation, threat to self-esteem or chances of heart burning/jealously etc., do intensify the conflict. To successfully resolve it, the core issues need to be resolved first.
3. Analyse and understand both sides of the given conflict rather issues involved. The timid and cunning members should be encouraged to express themselves. Avoid debates that are right or wrong. Focus on facts and behaviour and not feelings or personalities.

4. Help concerned members to identify similarities rather than differences and eliminate blaming segment on the part of either party as that may drive both sides to meet on common ground.
5. Explore each party's position in confidence and possibilities of consensus. Open discussions, after requisite enlightenment and conditioning of the parties, can result in a broadening of the information and alternatives available. This process can lead to more trusting and healthy relationships between the people involved.
6. Now it is time to look in the solution so *cajole* the parties to gain agreement and own responsibility for the desired resolution. The team members should be motivated to do a role reversal, each person presenting another's views. This is one way to help people to accept one another's perspective and joint responsibilities for reaching a workable solution.
7. Providing for the machinery to monitor the religious implementation of the agreement and schedule a follow-up session to review the resolution.

The above process/strategy is not exhaustive but only enumerative in nature, just by way of sharing experience, hence may not be considered as a universal remedy for all situations.

Remember: Conflict resolution is rarely easy. Successful conflict resolution requires time, thought, patience and courage of conviction.

Part III

Human Resource Development

20

Demystifying Human Resource Development

UDAI PAREEK

Human Resource Development (HRD) in the organisational context is a process by which the employees of an organisation are helped in a continuous and planned way to:

- acquire or sharpen capabilities required to perform various functions associated with their present or expected future roles;
- develop their general capabilities as individuals and discover and exploit their own inner potential for their own and for organisational development purposes; and
- develop an organisational culture in which senior-subordinate relationships, teamwork, and collaboration among sub-units are strong and contribute to the professional well-being, motivation, and pride of employees.

This definition of HRD is limited to the organisational context. In the context of a state or nation, it would differ.

HRD is a process, not merely a set of mechanisms and techniques. The mechanisms and techniques such as performance appraisal, counselling, training, and organisation development interventions are used to initiate, facilitate, and promote this process in a continuous way. Because the process has no limit, the mechanisms may need to be examined periodically to see whether they are promoting or hindering the process. Organisations can facilitate this process of development by planning for it, by allocating organisational resources for the purpose, and by exemplifying an HRD philosophy that values human beings and promotes their development.

Three emphases are involved in the concept of HRD. In the first place, persons working in organisations are regarded as valuable resources; implying that there is a need to invest time and effort in their development. Secondly, they are human resources which means that they have their own special characteristics and, therefore, cannot be treated like material resources. This focusses on the need to humanise organisational life, and introduce human values in the organisation. And thirdly, human resources do not merely focus on employees as individuals, but also on other human units and processes in the organisation. These include the role or the job a person has in the organisation, the dyadic unit consisting of the person and his boss, the various teams in which people work, inter-teams, and the total organisation. Thus, we have six units which are included in human resources. viz., persons, jobs or roles, dyads, teams, inter-teams, and the organisation. The concepts of the development of these units are briefly explained ahead.

The Individual Employee

The individual employee is the key unit in an organisation. HRD is primarily concerned with the development of persons working in the organisation so that they may be able to have their own fulfilment and contribute to the goals of the organisation. Development of persons or individuals has three different aspects as suggested below:

Self-Management

The person working in an organisation should develop competencies to manage his/her work effectively. This would involve learning to set realistic goals. The goals must, of course be challenging but not too high for the individual to achieve. The individual should also learn to analyse the performance results in terms of factors responsible for the success or failure in achieving performance results. Some of the factors are related to the employee while others may be concerned with external conditions. Finally, self-management would involve using such information and competency to improve one's performance in future.

Competence Building

The main contribution of HRD to the individual's development is in terms of building competencies required for better performance on the job. The individual employee comes with his/her educational background, and personal strengths and weaknesses, whereas he/she learns new skills in the organisation which help him/her to work effectively for achieving organisational goals.

Advancement

Every employee wishes to advance her/his career in the organisation. HRD can be helpful in the process of such advancement. We shall later see that advancement of employees involves identifying their potential for use in higher responsibilities in the organisation, and helping them to develop further potential to take up new challenges.

The Role

It would be pertinent, in this context, to pay attention to the roles which an individual employee performs in the organisation. Role is not synonymous with job, although both are very similar. Nor is role synonymous with status or position in the organisation. Role is the position which a person occupies as defined by expectations that different significant persons who have face-to-face relationship with the role occupant, have from him/her.

There are three main aspects of the development of role with which HRD must be concerned.

Optimum Stress

Each role must have enough challenge which may help the role occupant to stretch herself/himself to meet the challenge. The role in which the scope is limited to routine work and in which role occupants do not see any challenges, is not likely to inspire the role occupants to do their best. They will feel under-worked. While every role has routine elements, challenge must also be developed in every role. However, the challenge should not exceed a limit, otherwise it may produce dysfunctional stress, resulting in poorer performance and damage to the health of the employee. Building optimum stress in the role is like setting the strings of a musical instrument at a level where the strings are stretched enough to produce music, but not stretched so much as to break.

Linkages

While roles in organisations are occupied by individual employees, it is necessary to build linkages amongst the roles, as well as linkages of different organisational roles with challenging goals. If the roles get isolated and produce a feeling in the role occupants that their work is very narrow (and not much use for wider groups), it will have damaging effects on the individuals as well as the organisation.

Autonomy

If individuals, who occupy the various roles, feel that they have enough scope of taking initiative or solving problems or doing creative work, the role occupants as well as the organisation benefit a great deal. HRD must attempt to develop a sense of autonomy of this kind in every role, even at the lowest level in the organisation.

The Dyad

The dyadic groups (an employee and his supervisor) are the basic building blocks in an organisational structure. The stronger the dyads are, the stronger the organisation will be. The focus of development of dyads in an organisation would involve developing the following three aspects:

Trust

Effective work cannot be done in an organisation unless a trusting relationship is established between an employee and his supervisor. Trust does not develop easily; efforts should be made to develop such relationships.

Mutuality

Effective dyads will require free exchange of help between the employee and the supervisor. A helping relationship is not a one-way process. The supervisor should take help from his employees as much as he would give them the needed help. Mutuality in relationships will also involve support to each other.

Communication

Developing effective dyads will also involve improving communication between the members of the dyads. Both the employee and the supervisor should be able to give feedback to each other. The employee should improve his ability to receive feedback as the supervisor should improve his competence to guide the employee.

The Teams

Effective teams are quite important for the strength of the organisation. Primarily, two aspects should be the focus of HRD as far as team development is concerned. These are:

Cohesion

The teams should be cohesive. Well-knit teams produce synergy, and are able to utilise individual competencies.

Resource Utilisation

Effective teams maximise the use of resources available amongst members of the team. This would not only satisfy the members, because each will contribute whatever resources one has; but also help the team to produce effective results. Poor teams rely on and use resources only of a few members, resulting in limited opportunities for other members.

The Inter-Teams

The main emphasis of inter-teams is to develop cooperation amongst various groups in the organisation (e.g., departments, divisions, functions), so that they are able to work effectively towards common objectives. The main focus of such cooperation is to develop corporate identity. When the teams are strong and concentrate on their own goals only, the organisation becomes weak. While teams should work on their own goals, their linkages with the organisation and their identity with it should be achieved through various measures.

The Organisation

As far as the organisation is concerned, the following three aspects should deserve the attention of the HRD effort.

Growth

Obviously, the development of the organisation would involve increase in its size, activities and operations. Every organisation looks forward to its growth. Even if growth is not in terms of its size, the organisation may be concerned with providing qualitative services or maintaining leadership position in its field of operations.

Impact

Each organisation would like to have some impact on the outside organisation or customers etc. Impact may be in terms of developing new markets, developing services or products, introducing new technology which others can follow, etc.

Self-renewal

The organisation must examine its working from time to time and take steps to update its technology. It should also analyse the present and potential problems imminent on its growth and take steps to prepare itself to meet these challenges. Self-renewal competency is necessary for organisational effectiveness.

To summarise, HRD is concerned with development of the following human units of an organisation on the aspects shown against them:

1. The individual employee: Self-management, competence advancement.
2. The role: Optimum stress, linkages, autonomy.
3. The dyad: Trust, mutuality, communication.
4. The team: Cohesion, resource utilisation.
5. The inter-team: Identity, collaboration.
6. The organisation: Growth, impact, self-renewal.

The HRD Matrix

As discussed till now, there are six foci or targets of HRD (the person, the role, the dyad, the team, the inter-team, and the organisation). In other words, the scope of HRD is to develop (i.e., increase effectiveness and potential of) these human units. These foci or targets of HRD form one axis. The other axis is formed by HRD systems and activities. These two axes make what can be called the HRD matrix. Over the years, in India, several HRD practices have emerged. There is no single way to classify HRD activities and efforts. The classification system suggested here is based on both the new emerging trends in the HRD work in India, as well as a conceptual understanding of the main focus of HRD. HRD activities should be concerned with developing systems to make individuals and their roles alongside the organisation and the teams more effective. The systems primarily concerned with individual employees and their roles relate to their appraisal, advancement and training. The systems concerned with development of the organisation and its teams would relate to management of work, management of culture, and renewal of the organisation. Here, the following six HRD systems are suggested:

Appraisal Systems

Appraisal systems have attracted the most attention in recent years in India. There are three main appraisal systems: performance appraisal, potential appraisal, and performance coaching. Out of these, much more attention has been given to performance appraisal. In many cases, in the absence of attention to performance coaching, performance appraisal has become a mechanical exercise. Very little attention has been given to potential appraisal.

Increasingly, more and more attention needs to be given to performance review and coaching.

Career Systems

Career systems are concerned with the advancement of the individual employees in their careers in the organisation. The first step is taken in introducing career development plans so that employees joining at an entry point are helped to go through various experiences, which may help them to move up in the organisation, and may give them opportunities to prove themselves for higher responsibilities. Career planning, on the other hand, is concerned with charting specific career paths for the individual employees who have spent enough time in the organisation and have proved their competence. The third element which has been used only in a few organisations in India, is mentoring. Mentoring ensures individual attention to young potential employees for their possible fast growth in the organisation.

Training System

Training system is the oldest element of HRD and does not require much discussion. However, it is being very inadequately treated in most organisations. Attention to identification of training needs, preparation of a training strategy, development of a training system, curriculum designing to meet specific needs, follow-up and evaluation, and post-training support would be needed.

Work Systems

Generally, work systems have not attracted attention in HRD effort in India. Moreover, HRD has remained mostly confined to managerial levels. HRD must deal with work-related issues. Four aspects deserve attention in this regard.

Task analysis remains a neglected aspect in HRD. It can provide better understanding of the key contribution each job should make to the organisational aspects.

Although, some work has been done on *quality of work life*, more attention to this important aspect is needed. This will include workplace democracy, autonomous work-groups, participating management, etc. Improvements in the quality of work life, primarily characterised by autonomy and diversity, are very important.

HRD should also be concerned with *productivity and improvements in the quality of products*. Improvements in the quality of products enhance, and are to be made through effectiveness of individuals and teams in the organisation. HRD attention to these aspects cannot be over-emphasised.

More emphasis is being increasingly given in many Indian organisations on stress management. With increasing complexity of organisational life, attention to work-related stress and role-stress is increasing. Some organisations have started programmes to deal with stress. Stress audit and stress management programmes help both the individuals and the organisation.

Cultural Systems

Cultural systems are the most neglected part of HRD. Three aspects deserve attention in this regard. HRD should focus on the development of an *organisational culture* which will sustain the kind of effort HRD has developed. Emphasis on development of appropriate organisational climate is equally important. Some work has already started in some organisations on HRD climate. More work needs to be taken up in this regard.

The second aspect deserving attention *is communication.* In most organisations, problems may arise because of lack of attention to various aspects of communication (top-down, bottom-up, horizontal, circular, external).

The third aspect is the *reward system.* Whatever is rewarded in an organisation gets reinforced. Reward system, including incentive-schemes, both for individuals and for teams, deserves careful attention. Rewards work both ways. They can facilitate and promote good work; but if they are not properly designed, it can also be harmful to the organisation.

Self-renewal Systems

An organisation should be concerned not only with its growth but also with its health. It needs to diagnose its problems from time to time and take steps to develop new competence to cope with the various problems and challenges it would be facing. This can be done through effective *organisation development* (OD) effort. Organisation development or action research is concerned with development of competence through effective teams to diagnose the problems and initiate the process of collaborative work to deal with such problems. In OD, the focus is on developing process-competency to increase organisational effectiveness. Organisation development aims at maintaining profiles of organisational health, monitoring organisational growth, assisting 'sick' departments, helping interested units and departments in self-renewal, conflict management, creation of strong teams, etc., and establishing processes that build a climate to promote enabling capabilities in the organisation.

In addition to OD, attention should also be paid to *organisational learning,* which is concerned with learning from the experiences, and utilisation of such learning for future effectiveness.

The third aspect of this system will be *research orientation in HRD,* which means consciously collecting data in order to understand the various issues, and designing interventions based on such data. For example, data should be collected on the working of appraisal system, benefit to and difficulties experienced by different groups. Such data will help to improve implementation of the appraisal system. HRD related research is important for HRD effectiveness; it helps in analysing data and information generated by the HRD sub-systems.

21

Approaches to Human Resource Development

ASHA HINGAR AND SANGEETA SHARMA

The productive development of an organisation is preconditioned by effective resource management. Multi-dimensional development of an organisation depends, among other things upon the extent to which it has been able to utilise various resources of both the 'commodial' as well as 'non-commodial' nature.[1]

The resources of commodial nature are easily manifested, measurable and manageable, whereas the human resources could be difficult to manage if not entirely unmanageable, as generally these involve several unpredictable facets of human relations. Humans who are basically the responding beings carry with themselves attitudes, beliefs, values and other personality variables. Though their exposure to the contextual environment would be considerably determining the ultimate effectiveness of 'human' as a 'resources', yet, despite these constraints, efforts should be made to utilise the available skills to their maximum.

A basic question could be why human beings are considered as resources.[2] A conceivable argument would be that a resource is a necessary enforcement of the system upon which ultimately depends the productivity of organisation, both in social as well as in economic terms. Furthermore, the tangibility of physical resources helps the organisation to foresee the results and manage thereafter accordingly, because these results are reducible to quantitative forms. On the contrary, human resources consisting of 'humans' who are reflexive of their feelings through exhibiting themselves overtly or covertly are many a time difficult to be adjudged though the necessary competent human resources certainly have a greater affinity to self-growth. Thus, the human resources management is of crucial concern. This certainly does not indicate that physical resource development is not required, in fact the economisation and utmost usage of all types of resources are a prerequisite for efficiency.

This could be further viewed from an ecological perspective, which assumes and explains dynamic interaction among various variables, thus, affecting the outcome of each other. Fuller exploration of physical resources would depend on the human potential, likewise the conducive environment of an organisation would in turn be affecting the overall output through maximum utilisation of physical resources. But then human beings are instrumental to organisational growth and, therefore, crucially important. Human resource development is an on-going process that starts with an individual's career from preparation for job applications at the pre-hiring stage to recruitment and selection, induction training, training on the job and occasionally off it, working in a congenial climate and conducive conditions for growth and development so that the individual attains results corresponding to his full potential.

Human resource development programmes refer to the systematic diagnosis of the available manpower and structuring appropriate strategy to activate human potential with necessary reinforcement mechanisms. This process identification and manifestation of human resources on a continuous basis is expected to operate within the organisation.

Sources of Human Problem in the Organisational Context

Human resource development involves the proper programming of strategy which begins with the identification of various arenas of human problems. Thus, it is pertinent to mention those probable factors which give rise to human problems within the organisation:

1. In the absence of a conducive and supporting working environment, there is a high degree of incongruence between job's requirement and the organisational process. Further, no proper arrangements are made to channelise and assimilate the individual's belief system with that of organisational functioning.
2. Non-equitable compensating policies create feelings of dissatisfaction among the members of the organisation, who are adversely affected by such measures. This has a demonstrating influence on the personnel in the organisation.
3. Lack of role specificity creates tensions among the members of an organisation and sometimes insecurity.
4. Not selecting the right person for the right job which is the consequence of choosing through faulty selection methods, is also a source of human problems in an organisation.
5. Problems also originate when the organisation inhibits the self-improvement of the individual and blocks the fulfilment of his social needs.

Further, the possible potential areas in human development which human resource development aims at have been observed as:

1. *Competence:* The human resource development must aim at increasing the individual's competence for his 'job' in particular and organisation in general.
2. *Capabilities:* Certain capabilities are to be developed particularly in the higher executive, for instance, his capability to make rational decisions, to regulate organisation procedures, to analyse environmental factors etc. Also certain leadership capabilities must be inculcated in the higher executives.
3. *Innovativeness:* The quest to learn innovative approaches must be one of the major foci of human resource development. This can be done by creating supportive mechanism to channelise one's innovation properly.
4. *Achievement-Oriented Values:* The cultivation of achievement-oriented values is a must for increasing organisational productivity.

5. *Time Management:* Time management is directly related to the successful achievement of organisational objectives. Hence, individuals must be taught to get the maximum of the time available.
6. *Meaningfulness of Tasks:* Through human resource development, a person's faith in the purposiveness and meaningfulness of the tasks that he performs can be evolved and enhanced.

Before discussing any approach to human resource development, it is essential to evolve a gestalistic approach which highlights that behaviour in an organisation is a function of the interaction between personality (i.e., ability, values, needs, expectancies, instrumentality and role demands) and the general environment (i.e., organisational contingencies, environmental constraints, supervision and available alternatives). In other words, the intrinsic and extrinsic aspects of jobs should be taken into consideration while evolving strategies of human resource development. Athreya (1984) underscores the eleven sub-systems in human resource development, viz., role, analysis, selection and placement, transfer and rotation, reward and punishment, performance and potential appraisal, feedback and counselling, training and development, career planning, succession planning, participative devices and human resource development data bank.[3] Further, he suggests that integration of these sub-systems into a synergistic whole is required by identifying and improving sub-systems.

In the following pages, certain important human resource development strategies are being examined in brief under the rubrics of 'structural approach', 'organisational climate approach' and the 'training approach'.

Structural Approach

In any dynamic organisation, its personnel department should be entrusted with the responsibility of understanding manpower planning in an effective manner. For this purpose, an annual planning exercise, taking a broad organisational viewpoint, would be helpful. It is not advisable to select personnel on an ad hoc basis, which may impair the whole system of working in the organisation resulting in an inadequate utilisation of its human resources.

Further, caution should be observed against over-employment and mismatch of qualifications. It has been observed that an overqualified person for a job where his knowledge is not being utilised fully, may feel frustrated and, thus, reduce the overall effectiveness of the organisation. In an organisation, formulation of appropriate rules and regulations helps in streamlining the roles of different functionaries but sometimes strict adherence to rules may also create a straight-jacket system. The lines of command and reporting should be properly spelled out in order to avoid confusion and conflict.

Further, an organisation should have a sound and rational system of performance appraisal. Therefore, a simple format focussing on the expectations and achievement of employees may be specified. In place of confidential reports, a more open and objective performance appraisal system should be considered ideal. An appraisal system should invariably act as a source of motivating employees.

It has been observed in governmental organisations that placement of an employee takes place on the whims of those who are generally not well-conversant with his skills and abilities. Therefore, it is suggested that efforts must be made to synchronise the transfer and placement policy with the capabilities and attitudes of individual employees. Sometimes, it becomes very difficult to break the existing organisational conventions and practices because of various forces resisting change. It may be pertinent to mention here that education about management of stress may help the managers to make well-balanced rational decisions at such times and shall also enable the senior management to receive helpful feedback concerning the attitudes to these changes. For introducing human resource development, one has to redesign jobs in the light of changing technology and working conditions. A sound system of resource accounting should be able to provide information necessary for making more rational decisions.

Therefore, it seems urgent to have proper planning of recruitment, training and placement for the maximum utilisation of existing human resources.

Organisational Climate Approach

There is built-in motivation in the administrative culture and value system which demand conformity with survival aud growth of every employee. Goals of the organisation must always be kept in mind and sense of duty towards organisational goals must be nurtured. Further, in any human resource development scheme, it is necessary to promote the positive aspects of organisational climate relating to leadership, inter-personal and intergroup relationships, communication, motivation, conflict management, creativity, and risk-taking, feedback and counselling and role analysis.

Similarly, identification of human potential with the help of aptitude, interest pattern and other tests is also essential for a systematic development of an organisation's human resources. Newly cultivated positive attitudes of employees need to be continually reinforced through purposive organisational climate.

Reward System

Reward refers to 'recognition', and 'appreciation' of good work. This is a very important factor for improving the climate of organisation and involvement of employees in the organisation. The following steps may be taken to institute a reward system in an organisation:

1. Recognition and appreciation of good work should be done through special circulars, on-the-spot appreciation, performance certificates, gifts like books and small write-ups in the in-house magazine.
2. A cash reward for any significant contribution to organisational productivity made by an employee can prove to be an effective motivational instrument.
3. Ensuring better working conditions for employees of all levels.
4. Linking rewards with the desired place of transfer and also with promotion.
5. To give the children of outstanding employees priority in employment within the organisation or its affiliated wings.

Hopefully, the above strategies of reward system would help to evolve and reinforce a motivational climate that would be favourable to the promotion of organisational effectiveness.

Other Motivating Factors

An organisation must facilitate the satisfaction of various needs of its employees. The needs may be physiological, security, social extension, esteem, power and achievement. To maintain a communication link with the employees for ascertaining their needs, a committee may be appointed which would periodically review the working conditions to facilitate benefits provided to the employees. Facilities for club formation and undertaking cultural activities may be made available. They are likely to make the employees feel well-integrated with the organisation that they serve. Feeling of belongingness and oneness may lead to high level of morale, motivation and job satisfaction. It will help in inculcating a feeling of self-worth which is a primary motivating factor.

If an organisation is actually keen in introducing human resource development in a systematic manner it has to start from the individual level itself, since an individual is a prime source of all the visible and invisible energy. The main task of human resource development administrator is to motivate a person to actualise one's talent and psychic energy. Therefore, an organisation needs to evolve a self-development programme which will help an individual to handle specific life crisis and provide him opportunity for self-awareness and self-growth. Besides he has to guide and train him to channelise and internalise these resources for the benefit of oneself and the growth of the organisation.

Training Approach

A training system in an organisation should aim at the development of human resources at all levels. The recognition of training as an important means of improving human potential and increasing the organisational efficiency has attracted a number of organisations to arrange training programmes for their employees. Such training programmes are designed to improve the capabilities of their employees, to introduce methods of work to attain efficiency, to update their professional knowledge, to modify their attitudes, and to prepare them for assuming higher responsibility. There is a growing awareness that training alone cannot fully develop human resources, since the human resource development activities, broadly speaking, involve expertly studied, designed and implemented programmes of planned change in work itself and the realignment of task and decision structure. Training is only one of the major tools of human resource development scheme.

In order to make employee training programmes more effective and meaningful, a deliberate training policy needs to be framed. Such a policy would be based on the organisations' requirements both in short-term as well as in long-term. It would help to provide broad guidelines for taking the organisation towards its specific goals and in the process, help to equip its manpower to achieve them.

The word 'need' implies that something is lacking or there is a lacuna somewhere. The function of training assumes that such lacuna can be overcome by systematic training efforts. Such needs can be intensified at the individual, organisational and occupational levels. The levels of database for identifying the needs and matching them with the task needs of the organisation and the content of programme is an important task. Further, a superior plays an important role in identification of subordinate needs and matching them with the choice of a particular programme.

Training Techniques

Though a training programme can be planned or organised in a systematic manner and it may have specific objectives and resources for achieving them, yet a training programme may not become fruitful unless the media through which the participants are being instructed are appropriate for the level of participants. The methods which are commonly used by various training institutions are lecture method, group discussion, seminar, panel discussion, workshops, conferences, syndicate method, case study method, incident method, in-basket exercises, role playing, sensitivity training, transactional analysis, behaviour modifications, management games, brainstorming and audio-visual aids. Knowledge of transactional analysis stimulates managers to accept the 'principle of self responsibility' which is required for the development of an organisation. However, it has been found that Grid O.D. has significantly positive effects on the capacity of organisations to increase their productivity and efficiency. This helps in team-building, intergroup development, systematic implementation and stabilisation. These methods are for providing information, developing insight into the problem and their solution evolving practical skills and methods for improving human relations.

Chart

Strategies of Human Resource Development

Structural Approach	*Organisational Climate Approach*	*Training Approach*
Formal Structure	Personnel Profiles	Diagnosis of the Problem Identification of Training Needs
Policies	Strengthening Rewards and Punishment System	Training Plan/Policy Training Techniques
Rules and Regulations Decision-Making	Identification of Aptitudes and Interest	(A) Methods for Providing Information (a) Lecture Method
Manpower Planning	Potential Appraisal	(B) Methods for Developing Insight into the Problems and their Solutions
Recruitment	HRD Data Bank	(a) Group Discussions (b) Seminars (c) Conferences (d) Syndicates (e) Simulation (f) Brainstorming
Placement	Participative Devices	
Performance Appraisal	Career Planning	
Transfer and Rotation	Feedback and Counselling	(C) Methods for Developing Practical Skills
Succession Planning	Role Analysis	(a) Case Study (b) Incident Method (c) Workshops (d) In-basket Method (e) Audio-Visual Aids
		(D) Methods for Developing Human Relations (a) Role Playing (b) Image Sharing (c) Transactional Analysis (d) Behaviour Modification (e) Sensitivity Training (f) Management Games (g) Leadership Training (h) Grid Training
		Evaluation of Training

These methods of training are used in different combinations in a single training programme to achieve the purpose of the programme. Every method has its own merits and limitations in a variety of situations.

Some are useful for providing knowledge and understanding, whereas others are functional for enhancing problem solving capabilities. Further, there are certain techniques that are pertinent to small groups while others may be suitable to the training of larger groups. Therefore, the role of trainer becomes more important particularly in selecting the training techniques, keeping in view the nature of the group, the training need and the general organisational environment.

The capsule training programme at organisational induction stage and the in-service training courses prepare an employee to adjust himself psychologically and administratively to the organisational demands and climate.

Training Agenda for Action

1. Formulation of a comprehensive and rational training policy and making everyone aware of it.
2. Preparation of perspective and long-term training plans.
3. Rectifying the imbalance in training system by introducing and imparting training at all levels of the organisation.
4. Nomination should be based on "will" and not on "force". The zeal for learning is a must. In other words, pre-training preparation of trainee is essential.
5. Mixed level training may help in introducing attitudinal change followed by better adjustment in the organisation.
6. There should be a proper linkage between general management training and organisation-specific training.
7. Participative experiential training technique may be fruitful.
8. Training of trainers needs special attention.
9. Sound scientific system for the evaluation of training is needed. The constraints such as lack of information, difficulty of stating goals in quantifiable terms or unstated values, lack of trained and experienced evaluators and time limitations hinder the proper evaluation of training.
10. Self-analysis of the training institute itself is needed.

In the preceding discussion, an attempt is made to highlight certain techniques of human resource development which could help in solving certain organisational problems. Through human resource development, different areas of human potentialities are generally explored, developed and diversified, so as to have the maximal utilisation of 'human' as the 'resource'. We should not copy the Western model, we have our own culture and value system and human resource development personnel should play a catalytic role of getting these values stated and developing a culture that is suitable to its organisation. If these probable potential areas remain unexplored, the human resources in turn may also remain either unutilised or underutilised which an efficient organisation cannot afford. The potential areas could be isolated primarily on the basis of the idea, "what an organisation wants (aims) to develop in human".

Epitomisation

Manpower planning and forecasting at the micro-level needs to be linked with the macro-level manpower forecasting. There should be a proper system for feedback to the top management. Action research may help in redesigning the work systems. The personnel profiles are needed in the absence of which the personnel actions are likely to be delayed and also decisions based on remembrance may be faulty. It is agreed that one should not develop a sense of dependence on the western countries models but it is also not to adopt better applied and experimented aspects simply for the sake of resistance to borrowing. One can modify and learn from the Japanese, USSR, USA and British models of human resource development and then apply them according to the demands of our own system. Thampuran in his book entitled *Indian Philosophy and Culture for Modern Management,* highlighted that these concepts are not new to our culture, they are deep-rooted in Indian philosophy. There is an urgent need for evolving a national human resource development policy taking into consideration the inherent potential in every human being. The success of above-mentioned approaches depends upon the decision makers who are the system, the degree of accuracy of the input data, flexibility in administration and psychological preparedness of those who are going to be affected by the system.

Notes

1. The word 'commodial'; has been derived from the word 'commodity' which constitutes 'something' that can be easily bargained and sold off in the market.
2. Tread Mills, "Human Resources: Why the New Concern?" in Robert Golombiesky, et al. (eds.) *Public Administration: Readings in Institutions, Processes, Behaviour Policy,* 3rd ed. (Chicago, Rand, 1976), p. 450
3. Asha Hingar, "Identification of Training Needs in the Government of Rajasthan", *Training for Development Administration* (Jaipur: HCM RIPA, 1977).

   M.B. Athreya, paper presented at the NIPM, Hyderabad Conference on "Maximizing the R.O.I. through Management of People", November 11, 1984.

   T.V. Rao, "Role of Training in Human Resource Development", *Indian Journal of Training and Development,* Vol. XIV, No. 3, July-September, 1984, pp. 118–23.

   K.V. K. Thampuran, *Indian Philosophy and Culture for Modern Management* (Bangalore: Chinmaya Institute of Management).

22

HRD Climate in Public Enterprises
A Case Study

C.M. MAHAJAN

With the initiation of the process of globalisation and opening up of Indian economy, there have suddenly been major changes in the prima donna status of the public enterprises. They are now reeling under the threat of privatisation. The persistent losses and inefficient working have forced the government to rethink about the revival of or to say goodbye to sick units. This trend is prevailing not only in India but world over.

In this context, the public enterprises have to cope up with the emerging environment. They must run fast. They must shed the stigma of being inefficient and being a burden on the national exchequer. Different countries in the world have chosen different strategies, own paths and management styles to face this challenge. Japan has emerged as the leading nation with the unique style of management—thanks to its overwhelming reliance on the use of major asset, viz., the human resource. The key to the whole matter in public enterprises in India is also to develop and position our human resources in such a way that organisations become strategic. Thus, there is a need to institutionalise the system of human resource development (HRD) in all public enterprises in order to improve their working as well as make them operationally more productive. According to Y.S. Mahajan, "human resource being the most vital factor of production and labour productivity, a positive, forward looking, human resource development policy is a *sine quo non* for the efficiency and effectiveness of public sector employees".[1]

The HRD programme, however, has to be designed after careful assessment of employees' profiles and organisational needs. In other words, the first primary challenge for the successful implementation of HRD policy is to develop the 'HRD climate in an organisation which is also termed as the 'development climate'. Rao and Abraham have mentioned that an optional level of development climate is essential for facilitating HRD.[2] To Finkel also, the management of an organisation must create specific surroundings that will best need the participation and the requirement of HRD.[3]

The HRD climate is, thus, fundamental to an organisation. It also facilitates HRD programmes. In the present paper, an attempt has been made to capture the wider dimension of the HRD climate as prevailing in the organisation under study. It is based on the study which was planned to work out the extent to which such a climate exists in the Nangal unit of the National Fertilizers Limited. The main objective of the study is to prepare a profile of the HRD climate and to design interventions for its improvements.

The study is exploratory in nature, since it looked at an area where very little research has been done earlier. A correlation design has been used for explaining interdependency among various items. The sample of the study (Table 1), which consists of 182 employees, was drawn taking care that all categories of

Table 1

Patterns of Distribution/Receipts of Responses

Level of management	*Total*	*Distributed*	*Received*
Top management	24	15	12
Middle management	75	47	35
Lower middle management	377	85	65
Skilled workers*	1,746	100	70
Total	2,222	245	182

* Do not include the employees working in schools, hospitals, canteens and estate office of the unit.

employees including the top management were fairly represented. Informal interviews were also conducted to seek some clarifications in regard to prevailing HRD trends.

A comprehensive questionnaire consisting of 38 items was administered to seek views and reactions for the various aspects of the HRD climate.[4] A five-point scale (almost always true–5, mostly true–4, sometime true–3, a little true–2, not at all true–1) was used for scoring. After scoring, the data were computerised. Mean scores and percentages were found to make interpretations easier. The major findings of the study have been recapitulated in the later part of the paper.

HRD Climate: Conceptual Concerns

An organisation nurtures and establishes its own climate over a span of period. The climate signifies commonly shared beliefs, values, expectations, working styles, leadership and commitment and goes a long way towards influencing performance and ensuring Job satisfaction.[5] However, the HRD climate is much more comprehensive and is essential for executing HRD mechanism. Rao and Abraham have mentioned that the HRD climate is characterised as consisting of the following tendencies on the part of an organisation:[6]

- A tendency at all levels starting from top management to the lowest level to treat the people as the most important resources.
- A perception that developing the competencies in the employees is the job of every manager/supervisor.
- Faith in the capability of employees to change and acquire new competencies at any stage of life.
- A tendency to be open in communications and discussions rather than being secretive.
- Encouraging risk-taking and experimentation.
- Making efforts to help employees recognise their strength and weaknesses through feedback.
- A general climate of trust.
- A tendency on the part of employees to be generally helpful to each other and collaborate with each other.
- Team spirit.

- Tendency to discourage stereotypes and favouritism.
- Supportive personnel policies.
- Supportive HRD practices including performance appraisal, training, reward management, potential development, job rotation and career planning.

The HRD climate is, thus, essentially an integral part of an organisational climate and is additionally characterised by the presence of values of openness, confrontation, trust, authenticity, pro-activity, autonomy and collaboration.[7] Besides, a general supportive environment which includes commitment of the top management, positive attitudes and good personnel policies are necessary aspects of the HRD climate.

HRD Climate in Nangal Unit

The Nangal unit of the National Fertilizers Limited (NFL) is one of the premier and oldest fertiliser undertakings in the public sector. It is situated on the right bank of the river Satluj, a few miles away from the famous Bhakra Dam. The factory is running successfully and its performance is getting better year after year. It is well aware of the significance of the human resources and lays due emphasis on human resource development.

Following from its corporate office, the Nangal unit takes care of its more than 2,800 employees. For HRD, it imparts intensive training to its employees, both at entry and post-entry levels.

During a number of visits to the unit it was found that there exists a good and peaceful working atmosphere. Most of the staff has mutual understanding and there also prevail better working relations. Notwithstanding, the peaceful atmosphere of the company, a survey was conducted to determine the 'development climate' with reference to facilitating HRD programmes. It is significant to mention here that so far no effort has been made by the management to know, discuss and prepare a profile of the development climate of the unit. Whereas it has been pointed out that an HRD-oriented organisation should conduct annual surveys of such climate and profile should be maintained accordingly for future interventions.[8]

The climate of the Nangal unit has been analysed on the basis of itemwise mean scores and overall mean scores, across all items as presented in Table 2.

Table 2

Itemwise Mean Standard Deviation and Percentage of the Total Sample

Item No.	*Mean*	*Standard deviation*	*Percentage*
1.	3.5	0.787	62
2.	4.0	0.920	75
3.	3.5	0.897	62
4.	3.6	0.817	65
5.	3.4	0.919	59
6.	3.6	0.719	65
7.	3.3	0.916	58
8.	3.3	0.890	57
9.	3.8	0.788	70
10.	3.6	0.776	66
11.	3.9	0.738	73
12.	3.5	0.703	63
13.	3.3	0.871	58
14.	3.2	0.961	56
15.	3.6	0.804	64
16.	3.4	0.782	60
17.	3.4	0.902	59
19.	3.1	0.843	53
19.	3.4	0.839	60
20	3.5	0.843	62
21.	3.5	0.913	62
22.	3.1	0.875	53
23.	3.0	0.831	51
24.	3.3	0.965	58
25.	3.2	0.878	56
26.	3.4	0.823	61
27.	3.6	0.753	66
28.	3.4	0.817	60
29.	3.4	0.885	59
30.	3.1	0.917	52
31.	3.0	0.896	50
32.	3.2	0.890	56
33.	3.7	0.846	67
34.	3.6	0.670	66
35.	3.3	0.890	57
36.	3.3	0.899	58
37.	3.5	0.787	62
38.	3.2	0.915	54
Average	3.41		60.39

It is well evident that there prevails 'an average' level of HRD climate (overall mean score 3.41 and percentage score is 60.39) in the Nangal unit. It means that the NFL has achieved the minimum desirable climate for facilitating HRD designs, but at the same time, there is a good scope for further improvements. It is important to say here that in this regard the Nangal unit is not an exception. It is like most of the Indian organisations* in which the HRD climate is just an average level.

Positive Factors

The survey highlights certain factors as positive contributors to the prevailing HRD climate. Some of these are:

1. The top management of the organisation believes that human resources are the most important resource and they must be treated more humanly.
2. There is a healthy tendency among the employees to be generally helpful to each other.
3. Employees do not hesitate to discuss their personal problems with their supervisors.
4. Mistakes are treated with understanding.
5. A tendency on the part of the organisation to ensure employees' welfare.
6. Seniors guide their juniors.
7. The psychological climate prevailing in the organisation found to be conducive for the employees interested in developing themselves.
8. Active interest on the part of executives in their juniors.

The scores of the above factors lie between 60 and 75. While these elements of the HRD climate are well present in the Nangal unit, but certainly there is scope for further improvement.

Critical Factors

A number of factors were found to be responsible for an 'average' HRD climate. These were the items which were low scored

* In a study carried out by Rao and Abraham the organisations surveyed have scored very near to the NFL's score, i.e., percentage scores 54 and the mean scores 3.16. Further, among 41 companies, nine scored 75 per cent and only other eight scored above 60 per cent on their overall HRD climate scores. Another eight companies scored even less than 50 per cent scores.

(percentage scores lie between 50 and 60). The survey indicates the following items as the most critical ones:

1. One of the most significant critical factors was found to be the lack of delegation of authority. This has discouraged juniors to handle higher responsibilities.
2. The second significant factor has been the general indifference on the part of employees to their own development which could take place through making efforts to recognise their own strength and weaknesses.
3. The third important factor was that the employees are not encouraged to take initiative. They are also not allowed to do things on their own.
4. The employees do not have much fixed mental impressions about each other.
5. The behaviour feedback is not taken seriously by the employees.
6. Job rotation exercise is very rare and it does not facilitate employee's development.
7. There is no tendency to be open in communication and free expression of feelings.
8. There is a general feeling that employees' behaviour cannot be changed and they can never be developed at any stage of their life.
9. Not many efforts are made to identify and utilise the potential of the employees.
10. Last, but not the least, is the fact that juniors in the organisation also do not utilise delegated authority for development.

Conclusions

The above-mentioned elements of the HRD climate exist only up to a limited extent in the company. Therefore, the NFL must concentrate on these items in order to raise and improve its HRD climate. It should think of better delegation of authority, patronising the employees to take initiative, recognising their potentials and strengths, proper job rotation exercise and free expression of feelings. Juniors must be encouraged to utilise delegated authority in a better way and senior managers should take interest in their developmental activities.

On the whole, an organisation must recognise the complete role of development climate to the success of a programme. The unit under study should create a more responsive HRD environment that will best meet the needs of HRD programmes and the requirements of developing people at work.

Notes

1. Y.S. Mahajan and M.R. Virmani (eds.), *Human Resources Development in Public Enterprises,* Centre for Public Sector Studies, New Delhi, 1988, p. 7.
2. T.V. Rao and E. Abrahman, "Human Resource Development Climate in Indian Organization" in T.V. Rao and D.F. Pereria (eds.), *Recent Experiences in Human Resource Development,* Oxford & IBH, New Delhi, 1986, p. 70.
3. Coleman Finkel, "The Learning Environment: Its Critical Importance to Successful Meetings" in Leonard Nadler (ed.), *The Handbook of Human Resource Development,* John Wiley and Sons Inc., 1984, p. 47.
4. For details of questionnaire, see T.V. Rao, *The Hard Missionary,* Oxford & IBH, New Delhi, 1990.
5. N. Raja Reddy, "Motivational Climate: A Case Study of Commercial Banks". *The Journal of Institute of Public Enterprises,* Osmania University, Hyderabad, Vol. 14, June 1991, p. 163.
6. T.V. Rao and E. Abraham, op. cit., pp. 70–71.
7. For details, see Udai Pareek and T.V. Rao, *Designing and Managing Human Resources Systems,* Oxford & IBH, New Delhi, 1992, pp. 24–26.
8. T.V. Rao and E. Abraham, op. cit., p. 61.

23

Job Selection, Job Satisfaction and Career Commitment

R.P. JAISWAL

Job Selection

The entry into an occupation is not an accidental phenomenon, rather it is an exclusive process where many factors impinge upon the final selection of an occupation. Each job demands specific aptitude, skill and specialised training. A long educational and professional training programme is required as a preparation for a particular job position. Therefore, occupational choice of an individual who wishes to enter any specialised profession has to be stated quite early in his/her age and educational career. Immediately after the completion of the school level of education, the young boys and girls have to select from amongst the different alternatives available to them according to their past performance, aptitude, academic and professional aspirations, and competitiveness. However, at the time of actual job selection, many other factors become paramount which range from purely psychological to the socio-economic. Therefore, the process of job selection, the motivating factors, agents in the selection process, the reasons for selecting a particular type of job are factors which should be explored in order to have a comprehensive profile of the individuals in the occupation.

Reasons for Job Selection

Reasons for working for men and women differ significantly. Economic need has been repeatedly cited as one of the most important factors impelling women to join work (Sobol, 1963; Rosenfeld and Perella, 1965; Weller, 1968; Nath, 1968; Gordon, 1979). Women have also been stated as secondary breadwinners in the family. If their parents' or husbands' income is sufficiently high they need not augment the family income, but if the wages are low, one person's income may not be sufficient for the whole family (Sethi, 1976; Gordon, 1979; Raju, 1981). Schoenberg and Douglas (1937) have shown that during 1910–11 in Britain, low wages were associated with high proportion of women at work; and in the USA, high wages were associated with low proportion of women at work. But this purely economic view fails to explain the paradox of those cases where increasing prosperity is accompanied by corresponding increase in the female work participation rate. For example, Rowntree and Laver (1951) have reported that in Britain, a large number of married women come out to work at the time when the wages had touched a high level where they had never reached before. Srivastava (1978) has also found that in certain situations, the rate of female participation in the labour force increases with the general prosperity. In view of such conflicting views, it may be said that economic factors are important, but not a sufficient condition for women to join the labour force. Although marriage, number and age of children, and dependency status are other factors which determine their work participation, higher educational qualifications may impel women to seek employment, especially those having professional degrees. A change in the occupational composition may also bring about a change in the female labour force participation. Industrialisation and urbanisation also create conditions that are favourable for the employment of women (Gulati, 1975).

Thus, attraction of income and work is an important factor for women's work participation. Once a woman joins the job, she may command of it high prestige and power. She may, therefore, be deriving a kind of satisfaction from her work which further gives her a feeling of achievement in life. She may also feel that by working she is utilising her time and training in a productive manner, or she may be enjoying enhanced prestige in the eyes of her family members and friends. This may be rewarding for her in life rather than to be completely engaged in the household routine. Turner (1964) points out that women seek intrinsic rewards through their education and occupation. Their station in life and corresponding level of living is determined by their husbands' occupation but their life is idle unless they themselves are engaged in some work. Professional women may perceive the cause of their work more often in terms of personal satisfaction rather than economic factors.

Morgan et al., (1966) have given a number of reasons which are associated with the employment of women. These include economic pressures, employability and earning potential, family situation, and some psychological variables too. Thus, economic, social and psychological reasons have been stated to contribute to women's participation in modern occupations and professions.

Strong men-women differences also exist in the reasons for the selection of job. Although the economic reason has been the dominant factor for both men and women in joining the professions, yet within the broad economic category, the motives of men and women differ. In a study of men and women in science and engineering professions conducted by the author, it was found that the most important reason for selection of the job had been the economic one, which is followed by cognitive, occupational and altruistic. The study further reveals that whereas most of the men (36.89%) have joined the profession to eke out a living, most of the women have taken up the present job either to supplement the family income (31.01%) or to become economically independent (10.12%). As regards the cognitive factor, it is significant to note that 16.45 per cent women and 15.57 per cent men have selected the present job to satisfy their quest for knowledge. More women (14.55%) than men (10.65%) have selected the present job because of their deep interest in science subjects. Thus, occupational factor is more dominant among men than women. It is seen that 9.06 per cent men as against 71.59 per cent women have selected the present job because it provided better career prospects. There are 7.37 per cent men and 6.33 per cent women who have selected the present job because of the high social prestige which it provides. As regards the altruistic reason, that is, service to community, more women (3.80%) than men (2.46%) have given it as a factor for their selecting the present job.

Motivating Agent for Job Selection

Job selection is a complex process. Many factors and persons may contribute to the choice of a particular job. Those who influence the selection of a particular job may belong to the family or may be from outside the family. Such persons influence the decision-making process of the individual in selecting the job. The importance of role models for career aspirations and selection among youth is well-documented (Almquist and Angrist, 1972; Husbands, 1972; Theodore, 1972; Fox, 1974). Again, the sex of the role model is a critical factor in career aspiration and career choice. The presence of a female role model in the family and among acquaintances can provide examples of achievement and success. They can lend support and encouragement to young women (Epstein, 1970; Roby, 1972; Rossi, 1970). To take a decision about joining the men dominated professions like science and engineering is not a simple task. Parents, siblings, close relatives, teachers, friends, and acquaintances may serve as role models. In traditional societies where family, kinship and caste networks were dominant, the individual's choice was largely influenced by these networks. However, in contemporary achievement-oriented society, individualism is on the rise. Instead of traditional networks, an individual himself takes important decisions about his future. But despite many changes in the modern society, such independent judgement is more characteristic of men than that of women.

Exploring the impact of individual versus traditional networks on the choice of occupational career, the findings of the above-mentioned study, conducted by the author, indicate that the majority of the respondents have taken independent decision about the choice of their occupational career. Among those who have been influenced by others, the impact of family and kinship networks is relatively more pronounced than the impact of other persons. Similarly, sex-wise distribution of the data reveals that though both respondent men and women have taken independent decisions about their occupational career, yet the proportion of men is comparatively higher than the proportion of women.

Job Satisfaction

Job satisfaction is difficult to define. According to Blum (1956), it is the result of various attitudes the person holds towards his job, towards related factors, and towards life in general. Job satisfaction has many interrelated factors, namely, working conditions, job security, job structure, compensation and supervision etc. It is also a function of an individual's level of aspiration. Human behaviour is caused by two types of factors—external and internal. The conditions of work, tools, equipment are external factors, while motivation and frustration are internal factors (Srivastava, 1983). Bullock (1952) states that "job satisfaction is the result of various attitudes possessed by an employee towards his job". These attitudes are related to specific factors such as wages, conditions of work, advancement opportunities, prompt settlement of grievances, fair treatment by employers and other fringe benefits. Job satisfaction can, thus, be defined as an attitude which results from a balancing and summation of many specific likes and dislikes experienced in connection with the job.

The satisfaction of an employee with his job is governed by many factors. It may come from the very altruistic factor which may relate to satisfaction with the nature of activities being performed at a particular job position or with the academic interest in the job-related activities. On the other hand, the satisfaction may depend upon the several materialistic conditions attached to the job position, viz., the nature of work organisation, the nature of job position, the salary, the increments, the fringe benefits, the pensionary benefits and the rules related to promotion, transfer and retirement, etc. Apart from these job-related material factors, there are other factors as well which indirectly affect the satisfaction of employees. These are the physical layout of the work place, seating arrangement, tools, vehicles and instruments provided for the performance of occupational roles, and the recreational facilities. All these factors affect not only the productivity and performance of the employees but also his commitment to, and the involvement in the work organisation.

Satisfaction with Working Hours

One of the major areas which affect the job satisfaction of a worker in various ways is related to working hours. On one hand, it may interfere with the domestic responsibilities of the individual especially women, and on the other, it may intervene in his/her other social obligations. If the worker happens to be a woman then many areas of conflict may arise because of her long and busy work schedule. Certain other problems such as availability of transport facility are also related to it. Overstay in the office, extra work on holidays, and inconvenient shifts also affect the female employees more adversely than male employees. These adverse effects may include low productivity and non-commitment to work.

Satisfaction with Placement in the Job

Job satisfaction is also related to the placement of the incumbents in their job positions. In most of the organisations, it is seen that persons with same designation and pay scale are expected to perform different types of functions in different job positions. Some of these positions are highly valued in terms of power, prestige and other fringe benefits. while others possess relatively lesser amount of power, prestige and related benefits. Even some of the job positions are considered punishment postings where authority, social prestige and other benefits are minimum. Similarly, some of the job positions provide good opportunities for overtime allowances, travelling allowances and other pecuniary benefits. Thus, it is not necessary that all positions with the same designation and the same pay scale may have similar benefits.

The placement in job has got another significance too. It is an area where discrimination and favour can be showered upon the employees, particularly women. Men may be given highly prestigious, extremely powerful and more paying job positions, while women with equal rank and pay scale may be put in such job positions which are less valued, less rewarding or even sometimes punishing. Therefore, an employee's satisfaction with the job is dependent upon the nature of his/her placement in the job which may either be rewarding or disappointing to him/her.

Satisfaction with Facilities at Work Place

Adequate facilities at work place are important not only for the satisfaction of the workers but also for the proper performance of work roles. These facilities range from simple amenities like stationery, furniture, ventilation, light arrangement, seating accommodation etc., to the sophisticated ones like instruments, gadgets, apparatuses etc. Apart from the physical facilities, the general atmosphere of the work place, incentives and recognition for hard work and innovation are also necessary for the smooth performance of the work roles.

Interrelatedness of Job Activity and Qualification

One of the reasons which contributes to the dissatisfaction with the job relates to the association between the job activities and the area of specialisation. Top jobs are geared to the performance of certain specific work roles for which necessary training and qualifications are required. In the study referred above, most of the respondents (86.07%) have stated that the principal activity on their job is related to their specialisation. However, only a few of them (13.21%) have stated that their job activity is not related to their educational qualification and training. These respondents are likely to be more dissatisfied with their jobs than the others.

Compatibility of Salary with Qualification and Experience

The outcome of the above study explains that the men respondents, owing to their higher ambition and larger range of job opportunities, are more dissatisfied with the existing pay structure than women who have relatively shorter range of job opportunities and lower level of aspiration. Women have fewer job opportunities within the male dominated science and engineering professions. Moreover, within these professions, they themselves opt for such job positions as are physically less demanding and more suitable to their feminine role. Therefore, their inspirational level is likely to be low and they are likely to have less dissatisfaction even if their salary is incompatible with their qualification.

Status Self-Evaluation

In modern work organisations, where both men and women are working together, the status self-perception has assumed new dimensions. Unlike the unisex organisations where merit, experience and performance are counted most in the career profile of the incumbents, the organisations consisting of both the sexes add one more dimension, i.e., the sex status of the incumbents in status self-evaluation. Men may have a feeling that the benefits in placement, transfer and promotion are given to the women, and men with equal qualification and experience are put at a disadvantage. On the other hand women may feel that the organisation belongs to men and they are not given equal and fair treatment as is given to their men counterparts.

Career Commitment

Commitment on the part of employees is important in all work situations. However, it may vary in organisations, jobs, occupations etc. Commitment symbolises a complex form of human behaviour resulting from the interplay of several forces (human, organisational, social etc.) which vary in intensity, but are operative at the same time. Many of the available paradigms while accepting this as reality, find it hard to identify causal links between the force and commitment types (Buchanan, 1974; Porter et al., 1974; Steers, 1977; Stevens et al., 1979; and Hongland and Wood, 1980).

The concept of commitment has assumed various dimensions. Theorists have made a distinction between the employee's commitment to his organisation, to his job, or to the occupation/profession. Conceptualisation of commitment is also known to be culture-bound (Dore, 1973; Marsh and Manari, 1977). The prevalent socio-organisational norms determine, to a significant extent, the nature and type of employee's commitment. In societies having deep-rooted traditions, as in India, a larger discrepancy exists across the social, organisational, job and occupational norms.

Organisational commitment is more like a loyalty which may change with a change in the organisation itself, or level of job, or work groups. Job commitment is restricted to a position in the role hierarchy and may change with a change in the situation.

Career commitment is work group or class-oriented, extending beyond the present job and the organisation. It is not a uniform level across the hierarchy of occupations. Occupations which require their members to learn specialised skills and discreetly use them (jurists, doctors, nurses) make relatively more rigid demands on them. Given the professional orientation of their training, they develop interests, attitudes and values which give them positive self-esteem as members of the occupation.

It is a well-known fact that no occupational role could be satisfactorily performed unless the individuals have the requisite interest and identification with their occupational roles. Educational achievement or professional training is not enough to create an interest in the job. The interest comes either through the dedication to the type of work being performed, or through the climate of work which is prevalent in any work organisation. Facilities related to salary, promotion, transfer, placement, interpersonal relationship with seniors and subordinates also contribute to a large extent in making a person committed to his work.

The career commitment differs individually from one person to another depending on the differences in the interest, aptitude, and professional training, etc. However, taking all these variables into consideration, the career commitment may differ among men and women as well. Men and women with equal educational achievement and training, and with equal placement in the job may possess different commitment to their occupational goals and obligations.

References

Almquist, E.M. and Angrist, S.S. (1972), "Role Model Influences on College Women's Career Aspirations" in A. Theodore (ed.) *The Professional Women,* Scherkman, Cambridge, pp. 301–23.

Epstein, Cynthia F. (1970), *Women's Place: Options and Limits in Professional Careers,* University of California Press, Berkeley.

Fox, G.L. (1974), "Some Observations and Data on the Availability of Same Sex Role Model as a Factor in Under-Graduate Career Choice", *Sociological Focus,* Vol. 7, No. 4, Fall, pp. 15–20.

Gordon, Margaret S. (1979), "Women and Work: Priorities for Future" in C. Kerr and J.M. Rosow (eds.). *Work in America,* Van Nastrand Reinhold and Co., New York, pp. 111–27.

Gulati, Leela (1975), "Female Work Participation: A Study of Inter-State Differences", *Economic and Political Weekly,* Vol. 10, No. I and 2, pp. 35–42.

Husbands, S.A. (1972), "Women's Place in Higher Education", *School Review,* Vol. 80, No. 1, pp. 261–74.

Margann, C.T. et al., (1966), *Productive American: A Study to How Individuals Contribute, to Economic Growth,* Institute of Social Growth, Ann-Arbon, University of Michigan, Michigan.

Nath, Kamla (1968), "Women in Working Force in India", *Economic and Political Weekly,* Vol. 3, No. 31, pp. 1205–13.

Raju, Saraswati (1981), "Sita in the City: A Socio-geographical Analysis of Employment in Urban India", Discussion Paper, University of Syracuse, Syracuse.

Rosenfeld, C. and Perella, F.C. (1965), "Why Women Start and Stop Working: A Study in Mobility", *Monthly Labour Review,* Vol. 88, pp. 1077–82.

Rowntree, S.B. and Laver, G.B. (1951), *Poverty and the Welfare State,* MacMillan, London.

Schoenberg, E.H. and Douglas, P.H. (1937), "Studies in the Supply Curve of Labour", *Journal of Political Economy,* Vol. 45, No. 1, pp. 61–67.

Sethi, Raj Mohini (1978), *Modernization of Working in Developing Societies,* National, New Delhi.

Sobol, M.G. (1963), "Commitment to Work" in F.L. Nye and L.W. Hoffman (eds.), *The Employed Mothers in America,* Rand McNally, Chicago.

Srinivas, M.N. (1978), *The Changing Position of Indian Women,* Oxford University Press, Bombay.

Theodore, A. (1972), *The Professional Women,* Scherkman, Cambridge.

Turner, Ralph H. (1964), "Some Aspects of Women's Ambitions", *American Journal of Sociology,* Vol. 70, pp. 279–93.

Weller, R.H. (1968), "A Historical Analysis of Female Labour Force Participation in Puerto Rico", *Social and Economic Studies,* Vol. 17, pp. 60–69.

24

Role of Academic Institutions in Human Resource Development

MEENA SOGANI AND SANGEETA SHARMA

The contrived nature of organisations explains why they inherit imperfections in one form or the other. The manifestation of these can be at various levels but through proper strategic human efforts, their negative impact can be reduced considerably. Since human endeavour involves multifarious human activities at various levels, an inbuilt mechanism of coherent system is required. This in turn highlights the need for effective resource management. Of many resources, human resources are the most important since they have distinct role in the process of conversion of inputs into outputs. The management of human resources is affected by its basic fundamentals, viz., availability, generation and recycling optimal utilisation.

In a developing country like India, where multiplicity of problems exist, unskilled and untrained human beings are available in abundance. It, therefore, requires serious and rigorous exercise to plan for managing millions of men and women to avoid obsolescence. Hence, it would be pertinent here to explore various dimensions and phases of human development in the context of the role played by academic institutions at different levels. A planned intervention through academic institutions would help a system to reorient itself. Thus, these institutions occupy a pivotal place as these act as motivators of individual's growth.

Requirements of Tomorrow's Man

The inevitability of change focuses on the need to adopt prospective manpower planning as a tool of attaining objectives where combination of few conventional and modern techniques help an organisation to maintain continuity of growth.

What kind of 'man' we want is determined, among other things, by new socio-economic forces that are shaping today as a result of the emergence of global thrust and the need to explore new world market. This indicates that in the coming years, capital-intensive and wealth-generating organisation in society will become more important. Thus, the role of service institutions will be complementary in the sense of providing cohesive force to develop infrastructure. This gets reflected in various policies, such as industrial, EXIM, WTO, intellectual rights, etc., all of which bring us nearer to the policy of desegregation and unification.

Apart from economic reasons, erosion of social values is also an important factor to be taken care of; hence, education through academic institutions must have social relevance.

These trends indicate that for future manpower planning, important factors that one must keep in mind will be: competitiveness, strong value system, work ethics and right job placement. Hence, we have to re-focus on human requirements. The changes have to be introduced at two levels, viz., cognitive, and attitudinal and behavioural requirements, respectively. Important among these can be categorised as follows:

Cognitive Requirements	*Attitudinal and Behavioural Requirements*
– clear conception and thoughts	– commitment
– knowledge	– emphatic approach
– innovative capacity to design interventions	– willingness
– learning ability	– spirit of collaboration
– constructive suggestions	– positive attitude
– crystallised perceptions	– risk taking
– operational creativity	– time management
– quality thrust	– quick in response
– precision	– persuasive

Intervention Through Academic Institutions

In order to have proper liaison between the above requirements and human resource development (HRD), the role of academic institutions needs to be re-assessed. The foregoing brief analysis indicates that the two categories of values are needed: one, which are virtuous and fundamental, and two, which are modern and adaptive. Accordingly, we can envisage two types of academic institutions playing their respective roles: (a) formative, and (b) post-formative.

Formative Academic Institutions

These have important functions perpetuating fundamental values of being an asset to the organisation in particular and society in general. Irrespective of the nature of the job, values like perseverance, commitment, honesty, resilience, firmness, caring, etc., must be internalised from the very beginning as these are the fabrics with which society is made. In this category are included institutions of early learning, i.e., schools, colleges, etc.

These are nurturing institutions in order to mould individuals according to the demands and requirements that they are supposed to meet. An extra effort is called for to achieve this. The infrastructure and the trained personnel who make a direct impact on learners must be developed. Aptitude can also be assessed and given proper direction so as to increase the potentiality. Hence, apart from imparting knowledge required of various subjects the learners must be told how to perform any work systematically.

These institutions generate human resource for future, therefore, various capabilities can be identified here and nurtured accordingly. Identification of particular traits at an early stage can shape the right person. Even knowledge of coping mechanisms can also help them to manage stress in life and work.

Post-Formative Academic Institutions

Values without skill will make combination unbalanced. A right intervention through post-formative institutions of higher learning can promote professional excellence.

The management education must be imparted to all those who are interested in different professional jobs irrespective of their nature. For instance, those going for medical profession would find management education relevant and rewarding. In this category, we can have two types of institutions: (i) professional institutions, such as Indian Institutes of Management, Indian Institutes of Technology, All India Institute of Medical Sciences, Institute of Chartered Accountants, and Institutes of Textile Designing, etc.; and (ii) research institutions, such as National Council of Educational Research and Training, Indian Council of Agriculture Research, Indian Council of Social Science Research, and other state level institutions. As centres of technical and professional excellence, they have a responsibility to convert raw human resource into skilled ones, which are productively vibrant and useful. This is more important because knowledge and information become outdated very fast. It is through these post-formative academic institutions that a continuous updating is possible so as to respond effectively to the changing environment.

Policy Interventions and Suggestive Strategies

To meet the challenges of the 21st century, countries like India need to modify thrust of academic institutions from being centres of imparting information to the centres of creativity and excellence.

In the coming years, we expect to mould human beings according to the requirement of more useful human resource in a growth-oriented, highly competitive and efficiency-based socio-economic system. To initiate and introduce changes policy interventions are necessary. Two types of policy interventions will be required to restructure our conventional system of education: one, through making an integrated educational policy separately for early and higher learning; and two, through specific strategies to meet out distinct objectives of different institutions. What specific action plan can be drawn to prepare individuals for the next century is the basic question to ponder. Institutions need to be planned and structured which can free individuals from capacity of their ideas to form an integral perspective.

Integrated Educational Policy

To meet the general objective of changing thrust, a macro-level policy would be an ideal choice. Following suggestions may be offered in this respect:

1. *Re-analysis of contents of syllabi:* Contents of formative and post-formative institutions need to be grossly revised. Information, knowledge and values specified earlier must be introduced rightly. The centres of higher learning must become viable source of generating ideas. Thus, basic contents and creative contents must be clearly spelled out.
2. *Revision of text:* Planning the contents of texts is an important step in this direction. Books for different levels have to be goal-oriented. Such books may include books for general masses, professionals, and for promoting creative ideas. Hence, a careful scanning of material to be provided to learners has to be done.
3. *Developing infrastructure:* Who are going to communicate with learners and how again must be in accordance with the above-stated suggestions. Well-coordinated structures with proper linkages must be constructed. These will have to be supported by appropriate audio-visual aids. For this funding should not become an obstacle.

Specific Strategies

In addition to the general policy drafting, few specific strategies would facilitate the moulding of individuals. These are as under:

1. *Commercialisation of research products:* After undergoing earlier grooming, creative people ought to be prepared and persuaded for conducting research in various fields like medicine, agriculture, industry etc., on highly selective basis. Hence, there is need to create more research institutes of higher learning with applied thrust. With the forces of liberalisation and free market economy coming up, a need to commercialise research product and capture global market is evident. Researches must be utilised for the welfare of people and economic development. At this phase of development, none can afford to waste research.
2. *Establishing HRD consultancy:* For having proper utilisation of vast human resource, consultancy must become an integral part in the present higher education system. Consultative teams of experts should be constituted from different fields. A detailed information regarding availability of jobs, job requirements and possibilities of job placement must be

made available to institutions. A proper testing mechanism must be evolved to match the jobs and aspirants' qualifications. They should also ensure absorption of this skilled human resource.

3. *Creating job market:* This should be complemented by a parallel effort to streamline and restructure job market. A young brilliant entrepreneur should be able to grow up continuously and make his best contribution to nation-building, rather than serving as cog in the wheel. Nation's best resource must not be sacrificed because of whims of leaders who lack vision, idealism or zeal for excellence.
4. *Developing a system of evaluation:* Placement of people is not the end of the human resource management but there is a need to develop in-built mechanisms of evaluation so that weaknesses can be identified and strengths multiplied for improvements.

The role of media in making people aware of different career opportunities is gaining currency but this is only a beginning. Conversely, we need to develop human beings who have mix of emotions and creativity on one hand and are technically and qualitatively well developed on the other. We must convert individual into a complete man imbibing in him values and excellence required for balanced growth.

25

HRD-OD Interface

J.P. SINGH

As Human Resource Development (HRD) gains in popularity, an increasing number of people are enquiring: What is the difference between HRD and Organisation Development (OD)? Is this just a new terminology for the same age-old 'human relations' wine? Where does one begin and the other finish? These questions are not only limited to the enlightened manager, they are also being asked by professionals dealing with the human resources. The question was raised even in the National Conference of HRD Network and, therefore, needs a close scrutiny.

What is HRD?

HRD has been defined as a process by which employees of an organisation are helped in a planned and continuous way to:

1. acquire or sharpen capabilities required to perform various functions associated with their present or expected future roles;
2. develop their general capabilities as individuals and discover and exploit their inner potential for their own and/or organisational purposes; and

3. develop an organisational culture in which senior-subordinate relationships, teamwork and collaboration among sub-units are strong and contribute to the professional well-being, motivation and pride of employees.

In short, it can be said that the focus of HRD is on the use of human potential for individual and organisational gains. Let us now briefly examine OD also.

What is OD?

The most widely accepted definition states OD is an effort planned organisation wide and managed from the top to increase organisational effectiveness and health through planned interventions in organisation's processes using behavioural science knowledge. A close analysis of this definition and study of OD practices reveal the following characteristics of OD:

1. It is a planned effort involving the total organisation.
2. It is a long-term effort often spread over three to five years.
3. It implies a collaborative relationship between a change agent and the client group.
4. Changes sought to be introduced pertain to organisational growth, effectiveness and human satisfaction.
5. It focusses on intact organisational teams, although working at the individual level is also often needed.
6. The activities undertaken are action-oriented.

Some Commonalities

A preliminary comparison of the two concepts indicates the following commonalities between OD and HRD:

1. Both focus on behaviour of people in organisations.
2. Both rely on the behavioural science knowledge about people.
3. Both make the assumptions that people like to change.
4. Both aim at bringing about behavioural change in the organisation.

If above are the commonalities among people it is no wonder that even practitioners are not clear about the differences between OD and HRD. Let us, therefore, take a deeper look at the two and identify the points of departure between the two.

A Deeper Look

For purposes of a deeper analysis, let us examine HRD and OD against a conceptual model of a system. A system is a set of inter-connected components with a repetitive pattern of interaction. A simple and widely understood system is the Input-Throughput-Output System with a feedback loop. Thus, one can view an organisation as a system which imports resources from the environment (input), processes them through technological and managerial guidelines (throughput), and exports the end result of products and services to the environment (output). Both HRD and OD can be examined against the above conceptual backdrop of a system since both use some inputs to convert them into an output, e.g., a changed pattern of behaviour. The description below focusses on these three components separately.

Input

Since both HRD and OD use people as resources for bringing about change, there does not seem to be any difference in the two at the input stage. The additional input used by both is the scientific knowledge of the way people behave. This knowledge is gained from behavioural science discipline and is common for both. The only difference that appears to be operating at the input stage is that, whereas OD emphasises the use of prior diagnosis as a necessary input to any OD exercise, HRD is not very emphatic about it. Obviously, such diagnosis prior to any change effort is not inimical to an HRD effort and is often used gainfully. The content of diagnosis also differs with emphasis on human resource management systems and mechanisms like induction, training, appraisal etc., in HRD. The emphasis of diagnosis in OD, on the other hand, is on human organisational processes like communication, conflict, team-building and leadership etc. The difference, therefore, is merely of emphasis and not of substance.

Throughput

All OD efforts operate through interventions, whereas HRD, as has been argued, has no interventions. HRD has only mechanisms and relies on participative involvement and effective use of new systems. An HRD effort will, thus, focus on one or more of these mechanisms and reorient them to greater responsiveness towards individual and organisational needs. None of these are the traditional intervention strategies of an OD effort.

Interventions in OD form a set of structured activities in which selected organisational units (target groups or individuals) engage, where the goals are related directly or indirectly to organisational improvements, OD interventions are characterised by joint action between the consultant and client and are invariably focussed on process dimensions apart from the substantive content. Additionally, OD interventions, generally, focus on work teams in the organisation, individual level focus being brought in only as supplemental to the group effort. Thus, it would seem that the major difference between HRD and OD relates to the throughput—the way behavioural science knowledge about people is processed in bringing about change in behaviour of people and organisations. It is also obvious that HRD operates with more tangible human systems in the organisation; whereas OD, apart from looking at substantive issues, also focusses on the softer aspects, the so-called intangible aspects of organisational functioning.

Output

The analysis at the throughput level also points out the major differences at the output level. Whereas HRD focusses on change at the individual level (and at the organisational level through the individual), OD focusses primarily at the organisational level change (and at the individual level only as supplemental to organisational level).

Let us examine this aspect a bit in detail and further analyse the various output variables of HRD and OD. The HRD outcome variables as mentioned in the literature are:

- More competent people
- Better-developed roles
- Higher work commitment and job involvement
- More problem solving
- Better utilisation of human resources
- Higher job satisfaction and work motivation
- Better generation of internal resources
- More teamwork synergy and respect for each other

- The OD outcome variables are basically two: organisational effectiveness; and quality of work life.

Various authors have labelled these outcome variables differently. Some talk of organisational performance and health while others talk of performance and satisfaction. An additional outcome often emphasised, and generally treated as a final measure of the success of the OD effort, is the enhancement of an organisation's ability to cope with future change. This is not part of performance which is often limited to variables like output, quality, profits, growth etc., but nonetheless is a part of organisational effectiveness.

Figure 1

Comparison of HRD and OD on Systems Model

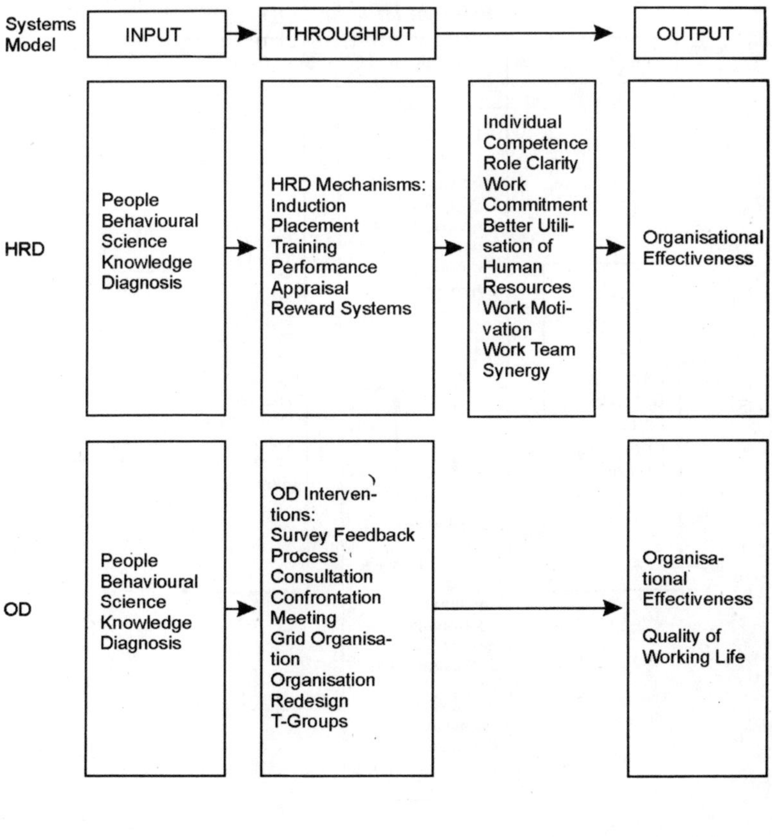

The figure below sums up the comparison of HRD and OD on the Input-Throughput-Output Model.

The diagram clearly indicates the commonalities and differences between OD and HRD. The analysis is obviously meant for the professional dealing with the human resources management to help him acquire a clarity for himself. An HRD professional, however, also has a responsibility to ensure a greater awareness for his organisation's top team in particular and total employee group in general about developments in his profession and their applicability to the work sphere. What direction does he give to the human resources management in his organisation in light of this clarity is a moot question.

Figure 2

Fusion of HRD and OD

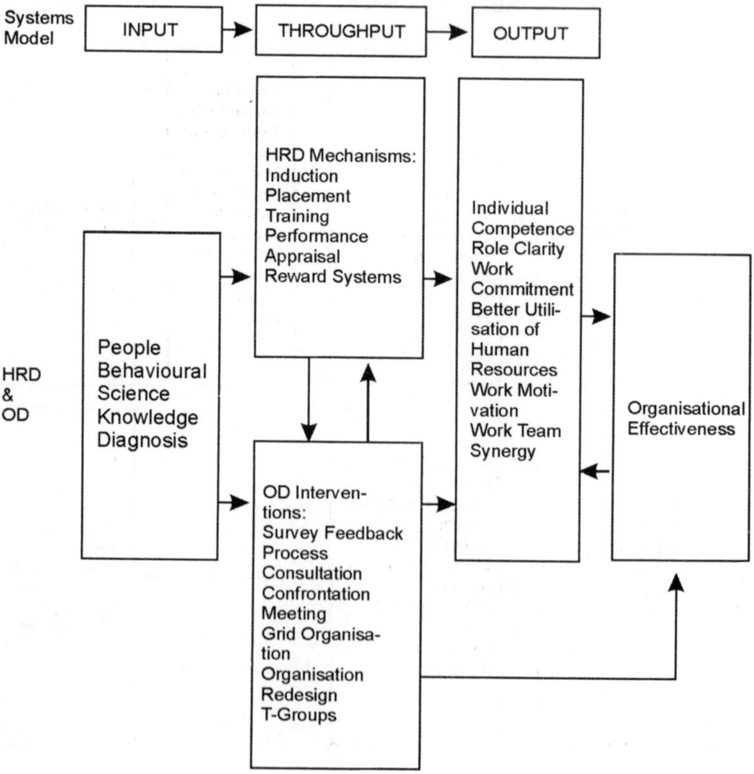

The Fusion

Let us for a little while forget that we are trying to differentiate between HRD and OD. Instead, assume that we are trying to achieve a fusion between the two. Such a stance should be possible since both HRD and OD are people-oriented and aim at fuller utilisation of human potential. Let us attempt this fusion again with the help of the systems model of input-throughput-output. Figure 2 presents a model which represents a fusion of HRD and OD.

As noted earlier, the first stage in the two approaches of HRD and OD is similar with common inputs of human resources and behavioural science knowledge and diagnosis. The only difference it may be noted is that in HRD, the diagnosis is aimed at analysis of human resource systems namely, induction, training, appraisal and rewards, etc., whereas in OD, it is aimed at the organisational human processes, namely, communication, leadership, teamwork, conflicts, etc. It is not difficult to think of a situation where a specialist or a consultant might wish to diagnose both of them simultaneously, although most specialists would look at them in stages.

The throughput and output obviously depend upon the diagnosis and follow accordingly. If the focus is on human resource management systems, one would need to evolve participative systems leading to what has been shown as the Level-I outcomes. On the other hand, if the focus is on the human organisational processes, OD interventions are the natural follow-up aiming directly at Level-II outcomes of organisational effectiveness and quality of work life. The solid arrows in the model show the natural flow of activities in HRD and OD. The broken arrows indicate the additional issues that are likely to crop up leading to enlargement of focus. They, therefore, also indicate various interface stages between HRD and OD both at throughput and at output levels.

What should an Organisation Do?

It is obvious that in light of the current climate, a greater emphasis on utilising latent human potential is inescapable. Whether this takes the form of 'exploiting' human potential or 'fulfilling' higher order needs is part of the managerial philosophy of an organisation. Similarly, whether this is done through a focus on the individual or on work teams is a managerial choice. Both HRD and OD subscribe to the values of human dignity at work, and to that extent aim at fulfilling higher level needs. To that extent, HRD and OD are mutually compatible and can even be complementary. The question, therefore, one should answer is: Where can one make a start; rather than whether to choose HRD or OD. If that be the case, the start can be made only at the level of current awareness in the organisation. Many organisations do not understand OD. It is more often confused with the sensitivity training and often evokes both founded and unfounded fears, even though sensitivity training constitutes only one of the scores of OD intervention strategies. The choice of making a start, therefore, depends on the best judgment of the human resource professional about his organisation. It is the responsibility of a human resource manager to assess what is feasible in his organisation and make a start in the desired direction. Eventually, a focus on the process dimensions of organisational functioning is inevitable. Good organisations do it all the time.

List of Contributors

Anita, Professor, Indira Gandhi Panchayati Raj Sansthan, Jaipur.

Ramesh K. Arora, Visiting Professor, HCM Rajasthan State Institute of Public Administration, Jaipur.

Hans C. Blaise, Former Regional Advisor for Public Administration, Ford Foundation, Bangkok.

Kamlesh Gupta, Research Scholar, University of Rajasthan, Jaipur.

Asha Hingar, Professor of Psychology, University of Rajasthan, Jaipur.

Rakesh Hooja, Director, HCM Rajasthan State Institute of Public Administration, Jaipur.

R.P. Jaiswal, DAV College, Varanasi.

R.H. Joshi, Deputy Director (Management), Water & Land Management Institute, Anand.

Pradip N. Khandwalla, Former Director, Indian Institute of Management, Ahmedabad.

N.K. Kulshrestha, Former Professor of Management, HCM Rajasthan State Institute of Public Administration, Jaipur.

Jagdish C. Kukar, Former Professor of Behavioural Science, HCM Rajasthan State Institute of Public Administration, Jaipur.

C.M. Mahajan, PG Department of Public Administration, Shivalik College, Naya Nangal (Panjab).

M.L. Mehta, Former Chief Secretary of Rajasthan, Jaipur.

Udai Pareek, Former Director, Indian Institute of Management, Ahmedabad.

G.P. Pilania, Member of Parliament, Rajya Sabha, New Delhi.

K.B.C. Saxena, Management Development Institute, Gurgaon.

Sangeeta Sharma, Associate Professor of Public Administration, University of Rajasthan, Jaipur.

J.P. Singh, Former Professor in Organizational Behaviour, Indian Institute of Management, Ahmedabad.

Meena Sogani, Professor in Psychology, University of Rajasthan, Jaipur.

Girish K. Srivastava, Professor of Management, HCM Rajasthan State Institute of Public Administration, Jaipur.

I.C. Srivastava, Former Chairman and Managing Director, Rajasthan State Mineral Development Corporation, Jaipur.

H.C. Suman, RPG Transmission Limited, Jabalpur.

B.R. Virmani, Former Chairman, Management Development Programmes, Administrative Staff College, Hyderabad.

N. Vittal, Former Secretary, Department of Electronics, Government of India, New Delhi.